Subfiles in RPG IV

Subfiles in RPG IV

Rules, Examples,
Techniques, and Other Cool Stuff

Kevin Vandever

MIDRANGE COMPUTING
IIR PUBLICATIONS INC.

First Edition

First Printing—June 2000

© 2000 Midrange Computing
ISBN: 1-58347-003-4

Midrange Computing
5650 El Camino Real, Suite 225
Carlsbad, CA 92008–9711 USA
www.midrangecomputing.com

For information on translations or book distributors outside the USA or to arrange bulk-purchase discounts for sales promotions, premiums, or fund-raisers, please contact Midrange Computing at the above address.

V4R4

To Corina: Thank you so much for the support, patience, and encouragement you devoted to me during this project. I am not surprised because it has been this way for all the personal and professional adventures I have embarked upon. My friends were right. I married way out of my league.

To my loving daughters Felicia and Kalia: Thanks for keeping Mommy company while I was busy writing this book. She couldn't ask for better companions and I am truly blessed to have such wonderful girls.

ACKNOWLEDGMENTS

I would like to thank the many talented people who assisted on the production of this book for their contributions, guidance, and support. Without their editing, graphic design, and layout skills, this book would never have made it to market. Three cheers to the following:

Merrikay Lee
Steven Bolt
Jim Utsler

I would also like to express gratitude to the AS/400 gurus who provided their technical expertise in one form or another. Thanks to:

Mark McCall for his thorough and insightful technical edit of the book.

Gary Patterson and Srinivas R.Vandanapu for supplying a couple of well-written and well-documented programs for my use.

Jim Coker for forcing me, in the mid-'80s, to learn subfile programming from him when I could have been out sucking down beers and chasing women. I've always hated him for that.

Robin Klima and Richard Shaler for writing the book *The RPG Programmer's Guide to RPG IV and ILE*. I especially like the appendix on recursion.

Last, but certainly not least, I would like to thank Boise Cascade Office Products, specifically Doug Mewmaw, for providing a V4R4 machine to code and test the programs that accompany the book.

Contents

INTRODUCTION

Y ou may ask yourself, "Why another book on subfiles? Have subfiles
changed since their inception on the System/38, in 1981? Can't I read the
IBM manuals and previously written subfile books and get along just fine?" Of
course you can! The basic concepts of subfiles haven't changed much, and yes,
you can read the IBM manuals and previously written materials to learn about
subfiles.

"So what's with the new book?" you might ask. Well, even though the basic concepts of subfiles haven't changed much over the years, there have been some additions and improvements, including new Data Description Specification (DDS)
keywords and their related implementation techniques. Also, the language sur-
rounding subfiles has changed drastically over the last couple of years. The re-
construction of RPG in the form of RPG IV, along with the introduction of the
Integrated Language Environment (ILE), have drastically changed how we create

applications and pushed the AS/400 development environment closer to more of an object-oriented approach.

What follows from the changes to the AS/400, RPG, and subfiles are new design fashions and programming techniques that must be consumed to fully take advantage of the environment, allowing us to create the best possible software solutions. A subset of this understanding is learning how to best employ subfiles in this new environment. It's one thing to learn the basic concepts of subfile programming, but it's quite another to learn how to program them in ways that allow them to work in harmony with today's surroundings. Reading previously written materials may satisfy part of the equation, but they won't teach you about what's new or about the most effective and efficient ways to incorporate subfile programming into today's development environment.

ABOUT THIS BOOK

So yes, this is another book on subfiles. But this one will provide you with the concepts, styles, and advanced topics of subfile programming, using RPG IV and ILE as its media. It will provide easy-to-understand explanations of subfile concepts, a bounty of practical examples, and some advanced techniques never before seen in previous subfile books.

This book will to take you on a journey from the very beginnings of subfile programming all the way to advanced techniques practiced by only those with a solid grasp of subfiles and the programming techniques and features of RPG IV and the ILE. More than simply getting you started with subfiles, it's meant to be a comprehensive resource that's used over and over again as you advance from very basic usage to guru-like practices.

This isn't a textbook—there are no exercises and exams at the end of each chapter to test what you've learned—but it certainly can be used as one. Each chapter builds upon the next so that you start with a solid base and build on that base as you proceed through the book. The purpose of this is to provide concepts, explanations, and practical examples you can use as templates for further development. The examples are included on an accompanying CD-ROM, so don't worry about having to rekey the code. Some basic knowledge of RPG IV and DDS is assumed. The contents of this book are there for the fine-tuning and enhancements of your skills.

WHAT DOES IT MEAN FOR YOUR CAREER?

Mastering subfiles has often been the defining moment in an RPG programmer's career. You could be the best RPG II programmer in the world coming off the System/36, but if you don't know subfiles, you'll probably be dismissed as an intermediate and told to learn subfiles. Whether this is justifiable is another issue, but it's a widely accepted fact that until you know subfile programming, you can't say you're an expert.

When I interviewed for new jobs, the big question was always, "Do you know subfiles?" Not until I could confidently answer yes to that question and eagerly await the subfile-related questions that would surely follow did I know I had arrived. Armed with the formidable subfile power, I couldn't wait to go on interviews. Once hired as a programmer with subfile experience, I was looked at in an entirely new light.

This phenomenon is less apparent now for three reasons. First, subfiles have been around for about 18 years and, with time, it's likely that programmers entering the AS/400 world today are being exposed to subfile programming. Second, because the AS/400 just celebrated its 10th birthday and in that time has swallowed up many a System/36 programmer, there are fewer programmers coming from a system where subfiles weren't available. Third, and most disturbing, is the *perception* that more RPG programmers know subfiles. I've worked in shops where this perceived knowledge spread throughout the programming staff like the plague. The problem was only partly the programmers' doing. They were assigned to programming projects that required subfiles and, using existing subfile programs as templates (as we've all done), would merrily code away. Well, simply cloning a subfile program doesn't make you knowledgeable in subfile programming. The other problem was with the code being used as a template. As you'll see later, there are a variety of subfile types, and each is used in a certain circumstance. Understanding this determination is paramount to writing good subfile programs.

What's happening today in some shops is that the proper subfile techniques aren't being used in the correct circumstances. Worst still, there's some bad code out there, even if it is employing the appropriate technique. If someone clones a subfile program but doesn't know subfiles, he may not know it's bad or inappropriate code. Once he uses bad or inappropriate subfile code as a template, some people might assume he knows subfile programming when all he really knows is how to clone bad subfile programs. The proliferation of subfile programs in this manner can be hazardous to your IT shop's health.

Don't follow in that vein. Come learn some basic and advanced techniques for yourself so you can stop bad subfile programming in its tracks. And take the time to learn how to use subfiles with other AS/400 tools such as recursion, data queues, and embedded SQL to create very powerful and efficient applications.

A Couple of Things to Mention

I tried to stay consistent with term use, but when discussing the finer points of maneuvering through a subfile, I use the terms *page down* and *roll up* interchangeably. These terms are synonymous, as are *page up* and *roll down*.

Throughout this book, I use the masculine pronouns: his, he, and him. This isn't meant to be sexist; rather, it's meant to help me avoid using the always awkward "his or her," "he or she," and "him or her" whenever I refer to someone in the third person. Let's call it form over political correctness.

THE SPECIFICS ON SUBFILES

According to IBM, a subfile is a group of records that have the same record format and are read from and written to a display station in one operation. As this definition suggests, a subfile is not a file; rather, it is a temporary place to store data of the same format to be used by a display file program.

WHY USE SUBFILES?

Figure 1.1 shows the typical use of a subfile. As you can see, subfiles are useful when you want to list multiple like records on a display. An additional benefit of subfiles is that you can define them so the number of displayed records fits on one screen or exceeds the number of lines available on the screen, allowing the user to scroll, or page, through the data. The latter capability is usually the reason you would decide to use subfiles in your display program. But because of their ease of use, I deploy them even when I know I will never display more than one screen. Additionally, subfiles are easy to change should your list of data someday require more than one screen, or page.

```
SFL001RG              Simple Subfile Program              7/14/00
                                                          12:50:26

Last Name             First Name           MI   Nick Name
Brown                 Adrian               C    Alphabet Man
Car                   Mack                 T    The Truck
Flowers               May                  B    Flower Child
Fort                  Frank                F    Hot Dog
Powers                Paul                 D    AB - Austin's Bro
Public                John                 Q    Invisible Man
Rain                  April                S    Mud
Sake                  Peter                F    Don't call me Pete!
Sampson               Othello              J    Don't call me OJ
Sampson               Sam                  S    Triple S
Smith                 Jim                  Z    The one and only
Smith                 Joe                  P    Joe for short
Stevenson             Steve                T    Nson
Vandever              Kelly                M    Bro
Vandever              Kevin                M    Fletch
Welcome               Matt                 A    Door Mat
Youmustbejoking       Shirley              N    Anyone see Airplane?
                                                             More...

F3=Exit    F12=Cancel
```

Figure 1.1: A typical subfile application that lists records from a file and allows the user to page through that list.

In addition to simply displaying multiple lines of data, using subfiles and their multiple line capabilities, you can add to, change in, and delete from data files very effectively.

You can also use subfiles in a non-display manner to create self-extending data structures and arrays in your RPG program. They work in the same manner as your multiple-occurrence data structures and arrays except that instead of having to hard code the number of elements, which have to be large enough to hold the maximum number of entries, you can use subfiles. You start with a small number of entries and allow them to dynamically expand as your data expands.

WHY SHOULD YOU CARE?

But haven't programmers been able to display data to a screen for years, without subfiles? The answer is yes, but subfiles allow you to display lists of like data that can extend beyond what fits on one screen. They make it easier for you to create display applications, which, in turn, will make you more productive. Subfiles programs are easy to write and maintain because much of the work is done for you in the Data Definition Specifications (DDS). Most of the time, you can change the characteristics of a subfile program without having to modify the RPG code driving it.

If that isn't enough, keep in mind that subfiles are often the barometers that measure an RPG programmer's worth. As I mentioned in the introduction, the merit of your skills is often measured by whether you can code subfiles. As an added benefit, when you're talking with a group of programmers at a users' group or technical conference, you can hold your head high, knowing that you're right up there with the rest of the subfile-savvy programmers.

Two DDS Formats Are Better Than One

As I stated earlier, most of the work in a subfile application is accomplished in the DDS. For every subfile you describe in your DDS, you're required to use two format types: a subfile record format (SFL) and a subfile control record format (SFLCTL). The subfile record format is used much as a record format is for a physical file. It defines the fields that are contained in a row of a subfile and the definition and attributes of those fields, and holds the actual data. Unlike a physical file, however, a subfile record format is used only in memory, and only for the duration of the job. Once the program using the subfile ends, the data in that subfile is gone. Individual subfile records are read from, written to, and updated to the subfile by accessing the subfile record format in your program. The subfile (SFL) keyword is required in your DDS to define a subfile record just as the record (RECORD) keyword is used for a typical display record format.

The subfile control record format is used to describe the heading information for the subfile and also controls how the subfile is going to perform. It's here that you define the size of the subfile, as well as the conditions under which the subfile will be cleared, initialized, displayed, and ended. The subfile control record format is unique because it controls aspects of a subfile in a way that other files aren't controlled. For example, you control the size of a physical file during compilation or by using the Change Physical File (CHGPF) command. You do not determine it in the DDS. Your program will operate the subfile control record format directly when it performs functions to the whole subfile, not individual records. Actions such as initializing, clearing, and displaying are accomplished in this fashion.

There are four keywords required in the subfile control record format:

- The subfile control (SFLCTL) keyword identifies the subfile control record format much as the record (RECORD) keyword does for a typical display record format. The SFLCTL keyword also identifies the subfile record format that must immediately precede it.

- The subfile size (SFLSIZ) keyword specifies the initial number of records the subfile may contain.

- The subfile page (SFLPAG) keyword specifies the number of records that one screen of data may contain.

- The subfile display (SFLDSP) keyword specifies when the subfile is displayed.

Note that the first bullet in the previous subfile control record requirements states that the SFLCTL keyword identifies the subfile record format that precedes it. This is a requirement. The SFL record format must immediately precede the SFLCTL format. The individual keywords available in each format can be placed in any order, but they must exist at the top of the format, before any constant or field definitions.

DDS AND RPG WORKING AS ONE

Once you code and compile the DDS for a subfile, you are ready to use that subfile in your RPG program. The first three actions you are going to undertake are initializing, loading, and displaying your subfile. There are other things you can, and will, do to a subfile, but let's start with the foundation and build up from there.

Before loading a subfile, you may want to clear or initialize it for use. In either case, clearing or initializing takes effect when you write to the subfile control record format with the appropriate conditioning indicator set on, using the RPG WRITE operation. This isn't a requirement for the introductory load in your program, but as you create more complex subfile applications, you'll need to know the difference between clearing and initializing a subfile.

Let's return to the DDS for a moment. To clear a subfile, use the subfile clear (SFLCLR) keyword. This removes all records from the subfile. However, it does not remove them from the display until the next time the subfile is written to the screen by your program. This is different than the subfile initialize (SFLINZ) keyword, which will set all the records in your subfile to their default value. If you have no default value set in your DDS, numeric fields will default to zeros and character fields will default to blanks. So instead of having an empty subfile, you will have 100 records in your subfile, each initialized with its default value, if your subfile size keyword is set to 100. I will talk more about SFLINZ later on so don't worry if you don't quite get it yet. In short, the decision about whether you should use SFLCLR or SFLINZ is determined by the role of your program.

You can load your subfile in a few different ways. The most common way is to retrieve data from one or more data files and write that data to the subfile record format using the RPG WRITE operation. You may also choose to write only enough records to fit on one page, as determined by SFLPAG, and write more only if the user requests more; write all the desired records to the subfile before displaying the screen to the user; or use a combination of both. As we go along in this book, I will show you examples of all the techniques because they are coded quite differently. I will also explain when to use which method.

A second way to load your subfile is to initialize the subfile first using the SFLINZ keyword, display the subfile with its default values to the screen, and allow the user to type data into the subfile from the screen.

Once your subfile is loaded or initialized, you're ready to display it. Depending on how you created your DDS, your subfile can take on many looks. But no matter which form it takes, one line of RPG code is all you need to display it.

Let's take a look at the code for a basic subfile program that displays a list of names, which could, for example, be customer names or salesman names. For our purpose, we'll just use generic names. Take notice of how much work is done with very little RPG code. Be careful, though: Once you understand this code, there's no turning back—you're on your way to becoming a subfile programmer.

OH GOODY! SOME CODE

I have provided the complete source for this example, including compile information for a physical file (SFL001PF), a logical file (SFL001LF), a display file (SFL001DF), and the RPG (SFL001RG), at the end of this chapter. The code is also included on the CD-ROM so you can load it on your machine and work with it. To make this example work, you need to compile the three source members in the following order: SFL001PF, SFL001DF, and SFL001RG. It might not always matter whether you compile the data file before the display file. In most cases, the data file will already exists. But in this example, I reference the physical file field information in my display file. As a result, the physical file needs to be created first. Figure 1.2 shows the code for the physical file.

```
A                                              UNIQUE
A          R PFR
A            DBIDNM        7  0
A            DBFNAM       20
A            DBLNAM       20
A            DBMINI        1
A            DBNNAM       20
A            DBADD1       30
A            DBADD2       30
A            DBADD3       30
A          K DBIDNM
```

Figure 1.2: DDS for physical file SFL001PF.

After creating the physical file, you'll need some sort of tool to get data into the file. One way to do this is to create a subfile program to enter the data (but if you could do that, you wouldn't be reading this book). In light of that fact, you can use the native Data File Utility (DFU) on the AS/400 or any third-party package your shop may already own. To start DFU, run the command UPDDTA

FILE(SFL001PF), or take Option 18 next to SFL001PF if you're using the Work with Objects using the Programmer Development Manager (PDM) view.

The DDS for the physical file is pretty self-explanatory so I will leave it alone. I'm going to start with the DDS for the display file. This is really where most of the work related to subfiles is accomplished. As I mentioned in the introduction, I'm assuming you have some basic knowledge of DDS. With that, I want to jump to the subfile record format signified by a record name of SFL1 and the record-level keyword of SFL. SFL1 is the subfile record format. It's where you will define the fields contained in each individual subfile record. It is also the format that will be written to in your RPG program. This is the format that will actually contain the subfile data. In the example shown in Figure 1.3, there are four fields being described: DBLNAM, DBFNAM, DBMINI, and DBNNAM. These fields are referenced from the physical file SFL001PF.

```
      A                                   DSPSIZ(24 80 *DS3)
      A                                   PRINT
      A                                   ERRSFL
      A                                   CA03
      A                                   CA12
      A*
      A         R SFL1                    SFL
      A*
      A           DBLNAM    R     O  5  2REFFLD(PFR/DBLNAM*LIBL/SFL001PF)
      A           DBFNAM    R     O  5 26REFFLD(PFR/DBFNAM *LIBL/SFL001PF)
      A           DBMINI    R     O  5 50REFFLD(PFR/DBMINI *LIBL/SFL001PF)
      A           DBNNAM    R     O  5 55REFFLD(PFR/DBNNAM *LIBL/SFL001PF)
```

Figure 1.3: DDS for subfile record format SFL1 in SFL001DF.

It's important to notice here that these fields are defined as output only ("O" in position 38) and are set to start on row 5. That means the list of data to be displayed on the screen will start on row 5. Each field has its own starting column number. DBLNAM starts in column 2, DBFNAM in column 26, and so on. The column settings let you place the fields across the row in whatever fashion you want, just as you would with a printed report. That's about it for the subfile record format.

You have defined your field's size and usage, and you have designed the layout of those fields. The next record format is the subfile control record format signified by the record name SF1CTL and the keyword SFLCTL. The subfile control format must come directly after the subfile record format. It's always distinguished by the SFLCTL keyword, and even though it has to come directly after the SFL format, you still must place the name of the subfile record format, in this case SFL1, within parentheses next to the SFLCTL keyword. The DDS for SF1CTL is shown in Figure 1.4.

```
A          R SF1CTL                     SFLCTL(SFL1)
A*
A                                       SFLSIZ(0500)
A                                       SFLPAG(0017)
A                                       OVERLAY
A N32                                   SFLDSP
A N31                                   SFLDSPCTL
A  31                                   SFLCLR
A  90                                   SFLEND(*MORE)
A          RRN1              4S 0H      SFLRCDNBR
A                                    4  2'Last Name'
A                                       DSPATR(HI)
A                                    4 26'First Name'
A                                       DSPATR(HI)
A                                    4 50'MI'
A                                       DSPATR(HI)
A                                    4 55'Nick Name'
A                                       DSPATR(HI)
A                                    1  2'SFL001RG'
A                                    1 27'Simple Subfile Program'
A                                       DSPATR(HI)
A                                    1 71DATE
A                                       EDTCDE(Y)
A                                    2 71TIME
```

Figure 1.4: DDS for subfile control record format SF1CTL in SFL001DF.

Whereas in the subfile record format you define everything about the individual record, the subfile control record format is where you define everything about the subfile as a whole. The two steps you are going to take in the subfile control record format are (1) define the subfile characteristics with a series of keywords and (2) define any fields that will exist in the heading of the subfile. The fields usually include column headings for the subfile records, as well as a title, program name, and date and time, but they can also include input-capable fields. I will discuss more about that in the next chapter. It's important to note that fields defined in the subfile control format are not part of the scrollable, subfile records.

There is no requirement for the content of the fields in the subfile control record format, but there is a limit as to where they can be placed. Remember that the SFL record format started on row 5. That means that fields defined in the SFLCTL record format must not be placed anywhere below row 4. Now, looking at the example, let's examine the keywords used. They can be placed in any order within the SFLCTL record format, but they must also be entered before any fields or constants are defined.

The first thing I do is define the subfile size (SFLSIZ) and subfile page size (SFLPAG). The SFLSIZ is set to 500. That means the initial number of records my subfile can contain is 500. I can extend the number contained in the SFLSIZ keyword, but I will cover that in the next chapter. The maximum number of records a subfile can contain is 9,999. The SFLPAG determines how many records can fit on one page. I set mine to 17, meaning that each screen of data will contain a maximum of 17 records. You're limited on this parameter only by the number that can physically be displayed on a screen.

The OVERLAY keyword is used to tell the display file to display the screen on top of what is already displayed—overlaying anything that is already there, but not erasing it. The subfile display (SFLDSP) keyword is used to display the subfile on the screen. It's conditioned, in this case, by N32, which means it will display only when indicator 32 is set off. You're not required to condition the SFLDSP keyword. I condition it in this example (and in most of my subfile programs, for that matter) because I want to stop the subfile from displaying if there are no records in it. You'll get a runtime error if you try to display a subfile with no records in it. There are a number of ways to handle the no-record situation, but I choose to set on indicator 32 when no records are loaded. This stops the subfile, and subsequent errors, from being displayed.

The next keyword you see is the subfile display control (SFLDSPCTL) keyword. This keyword allows you to display the control record format. The conditioning indicator on the SFLDSPCTL keyword, N31, conditions when the SFLCTL record format is to be displayed. In this case, the SFLCTL record format will be displayed only when it's told to do so by the RPG program and when indicator 31 is off. This keyword isn't required if there are no fields to display or function keys to control in the format. Many keywords change the characteristics of the subfile, but these changes aren't seen until either the SFLDSP or the SFLDSPCTL keyword is activated.

The next keyword is the subfile clear (SFLCLR) keyword, which is used to clear the subfile of its entries. It provides you with an empty subfile just waiting to have records written to it. Notice that I used the opposite conditioning indicator than when I was using the SFLDSPCTL keyword. I did this because the same RPG operation (WRITE) is used to display the control record format and clear the subfile. Because I probably don't want to clear the subfile at the same time I want to display it, I use the same indicator. When indicator 31 is off, I want to display the subfile. When it's on, I want to clear it.

The subfile end (SFLEND) keyword is used to indicate to the user that there are more records in the subfile. A conditioning indicator is required when you're using the SFLEND keyword. In this case, indicator 90 conditions the SFLEND keyword. The *MORE parameter is just one of the valid parameters used with the SFLEND keyword (the others will be discussed later). It will cause the screen to show the word "More..." at the bottom, right-hand corner of the last subfile record shown on the page. When the subfile is on its last page, the word "Bottom" will replace "More..." and indicate to the user that this is the end of the subfile. SFLEND specified by itself—that is, with no parameter—will cause the screen to display a "+" in the lower, right-hand corner when there are further pages to be displayed. When the subfile is on its last page, the "+" is replaced by a blank.

Now that all the keywords have been defined, you can define any fields you need for your subfile control record format. As you can see, I describe some basic column headings: a title, and the date and time. Because this is the same technique you would use to define headings on any display record format, it does not warrant discussion here.

I would like to point your attention to one field defined in the SFLCTL record format. RRN1 will be used as my subfile relative record number. I define it as a 4-signed numeric, with no decimal places (remember that there is a maximum of 9,999 records in a subfile). The "H" in position 38 indicates that this is a hidden field. I'm not going to display this field anywhere on the screen, but it's extremely important because it will keep track of which subfile record I'm working with.

The last record format defined in this DDS is the function key line. On line 23 of the display, I will list the function keys available to the user. This is the reason I use the OVERLAY keyword in the SFLCTL record format. I will first write the FKEY1 format, which will display on line 23, then OVERLAY the FKEY1 format, but not erase it. I use a separate record format to display the function keys because I want my function keys to appear at the bottom of the screen, as is standard with most AS/400 display screens. I cannot place the function key constants in the subfile record format because I don't want them repeated with each subfile record. I'm also restricted from placing the function key constants in the subfile control format because doing so would violate the rule of the subfile control format not overlapping the subfile record format. The only way I could get away with placing the function key constants in the subfile control format is if I wanted them to display at the top of the screen. The FKEY1 format is shown in Figure 1.5.

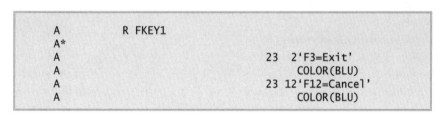

```
A               R FKEY1
A*
A                                    23  2'F3=Exit'
A                                        COLOR(BLU)
A                                    23 12'F12=Cancel'
A                                        COLOR(BLU)
```

Figure 1.5: DDS for function key record format FKEY1 in SFL001DF.

There, you have just built a basic subfile display file. More than a watered-down version appropriate only for learning, this is an example of a typical display file that would be used when you want to display a list of data to a user. You've done the hard part, believe it or not. Now let's look at the RPG code necessary to load and display this subfile.

```
Fsfl001df  cf   e              workstn
F                                         sfile(sfl1:rrn1)
Fsfl001lf  if   e              k disk
```

Figure 1.6: RPG F specs for RPG program SFL001RG.

Figure 1.6 shows the File specifications (F specs). Notice that there are two files described. SFL001DF is the display file we just learned about. I define it as a combined (C in column 17), full procedural (F in column 18), externally described (E in column 22) workstation (WORKSTN) file. I further define SFL001DF on the next line of code by using the SFILE keyword with two parameters separated by a colon. The SFILE keyword defines a subfile contained in the display file. If you want to use that subfile in your program, you would code a SFILE line for every subfile record format contained in your DDS. The first parameter of the SFILE keyword is the name of the subfile record format, and the second is the field that will contain the subfile relative record number. Remember that I defined the relative record number field (RRN1) as a hidden field in the SFLCTL record format. The important thing to note is that the hidden field defined in the subfile record format is the one placed in the second parameter of the SFILE keyword. We will use SFL001LF, the logical file built over SFL001PF, to load the subfile.

```
*****************************************************************
*  Main Routine
*****************************************************************
*
* Build the subfile
*
C                   exsr      sflbld
*
* Do loop to process the subfile until F3 or F12 is pressed
*
C                   dou       *inkc or *inkl
*
C                   write     fkey1
C                   exfmt     sflctl
*
C                   enddo
*
C                   eval      *inlr = *on
```

Figure 1.7: Mainline code for RPG program SFL001RG.

The body of the program consists only of a main routine and one subroutine. The main routine of this program (see Figure 1.7) is pretty simple. I first execute the subfile build routine (SFLBLD) and then code the DOU loop that will process the screen until either the F3 or F12 key has been pressed.

Let's examine the SFLBLD routine first because that code will be executed before the DOU loop. The subroutine SFLBLD is shown in Figure 1.8.

```
     ****************************************************************
     *   SFLBLD - Build the List
     ****************************************************************
     *
     C     sflbld        begsr
     *
     * Clear subfile
     *
     C                   eval      rrn1 = *zero
     C                   eval      *in31 = *on
     C                   write     sflctl
     C                   eval      *in31 = *off
     *
     * Load data to subfile
     *
     C     *loval        setll     sfl0011f
     C                   read      sfl0011f                            90

     C                   dow       (not *in90) and (rrn1 <= 500)
     C                   eval      rrn1 = rrn1 + 1
     C                   write     sfl1
     C                   read      sfl0011f                            90
     C                   enddo
     *
     * If no records were loaded, do not display the subfile
     *
     C                   if        rrn1 = *zero
     C                   eval      *in32 = *on
     C                   else
     C                   eval      rrn1 = 1
     C                   endif
     *
     C                   endsr
```

Figure 1.8: Subroutine used to build subfile in SFL001RG.

The first block of code is where I clear the subfile (SFLCLR in the DDS). Because it was conditioned on indicator 31, I set on indicator 31 and write to the SFLCTL record format, which performs the clear (the SFLDSPCTL isn't activated in this case because it's conditioned on indicator 31 being off). After I write the SFLCTL record format, I set indicator 31 off so the next write to the format will cause it to be displayed.

Now it's time to load data to the subfile. I do this by setting the file pointer to the beginning of the file and reading the first record of the data file. The three lines contained within the DOW loop are all that are necessary to load my subfile. I'm going to process the DOW loop until there are no more records in the file (while indicator 90 is off). Each time I read a record, I increment the subfile relative record number (RRN1) and write the record to the subfile record format. Because my subfile field names are the same as the data file field names, the MOVE, MOVEL, EVAL, or Z-ADD statements aren't necessary. Once the end of the file is reached, indicator 90 is set to on and I get out of the loop.

Indicator 90 is also the indicator I conditioned the SFLEND keyword on. This means that when the screen that contains the last record in the subfile is displayed, the word "Bottom" will appear on the lower, right-hand corner.

The IF statement below the loop is there to keep an error from ending the program. If no records were read from the file (RRN1 = 0), I set indicator 32 to on. Remember that the subfile display (SFLDSP) keyword is conditioned on 32 being off. If it's on, the subfile won't be displayed. Displaying a subfile with zero records will cause an error and end your program.

Back in the main routine (Figure 1.7), now that the subfile is loaded, I will display it. Within the DO loop, I write the function key format (FKEY1). This will display the function keys available to the user on line 23 of the screen. I then display the subfile with the execute format (EXFMT) keyword. When displaying a subfile, the EXFMT is always done on the SFLCTL record format. Because the operating system knows which subfile record format is associated with which subfile control record format, there's no need to explicitly perform an EXFMT to the SFL record format. I set indicator 31 off after the subfile was cleared, and with this write to the SFLCTL record format, the subfile control record will be displayed. If there are records in your subfile, indicator 32 will be off. As a result, the subfile should also be displayed.

Depending on how many records you added to your data file, you would see either the words "More..." or "Bottom" at the lower, right-hand corner of the screen. If you see "More...", you'll be able to press the Page Down key to display the next page of data. You can do this until you see the word "Bottom". If there's more than one page of data, you'll be able to use the Page Up key to scroll back to the top.

What's nice about this is that I didn't have to code a single line of RPG to handle the scrolling. OS/400 took care of it for me. Your program will sit on the EXFMT operation until a key is pressed that returns control back to the RPG program. In this case, the page-up and page-down keys are handled by OS/400 and won't return control back to the program.

This method of subfile programming is called the "load-all method." Using this method, you load the subfile one time and display it to the screen. OS/400 handles the paging for you. As you can see, it doesn't take a lot of code to get a load-all subfile up and running. In the next chapter, I will explain more about the load-all method, as well as introduce you to two more methods. I will also explain when to use which method.

HIP HOP SUBFILES CAN WRAP

There may be a time when one line of data doesn't cut. The subfile in Figure 1.1 displays first name, last name, middle initial, and nickname neatly on one line. But what if you want to show part of the address on the screen? There isn't enough room on the subfile line to squeeze in the address. What do you do? Do you abandon the subfile approach and try something else? The answer to the latter question, thankfully, is no. With just a little more code in the DDS and, optionally, a couple more lines in the RPG, your subfile can display multiple lines of data per subfile record. Figure 1.9 shows the output from previous subfile programs, with the addition of the address, city, and state on a second line.

```
SFL010RG              Simple Subfile Program              3/03/00
                                                         18:14:25

Last Name            First Name          MI   Nick Name
Anthony              Tony                A    Triple A
   123 Main Street                  Any Town, XX
Bert                 Al                  C    Alphabet Man
   1423 Lilac Lane                  Chicago, IL
Coker                Jim                 L    Da AS/400 Guru
   25345 W. Really Far Street       West of Egypt
Harrison             Harry               H    Happy
   777 Happy Lane                   Harrison, PN
Johnson              John                J    JJ
   876 W. East Street               New York, NY
Naisium              Jim                 B    Sweaty
   4987 N. Ball Street              Chapel Hill, NC
Patterson            Gary                R    The All-Knowing One
   Some Island Somewhere            Nobody Knows Where
Saint                Louis               A    Missouri
   234 1st Street                   Kansas City, MO
                                                         More...


F3=Exit   F11=Fold/Drop   F12=Cancel
```

Figure 1.9: Example of a subfile with drop.

JUST ADD THE FIELDS

Most of the work needed to create the multiple-line subfile record is accomplished in the DDS. In fact, the only reason I may decide to modify the RPG is to tighten up the technique a little. I could have easily left the RPG alone and still provided multiple-line subfile records. Figure 1.10 shows a new version of the subfile record format that includes two address fields and places them on a second line. All I've done is add two new fields on a second line of the subfile. The subfile starts on line 5 with the name fields and now will extend to a second line (line 6) with the addition of DBADD1 and DBADD2. This will cause your subfile to display two lines per record. OS/400 figures all this out for you once you define your subfile record format and determine how many records you want to display on a page (SFLPAG) in your record control format. You can see the complete DDS (SFL010DF) at the end of this chapter

This brings me to my next point. The one additional step you'll have to take to properly fit this new subfile on the screen is to change the SFLPAG keyword in the control record format. In our previous example, SFLPAG was set to 17. However, trying to fit 17 double-lined subfile records on a page will create some problems for you when you try to compile. To counter this, you'll have to modify the SFLPAG number to some appropriate number. Because I had 17 before and am now displaying 2 lines per record, I changed the SFLPAG keyword to 8. That means that the subfile will display eight two-line subfile records per page, which (and I know you can do the math) equates to 16 actual lines.

```
A          DBLNAM    R      O  5   2REFFLD(PFR/DBLNAM *LIBL/SFL001PF)
A          DBFNAM    R      O  5  26REFFLD(PFR/DBFNAM *LIBL/SFL001PF)
A          DBMINI    R      O  5  50REFFLD(PFR/DBMINI *LIBL/SFL001PF)
A          DBNNAM    R      O  5  55REFFLD(PFR/DBNNAM *LIBL/SFL001PF)
A          DBADD1    R      O  6   5REFFLD(PFR/DBADD1 *LIBL/SFL001PF)
A          DBADD2    R      O  6  37REFFLD(PFR/DBADD2 *LIBL/SFL001PF)
```

Figure 1.10: Subfile record format for a multiple-line subfile record.

SFLFOLD AND SFLDROP

By simply adding the two fields to the subfile record format, changing the SFLPAG keyword to 8, and recompiling both the display file and the RPG program, your subfile will now look something like that in Figure 1.9. Cool, right? Well, what if I want to toggle back and forth between one- and two-line subfile records? Maybe I don't always want to see the address information. Maybe I would like to display the subfile as in Figure 1.1 and press a function key to show me the address lines (Figure 1.9 shows that hint).

```
A N10                          SFLDROP(CA11)
A  10                          SFLFOLD(CA11)
A                              SFLMODE(&MODE)
A          MODE         1   H
```

Figure 1.11: Using SFLFOLD, SFLDROP, and SFLMODE together allows switching between display modes.

Am I asking too much? Of course not. With the addition of a few subfile keywords, you can actually toggle between single-line and multiple-line subfile records. Figure 1.11 shows the new additions to the subfile control format that make this happen. The SFLFOLD and SFLDROP keywords are used to toggle between displaying a full, multiple-line subfile record and its truncated, single-line version. Notice in Figure 1.11 that I use both keywords in my subfile control format. I will explain why momentarily. But first, let's talk about the difference between the two keywords.

FOLD? DROP? WHICH DOES WHICH?

Use SFLFOLD if you want to initially show the subfile in a folded format, displaying all the lines per subfile record. Use SFLDROP if you want to initially show the subfile in truncated form, where all but the first line in the subfile record is dropped. In parenthesis, place the function key you want to use to switch from folded mode to truncated mode and back again. I used function key 11 (CA11).

Because this is a display-only subfile, I can use the command attention (CA) indicators, which do not transfer data back to your program when the function key is pressed. If this had been an input-capable subfile (something we'll get to in chapter 3), I would have wanted to use the command function (CF) indicator CF11 as the SFLFOLD or SFLDROP parameter. The CF indicators allow the data from the screen to transfer to your program when the function key is pressed.

NOT JOINED AT THE HIP

You can use SFLFOLD and SFLDROP without necessarily having to use the other. If you want to initially display the subfile in truncated form but allow for multiple lines, you can use SFLDROP with CA11 as its parameter and not condition it on an indicator, as I did with N10 in Figure 1.11. What this would do is start and display the subfile in truncated mode each time it's thrown to the screen from the program. Pressing F1 allows the user to switch to folded mode and view the subsequent data in each subfile record. However, once control is passed back to the program and the screen is again displayed, the subfile, because of the use of SFLDROP, is displayed in truncated mode.

Conversely, you can use SFLFOLD by itself with the CA11 parameter and no conditioning indicator in positions 9 and 10 to initially display the subfile in folded, or multiple-line, format. Again, by pressing F11, you can easily switch back and forth between truncated and folded mode, but once control is passed back to your program and the screen is thrown again, it will, because of the use of SFLFOLD, display in folded mode.

SFLFOLD AND SFLDROP WORKING WITH SFLMODE

As you can see, you only need either SFLFOLD or SFLDROP to allow the user to switch back and forth between truncated and folded modes. And so far, no changes have been made to the original RPG program shown in Figure 1.1 to make this happen. I suggest you try it out using one or the other to see how it works. However, you've probably already noticed from Figure 1.11 that I use both SFLFOLD and SFLDROP, and that I condition one on indicator 10 and the other on N10 (not 10). I like to do this because when control is passed back to my program and the subfile is thrown to the screen again, the subfile might change modes, possibly confusing users.

For example, if I use SFLDROP in my DDS, but press F11 to toggle to folded mode, the subfile will switch back to dropped mode when thrown to the screen again. By using both keywords and conditioning indicators, I can stop this from happening. I can keep the subfile in one mode, regardless of whether control has passed back to the program, until I press F11 to change the mode.

SFLMODE is used to tell the program which mode the subfile was in when control was passed back to it. If the subfile is in folded mode, SFLMODE will contain a "0"; if it is in truncated mode, it will contain a "1". If SFLMODE is used without SFLDROP or SFLFOLD, it will return a "0".

The parameter, &MODE, the field that will contain the "0" or "1", must be defined in the control record format as a one-byte hidden field. Notice the "&" is used only in the parameter in the SFLMODE keyword and not when actually defined. When control now passes back to the program, I can tell the program which mode the subfile is in and ensure that it's thrown to the screen in that same mode.

A LITTLE RPG NEVER HURT ANYONE

The last step to my kicked-up SFLFOLD/SFLDROP technique is to add a little code
to the RPG program. (Figure 1.12 shows the necessary code.) After the EXFMT
operation, when control is returned to the program, I check the mode and set indicator 10 appropriately. If the mode is "0", or *OFF, which means the subfile was
in folded mode, I will set indicator 10 on so that when the subfile is displayed
again, it is displayed in folded mode. If the mode is "1", which means that the
subfile was in truncated mode, I will set 10 off (N10) to ensure that the subfile is
displayed in truncated mode the next time it is thrown to the screen. You can find
the complete RPG code for this program (SFL010RG) at the end of this chapter.

```
C                       if        mode = *off
C                       eval      *in10 = *on
C                       else
C                       eval      *in10 = *off
C                       endif
```

Figure 1.12: This code will allow the subfile mode to "stick" when the subfile is redisplayed.

A LITTLE WORK GOES A LONG WAY

By using SFLFOLD, SFLDROP, and SFLMODE together, I have not really done anything that can't be done by using either SFLDROP or SFLFOLD by itself without
SFLMODE and the RPG modifications. What I have done is provide the user with
a more consistently acting display and, because the mode will only change if the
F11 key is pressed, more control. In my opinion, it's worth the little extra work.

THE LAST WORD ON SFLFOLD AND SFLDROP

SFLFOLD and SFLDROP can only be used when SFLPAG and SFLSIZ aren't equal. If
SFLPAG and SFLSIZ are equal (something we'll look at in the next chapter),
SFLFOLD and SFLDROP are ignored. Also, when you're using both keywords in a
subfile control format, they must both use the same function key as a parameter.
It's a requirement.

THE FINE PRINT

Before we go on, I thought I would give you a taste of the DDS keywords and RPG operations you can use with subfiles. As you go along in this book, you'll see an example of most of the DDS keywords listed in Tables 1.1 and 1.2, and all of the RPG operations in Table 1.3. In some cases, I simply mention where a keyword might be used and what it will do, leaving it up to you to modify any chapter's given program or programs for use with that keyword. Having said that, however, I tried to provide an example of each keyword, unless it just didn't make sense to create a whole new program for that keyword.

Notice that only a smattering of what's available was used in previous examples. That's okay—and normal. I have never written a subfile program that used all the available DDS keywords and RPG operations. In most cases, I use only a smattering. The difference, depending on what I am trying to accomplish, is that my smattering varies from time to time. Note that you may use other, non-subfile keywords when defining your subfile. I used the OVERLAY keyword in my example. The list below contains only subfile-specific keywords.

Also notice that most of the DDS keywords mentioned in the list below are subfile specific, whereas only one RPG operation code is subfile-specific.

Table 1.1: Subfile Control Record Keywords (SFLCTL).

Keyword	Description
SFLCLR	Clears the subfile of all records
SFLMSG	Used for subfile messages
SFLDLT	Deletes the subfile
SFLMSGID	Used for subfile message identifications
SFLDROP	Enables a command key to fold or truncate subfile records
SFLPAG	The number of records to display on one page (screen) of data
SFLDSP	Controls when the subfile is displayed
SFLRCDNBR	Displays the page of a subfile based on the subfile record number
SFLDSPCTL	Controls when the subfile control record is displayed

Table 1.1: Subfile Control Record Keywords (SFLCTL) (continued).

Keyword	Description
SFLRNA	Allows for nonactive subfile records
SFLEND	Tells the users if they are at the end of a subfile or if there are more records to display
SFLROLVAL	Rolls records by specified number instead of by page
SFLENTER	Enables the enter key to work as the page-up key
SFLRTNSEL	Returns all selections chosen in a selection list when asked by the RPG program
SFLFOLD	Enables a command key to fold or truncate subfile records
SFLSCROLL	Returns to relative record number of the record at the top of the current page
SFLINZ	Initializes subfile records to their default values
SFLSIZ	Specifies the size of the subfile
SFLLIN	Specifies the number of spaces between subfile records located on the same line
SFLSNGCHC	Defines a single-choice selection list
SFLMLTCHC	Defines a multiple-choice selection list
ROLLUP	Allows the ability to scroll through the data (same as PAGEDOWN)
PAGEDOWN	Allows the ability to scroll through the data (same as ROLLUP)
ROLLDOWN	Allows the ability to scroll back through the data (same as PAGEUP)
PAGEUP	Allows the ability to scroll back through the data (same as ROLLDOWN)

Table 1.2: Subfile Record Keywords (SFL).

Keyword	Description
SFL	Identifies the subfile record format
SFLMODE	Determines whether the subfile was in folded or truncated mode
SFLCHCCTL	Controls the availability of choices in a selection list
SFLMSGKEY	Allows a subfile to contain messages from a program message queue

Table 1.2: Subfile Record Keywords (SFL) (continued).

Keyword	Description
SFLCSRPRG	Specifies cursor progression for a subfile
SFLMSGRCD	Also allows a subfile to contain messages from a program message queue
SFLCSRRRN	Determines where the cursor is located within the subfile
SFLNXTCHG	Returns the next changed subfile record when asked by the RPG program
SFLCTL	Identifies the subfile control record format
SFLPGMQ	Third in the trilogy of subfiles and program message queues

Table 1.3: RPG Operation Codes Used with the Subfile Control Record Format (SFLCTL).

Op code	Description
WRITE	Controls to subfile control record format
EXFMT	Displays the subfile to the screen and waits for a response from the user
READ	Reads from the subfile control record format

Table 1.4: RPG Operation Codes Used with the Subfile Record Format (SFL).

Op code	Description
WRITE	Writes to the subfile record format
CHAIN	Gets a subfile record by relative record number
UPDATE	Updates the contents of a subfile record
READC	Reads the next changed record from a subfile

SUBFILE TRIVIA FOR THAT SPECIAL MOMENT

A maximum of 24 subfiles can be active at any one time. A maximum of 12 subfiles can be displayed on the base screen or in a single window at any one time. I can't tell you how many times I've used this information to wow colleagues at work and impress friends at social gatherings. Actually, I can tell you—never! However, I would be wowed and impressed if someone came up with a valid application where these numbers were too limiting (remember that I said "valid").

SUMMARY AND CODE EXAMPLES

- The subfile control record format (SFLCTL) handles the whole subfile, whereas the subfile record format (SFL) handles individual subfile records.

- Most of the work in a subfile is done in the DDS and by OS/400.

- With just a few RPG operations, most of which you already know, you can process subfiles in your program.

- The four required DDS keywords are SFL, SFLCTL, SFLSIZ, and SFLPAG.

- SFLFOLD and SFLDROP are used to toggle between a display of a full, multiple-line subfile record and its truncated, single-line version.

SFL001PF: Physical file for Name Master

```
A                                       UNIQUE
A          R PFR
A            DBIDNM        7  0
A            DBFNAM       20
A            DBLNAM       20
A            DBMINI        1
A            DBNNAM       20
A            DBADD1       30
A            DBADD2       30
A            DBADD3       30
A          K DBIDNM
```

SFL001LF: Logical File over the Name Master

```
A                 R PFR                    PFILE(SFL001PF)
A                 K DBLNAM
A                 K DBFNAM
```

SFL001DF: Display File for Name Master Subfile Program

```
*=============================================================================
*
*   To compile:
*
*               CRTDSPF FILE(XXX/SFL001DF) SRCFILE(XXX/QDDSSRC)
*
*=============================================================================
A*
A                                          DSPSIZ(24 80 *DS3)
A                                          PRINT
A                                          ERRSFL
A                                          CA03
A                                          CA12
A*
A                 R SFL1                   SFL
A*
A                   DBLNAM     R       O  5  2REFFLD(PFR/DBLNAM *LIBL/SFL001PF)
A                   DBFNAM     R       O  5 26REFFLD(PFR/DBFNAM *LIBL/SFL001PF)
A                   DBMINI     R       O  5 50REFFLD(PFR/DBMINI *LIBL/SFL001PF)
A                   DBNNAM     R       O  5 55REFFLD(PFR/DBNNAM *LIBL/SFL001PF)
A*
A                 R SF1CTL                 SFLCTL(SFL1)
A*
A                                          SFLSIZ(0500)
A                                          SFLPAG(0017)
A                                          OVERLAY
A N32                                      SFLDSP
A N31                                      SFLDSPCTL
A   31                                     SFLCLR
A   90                                     SFLEND(*MORE)
A                   RRN1       4S OH       SFLRCDNBR
A                                        4  2'Last Name'
A                                          DSPATR(HI)
A                                        4 26'First Name'
A                                          DSPATR(HI)
A                                        4 50'MI'
A                                          DSPATR(HI)
A                                        4 55'Nick Name'
A                                          DSPATR(HI)
A                                        1  2'SFL001RG'
A                                        1 27'Simple Subfile Program'
A                                          DSPATR(HI)
```

SFL001DF: Display File for Name Master Subfile Program (continued)

```
A                                      1 71DATE
A                                        EDTCDE(Y)
A                                      2 71TIME
A*
A          R FKEY1
A*
A                                     23  2'F3=Exit'
A                                        COLOR(BLU)
A                                     23 12'F12=Cancel'
A                                        COLOR(BLU)
```

SFL001RG: RPG Program to Display Name Master File

```
*
*   To compile:
*
*              CRTRPGPGM PGM(XXX/SFL001RG) SRCFILE(XXX/QRPGLESRC)
*
*=======================================================================
Fsfl001df  cf   e            workstn
F                                      sfile(sfl1:rrn1)
Fsfl001lf  if   e            k disk
*
***********************************************************************
*  Main Routine
***********************************************************************
*
* Build the subfile
*
C                 exsr      sflbld
*
* Do loop to process the subfile until F3 or F12 is pressed
*
C                 dou       *inkc or *inkl
*
C                 write     fkey1
C                 exfmt     sf1ctl
*
C                 enddo
*
C                 eval      *inlr = *on
*
***********************************************************************
*   SFLBLD - Build the List
***********************************************************************
*
C     sflbld      begsr
*
```

SFL001RG: RPG Program to Display Name Master File (continued)

```
 *   Clear subfile
 *
C                eval      rrn1 = *zero
C                eval      *in31 = *on
C                write     sf1ctl
C                eval      *in31 = *off
 *
 * Load data to subfile
 *
C       *loval   setll     sfl0011f
C                read      sfl0011f                        90

C                dow       (not *in90) and (rrn1 <= 500)
C                eval      rrn1 = rrn1 + 1
C                write     sfl1
C                read      sfl0011f                        90
C                enddo
 *
 * If no records were loaded, do not display the subfile
 *
C                if        rrn1 = *zero
C                eval      *in32 = *on
C                else
C                eval      rrn1 = 1
C                endif
 *
C                endsr
```

SFL010DF: DDS for SFLFOLD/SFLDROP Toggle Program

```
 *===========================================================================
 *
 *   To compile:
 *
 *           CRTDSPF FILE(XXX/SFL010DF) SRCFILE(XXX/QDDSSRC)
 *
 *===========================================================================
A*
A                                DSPSIZ(24 80 *DS3)
A                                PRINT
A                                ERRSFL
A                                CA03
A                                CA12
A*
A       R SFL1                   SFL
A*
A         DBLNAM    R      O  5  2REFFLD(PFR/DBLNAM *LIBL/SFL001PF)
A         DBFNAM    R      O  5 26REFFLD(PFR/DBFNAM *LIBL/SFL001PF)  →
```

SFL010DF: DDS for SFLFOLD/SFLDROP Toggle Program (continued)

```
A              DBMINI    R        O  5 50REFFLD(PFR/DBMINI *LIBL/SFL001PF)
A              DBNNAM    R        O  5 55REFFLD(PFR/DBNNAM *LIBL/SFL001PF)
A              DBADD1    R        O  6  5REFFLD(PFR/DBADD1 *LIBL/SFL001PF)
A              DBADD2    R        O  6 37REFFLD(PFR/DBADD2 *LIBL/SFL001PF)
A*
A         R SF1CTL                   SFLCTL(SFL1)
A*
A                                    SFLSIZ(0500)
A                                    SFLPAG(0008)
A                                    OVERLAY
A N32                                SFLDSP
A N31                                SFLDSPCTL
A  31                                SFLCLR
A  90                                SFLEND(*MORE)
A N10                                SFLDROP(CA11)
A  10                                SFLFOLD(CA11)
A                                    SFLMODE(&MODE)
A              MODE        1   H
A              RRN1        4S OH     SFLRCDNBR
A                                  4  2'Last Name'
A                                    DSPATR(HI)
A                                  4 26'First Name'
A                                    DSPATR(HI)
A                                  4 50'MI'
A                                    DSPATR(HI)
A                                  4 55'Nick Name'
A                                    DSPATR(HI)
A                                  1  2'SFL010RG'
A                                  1 27'Simple Subfile Program'
A                                    DSPATR(HI)
A                                  1 71DATE
A                                    EDTCDE(Y)
A                                  2 71TIME
A*
A         R FKEY1
A*
A                                 23  2'F3=Exit'
A                                    COLOR(BLU)
A                                    +3'F11=Fold/Drop'
A                                    COLOR(BLU)
A                                    +3'F12=Cancel'
A                                    COLOR(BLU)
```

SFL010RG: RPG Program for SFLFOLD/SFLDROP Toggle

```
 *
 *  To compile:
 *
 *              CRTRPGPGM PGM(XXX/SFL001RG) SRCFILE(XXX/QRPGLESRC)
 *
 *========================================================================
Fsf1010df  cf   e                workstn
F                                       sfile(sfl1:rrn1)
Fsf1001lf  if   e           k disk
 *
 ****************************************************************
 *  Main Routine
 ****************************************************************
 *
 *  Build the subfile
 *
C                   exsr      sflbld
 *
 *  Do loop to process the subfile until F3 or F12 is pressed
 *
C                   dou       *inkc or *inkl
 *
C                   write     fkey1
C                   exfmt     sf1ctl
 *
C                   if        mode = *off
C                   eval      *in10 = *off
C                   else
C                   eval      *in10 = *on
C                   endif
 *
C                   enddo
 *
C                   eval      *inlr = *on
 *
 ****************************************************************
 *   SFLBLD - Build the List
 ****************************************************************
 *
C     sflbld        begsr
 *
 *  Clear subfile
 *
C                   eval      rrn1 = *zero
C                   eval      *in31 = *on
C                   write     sf1ctl
C                   eval      *in31 = *off
 *
 *  Load data to subfile
 *
```

SFL010RG: RPG Program for *SFLFOLD/SFLDROP* Toggle (continued)

```
C       *loval         setll     sfl0011f
C                      read      sfl0011f                              90

C                      dow       (not *in90) and (rrn1 <= 500)
C                      eval      rrn1 = rrn1 + 1
C                      write     sfl1
C                      read      sfl0011f                              90
C                      enddo
 *
 * If no records were loaded, do not display the subfile
 *
C                      if        rrn1 = *zero
C                      eval      *in32 = *on
C                      else
C                      z-add     1                 rrn1
C                      endif
 *
C                      endsr
```

2

A Subfile Type
for Every Occasion

As mentioned in chapter 1, there are three types of subfiles. The previous one was a load-all subfile, which allows the records to be loaded to the subfile at one time, before the subfile is displayed. What makes this program a load-all subfile is that OS/400 handles the paging for you, and all your records are displayed at the beginning of the program, before the data is displayed to the user. Notice in your RPG program that there's no code to allow you to page up or down through your subfile. You have only one routine that loads all the data from your data file until either the end-of-file is reached or the maximum number of records allowed in your subfile (500 in this example) is reached.

This type of subfile is very easy to code and can allow you to get a working application up and running rather quickly. It's great if you're certain about the number of records you want to display. Because OS/400 handles the paging for you, you can just load and display. The user can page through the data, and you don't even code for it in your RPG.

But as with everything, if something seems too good to be true, it probably is. The problem with load-all subfiles comes when the amount of data increases. Maybe there are more records that need to be loaded. The program will not blow up—we've coded for that in the DOW loop—but the data will not display. I could modify the DDS and change the SFLIZ keyword as high as 9,999, and then go into the RPG program and change the SUBFILE_SIZE constant to match the SFLSIZ keyword. Now all the data will be loaded—as long as the number of records doesn't exceed 9,999. But what about the poor user who has to scroll through seemingly endless pages of data to find what he's looking for?

That's another potential problem with the load-all subfile program and OS/400-controlled paging. The user might have to page through several pages to get to the data he wants. This can be time consuming, especially if the data is closer to the bottom of the list. One last pitfall to the load-all technique is the potential performance implications incurred when so much data is loaded at one time. Not only does it take some time to load thousands of records to a subfile, but the task also requires a considerable amount of system resources.

You have to be careful when using the load-all technique. You have to balance between how many records you want to display, how many potential pages you want the user to page through to get the desired information, and the potential performance issues of loading the maximum amount of data you're going to allow. So, let's say you are not sure how many records will be displayed. Or you know the number, but it's relatively high (for example, 1,000). How do you best write a subfile program that will both display all the records but also allow the user easier access? You do this by using the second of the three subfile types: self-extending subfiles.

SELF-EXTENDING SUBFILES

Because you still can't load more than 9,999 records (this is a not-so-subtle hint that there might be a way to load more than 9,999), the self-extending subfile works the same as a load-all subfile. However, it differs in a couple of other ways. A self-extending subfile allows the user to add records to the subfile only when they are needed. Normally, this is done one page at a time, although it doesn't have to be. One advantage the self-extending subfile has over its load-all counterpart is that the subfile performance will be more consistent. By loading only a specified amount of data each time, your subfile is more likely to perform as expected. A load-all subfile may load 50 records one time and 500 records the next, depending on your data. Another advantage is that by using a self-extending subfile and a position-to technique, I can make the navigation within the subfile more flexible.

Let's take a look at the DDS and the RPG program and compare them to the load-all technique discussed earlier. (The complete DDS and RPG for the programs used here can be found at the end of this chapter. I'll be showing you only the parts of the code that are pertinent or different from previous examples.) First, let's take a gander at the DDS. SFL002DF looks much like the load-all DDS, with the exception of a few changes. Figure 2.1 shows the subfile control record from the DDS, which is the only part of the DDS that has any changes.

```
A               R SF1CTL                    SFLCTL(SFL1)
A*
A                                           SFLSIZ(0018)
A                                           SFLPAG(0017)
A                                           OVERLAY
A                                           ROLLUP(27)
A N32                                       SFLDSP
A N31                                       SFLDSPCTL
A   31                                      SFLCLR
A   90                                      SFLEND(*MORE)
A               RRN1          4S 0H         SFLRCDNBR
A                                      4  2'Last Name'
A                                           DSPATR(HI)
A                                      4 26'First Name'
A                                           DSPATR(HI)
A                                      4 50'MI'
A                                           DSPATR(HI)
A                                      4 55'Nick Name'
A                                           DSPATR(HI)
A                                      1  2'SFL002RG'
A                                      1 71DATE
A                                           EDTCDE(Y)
A                                      2 71TIME
A                                      1 25'Self-Extending Subfile Program'
A                                           DSPATR(HI)
```

Figure 2.1: DDS control file record for a self-extending subfile (SFL002DF).

Notice that I changed the SFLSIZ from 500 to 18. This doesn't really mean much because both the load-all and self-extending subfiles require that the SFLSIZ be greater than the SFLPAG. Where it really matters is in how you load the subfile in your RPG code. I could have used 500 here too, but my standard for self-extending subfiles is to make SFLSIZ one greater than SFLPAG and only load one page of records at a time in my RPG program.

Next, notice that I added the ROLLUP keyword. This will allow my RPG program to control when more records are added to the subfile. With a self-extending subfile, it's important to note that the duties of paging through the data will be shared by your RPG program and OS/400. By adding the ROLLUP keyword, I've told OS/400 that whenever the last page of the subfile is displayed and the user presses the Page Down key to get more data, my program will take control and handle the paging. When the user isn't on the last page, or anytime he is paging back through the data, I want OS/400 to handle the paging. I will discuss this more when I get to the RPG code.

Now that we've looked at the DDS and seen that there weren't many changes necessary to making this a self-extending subfile, let's glance at the RPG program (SFL002RG) and see what's going on there. Figure 2.2 shows the F and D specs for the program.

```
     *=================================================================
     Fsfl002df  cf   e                   workstn
     F                                        sfile(sfl1:rrn1)
     Fsfl0011f  if   e             k disk

     Dsflpag          C                       const(17)

     Dlstrrn          S             4  0 inz(0)
```

Figure 2.2: Standard F and D specs in the subfile programs (SFL002RG).

Notice that I included a stand-alone field called LSTRRN. This field will be used to contain the last relative record number written to the subfile during the subfile load routine. When the user presses the Roll Up key, the program will know where in the subfile to start writing records.

Notice also that I have separated the clearing of the subfile from the loading of the subfile by placing the tasks in two separate subroutines. I do this in a self-extending subfile program because I don't want to clear the subfile every time I load records. Because I'm going to add records to the subfile when the user presses the Roll Up key, I don't want to clear it first. We'll get to the mainline of the program in a moment, but first let's look at the clear subfile routine, as shown in Figure 2.3.

```
     ********************************************************************
     *   CLRSFL - Clear the subfile
     ********************************************************************
     *
     C     clrsfl        begsr
     *
     * Clear relative record numbers and subfile
     *
     C                   eval      rrn1 = *zero
     C                   eval      lstrrn = *zero
     C                   eval      *in31 = *on
     C                   write     sflctl
     C                   eval      *in31 = *off
     C                   eval      *in32 = *off

     C                   endsr
```

Figure 2.3: Clear routine for the self-extending subfile (SFL002RG).

In the CLRSFL subroutine, I set my relative record number (RRN1) to 0 and also set a last relative record number (LSTRRN) to 0. I'll use LSTRRN to hold the last relative record of the subfile so that when I add records to the subfile, I'll know where I left off.

After setting on indicator 31, which conditions the SFLCLR keyword, I write to the subfile control record format to clear the subfile. Then I set indicator 31 off, which conditions the SFLDSPCTL keyword, and set off indicator 32, which conditions the SFLDSP keyword.

```
*****************************************************************
*  SFLBLD - Build the List
*****************************************************************
*
C       sflbld        begsr
*
* Make RRN1 = to the last relative record number of the subfile
* so that the load process will correctly add records to the bottom
*
C                     eval      rrn1 = lstrrn
*
* Load the subfile with one page of data or until end-of-file
*
C                     do        sflpag
C                     read      sfl0011f                        90
C                     if        *in90
C                     leave
C                     endif
C                     eval      rrn1 = rrn1 + 1
C                     write     sfl1
C                     enddo
*
C                     if        rrn1 = *zero
C                     eval      *in32 = *on
C                     endif
*
C                     eval      lstrrn = rrn1
*
C                     endsr
```

Figure 2.4: Load routine for the self-extending subfile (SFL002RG).

My subfile load routine (see Figure 2.4) is a little different than the load routine in the load-all subfile. This is mainly because I'm only going to load one page of data at a time, and not all the available records from my database file. In this case, field SFLPAG was set as a constant in my D specs and will contain the same number as used with the SFLPAG keyword in DDS. If you decide to change the keyword in the DDS, you'll have to change the D spec in your RPG. Don't let the fact that they have the same name fool you. I just like doing it that way.

If end-of-file is reached, indicator 90 will come on, and I will exit the loop. Indicator 90 also conditions SFLEND. Otherwise, I increment the relative record by one and write to the subfile record format. Once the loop has finished its work by either writing the prescribed number of records to the subfile (17 in this case) or hitting end-of-file, I check to determine whether I should display the subfile by conditioning indicator 32 and then set LSTRRN appropriately.

Now, let's go back to the main routine, where you'll see a more complex DOU loop than that contained in the load-all subfile. Figure 2.5 shows the mainline code.

```
 *
 * Clear then build the initial subfile
 *
C                      exsr      clrsfl
C                      exsr      sflbld
 *

 * Do loop to process the subfile until F3 or F12 is pressed
 *
C                      dou       (*inkc = *on) or (*inkl = *on)
 *
C                      write     fkey1
C                      exfmt     sflctl
 *
C                      select
 *
 * Add more records to the subfile if user is at the bottom
 *
C                      when      *in27 and not *in32
C                      exsr      sflbld

C                      endsl
C                      enddo

C                      eval      *inlr = *on

 *
```

Figure 2.5: Mainline routine for the self-extending subfile (SFL002RG).

This isn't very complex. I've added the code to handle the Roll Up key to the original load-all mainline. Remember that I used 27 with the ROLLUP keyword in the DDS, which means that when the Page Down (ROLLUP) key is pressed, indicator 27 will be set on. If indicator 27 is on and the subfile isn't empty (*IN32 is off), I simply execute the SFLBLD subroutine, which will add to the subfile from where it left off, without clearing it.

Let's go back to the EXFMT command for a minute. Remember that I said that with a self-extending subfile, paging duties are shared between your program and OS/400. This is where that decision takes place. Your program will sit on this line of code until a valid function key (as defined in your DDS) or the Enter key is pressed. However, when the Page Down key is pressed, OS/400 is smart enough to know whether it's about to page through data already in the subfile, in which case, it can handle the operation. If the last page of the subfile is already displayed, OS/400 knows to pass control back to your program.

OS/400 always handles the page-up (ROLLDOWN) duties in a self-extending subfile. Basically, this means that when you call your program for the first time, the first page of data will be displayed. If you press the Page Down key to get more records, control will pass back to your program and 17 more records will be written to the subfile. Now there will be 34 records in your subfile, and page two (records 18 through 34) will be displayed. If you press Page Up to get back to the first page of data, OS/400 will navigate that one for you and, because those records already exist in the subfile, your program will do nothing. If you decide to page down again to get to the second page, OS/400 will also handle that because records 18 through 34 already exist. If you decide to see a third page—you guessed it—control is passed to your program to add 17 new records to your subfile. The self-extending subfile is probably the most widely used type of subfile. It balances nicely between letting OS/400 handle a bit of the processing while allowing you to add some code to increase flexibility for the user.

ADD SOME OOMPH

Now that you have the self-extending basics down, I want to show you some techniques you can use to make your subfile programs more flexible for the user and easier to code and understand for the programmer.

One thing I like to do in my subfile programs is give the user an additional navigation tool. It could get tedious, for instance, if a user is interested in a name beginning with "V" and the file contains thousands of names listed in alphabetical order. It would be nice if the user could position to the names starting with "V" and page from there. Better yet, if the user knows the exact name, he could position to that location without using the page keys at all. The position-to field allows that flexibility. It isn't required, but I always use a position-to field in the subfile control record format whenever I create a subfile. To me, writing a subfile program without position-to capabilities is like being forced to stop on every floor of a high-rise building even if you live on the top floor. Adding the position-to capability gives you the ability to go directly to the floor at which you want to get off.

The position-to field provides the ability for the user to select the exact position in the subfile to which he wants to navigate. If the "A"s in my name list are displayed, I can enter a name, or partial name, starting with "Z" in my position-to field and the subfile will position to the "Z"s, or the name that is closest to "Z" if there are no "Z"s in the file. Let's take another look at the subfile control format from SFL002RG. This time, I've added a position-to field call PTNAME. Figure 2.6 shows the pumped-up control record format.

```
A             R SFICTL              SFLCTL(SFL1)
A*
A                                   SFLSIZ(0016)
A                                   SFLPAG(0015)
A                                   OVERLAY
A                                   ROLLUP
A N32                               SFLDSP
A N31                               SFLDSPCTL
A   31                              SFLCLR
A   90                              SFLEND(*MORE)
A             RRN1        4S OH     SFLRCDNBR
A                                 6  2'Last Name'
A                                    DSPATR(HI)
A                                 6 26'First Name'
A                                    DSPATR(HI)
A                                 6 50'MI'
A                                    DSPATR(HI)
A                                 6 55'Nick Name'
A                                    DSPATR(HI)
A                                 1  2'SFL002RG1'
A                                 1 71DATE
A                                    EDTCDE(Y)
A                                 2 71TIME
A                                 1 24'Subfile Program with Position To'
A                                    DSPATR(HI)
A                                 4  2'Position to Last Name . . .'
A             PTNAME      20  B   4 30CHECK(LC)
```

Figure 2.6: Subfile control format with position-to field PTNAME (SFL002DF1).

To make room for the position-to field, I changed the SFLPAG keyword from 17 to 15 and, in keeping with my standard of assigning SFLSIZ as one greater than SFLPAG for self-extending subfiles, I changed SFLSIZ from 18 to 16. Now I have room to add the position-to field, PTNAME, on line 4 of the screen. I define it as a 20-byte field, which matches the field length for the LAST NAME field in my data file, and allow entry in the field by placing a "B" in position 38. The CHECK keyword with the LC parameter allows the user to key in lowercase characters.

The only logic necessary in the RPG program to make this work is an IF block in the mainline routine that determines if something was entered in the position-to field. If something was entered, clear the subfile by executing the CLRSFL routine, position the data file with a SETLL operation using the PTNAME field, load the subfile by calling the SFLBLD routine, and clear the PTNAME field before displaying the subfile to the screen. Figure 2.7 shows an example of the block of code you might use for this.

```
C                      if        ptname   *blanks
C        ptname        setll     sfl001lf
C                      exsr      clrsfl
C                      exsr      sflbld
C                      clear                    ptname
C                      endif
```

Figure 2.7: Mainline logic to handle the position-to field (SFL002RG1).

No matter where you are in your subfile, the subfile will be cleared when you key something into the PTNAME field, and 15 new records will be written and displayed based on what was entered into the PTNAME field. Figures 2.8 and 2.9 show what happens when the position-to field is used.

Figure 2.8 shows the file beginning with the last name "Anthony." If you want to position the file to "Vandever," simply key that into the position-to field and press Enter. The list will be repositioned, as shown in Figure 2.9.

```
SFL002RG              Subfile Program with Position To              1/20/00
                                                                  18:08:30

Position to Last Name . . . Vandever

Last Name             First Name        MI   Nick Name
Anthony               Tony              A    Triple A
Bert                  Al                C    Alphabet Man
Coker                 Jim               L    Da AS/400 Guru
Harrison              Harry             H    Happy
Johnson               John              J    JJ
Naisium               Jim               B    Sweaty
Patterson             Gary              R    The All-Knowing One
Saint                 Louis             A    Missouri
Samuelson             Sam               S    The snake
Simpson               Othello           K    Don't call me OJ
Stevenson             Steve             S    Mike
Tessential            Quinn             C    Important
Thompson              Tom               T    Triple T
Vandever              Corina            B    Wife of Subfile Man
Vandever              Felicia           R    Cub
                                                            More...

F3=Exit    F12=Cancel
```

Figure 2.8: Subfile example with a list of names.

```
SFL002RG              Subfile Program with Position To              1/20/00
                                                                  18:10:31

Position to Last Name . . .

Last Name             First Name        MI   Nick Name
Vandever              Corina            B    Wife of Subfile Man
Vandever              Felicia           R    Cub
Vandever              Kalia             M    Koo
Vandever              Kelly             M    FaderHead
Vandever              Kevin             M    Subfile Man
Vannerberg            Kern              X    kevin
Williamson            William           W    The web
Zachery               Zak               Z    The snoozer




                                                            Bottom
F3=Exit    F12=Cancel
```

Figure 2.9: The file is repositioned to "Vandever."

EVEN MORE OOMPH

One last technique I want to show you before we move on is a better way to handle the Enter and function keys in your program. If you look back at Figure 2.5, you'll see that the F3 and F12 keys are represented by *INKC and *INKL, respectively, and the Roll Up key is represented by *IN27. Because these aren't very intuitive labels, they don't easily allow someone to follow what's going on in the code. You may also notice that the Enter key isn't represented at all. There's no keyword entry in DDS for the Enter key and no indicator to associate with it. Therefore, it's common in a display program to assume that Enter has been pressed only after all the other valid function keys and page keys have been checked. This isn't the most efficient way to process the display program because the Enter key is the key that is pressed most often. Wouldn't it be nice if you could provide more descriptive names for the function keys, as well as include a way to process the Enter key explicitly, before the other keys are checked? Well, you can do just that by including the file information data structure in your program and using the attention indictor byte from the data structure to determine which key has been pressed.

```
Fsfl002df1 cf   e                    workstn
F                                    sfile(sfl1:rrn1)
F                                    infds(info)
Fsfl001lf  if   e           k disk

Dinfo           ds
D cfkey                369    369

Dexit           C                    const(X'33')
Dcancel         C                    const(X'3C')
Denter          C                    const(X'F1')
Drollup         C                    const(X'F5')
Dsflpag         C                    const(15)
```

Figure 2.10: F and D specs for file information data structure with an attention indicator byte (SFL002RG1).

Let's make some more changes to our self-extending subfile to incorporate this new technique. First of all, the only change you need to make in the DDS is to remove the parameter 27 from the ROLLUP keyword. You will no longer need to associate an indicator with ROLLUP. Now let's take a look at additions made to the RPG program. Figure 2.10 shows how to define the attention indicator byte.

Notice the addition of D specs and an extra F spec. The additional F spec defines a data structure (INFO) as the file information data structure for the display file SFL002DF1. In the D specs, notice that the INFO data structure contains only one field, CFKEY. The file information data structure contains all kinds of data about its associated file, but I'm only interested in one byte of it. When the user presses a valid key and control returns back to the RPG program, CFKEY will contain a hexadecimal representation of the key pressed.

I next set up constants to define more meaningful names to the hexadecimal values. Now, instead of using INKC to condition code when F3 is pressed, I can use the word "exit." You'll see what I mean as we get into the code. Please note that the new F and D specs just explained are not specific to subfiles. If you already have a method of processing display files, use it. I just thought it might be thoughtful to share my programming techniques with you, even if they're not related specifically to subfiles.

Figure 2.11 shows the addition of the position-to field and use of the new constants to the original self-extending mainline routine. Notice the first use of the CFKEY value. After writing the function key line and throwing the subfile as you've seen before, I code a SELECT routine to handle the possible responses from the user. I like to use the SELECT and WHEN clauses because they make my program more modular—and therefore easier to read. Once a WHEN clause is satisfied, the remaining clauses are ignored. As a result, it makes sense to validate the keys in the order of their potential use. If you think Enter is going to be pressed most often, check for the Enter key in your first WHEN clause. That's one of the advantages of the attention indicator byte; it allows you to specifically check for the Enter key. The responses I care about in the SELECT logic are Enter, Roll Up, F3, and F12. When Enter is pressed, I also want to know if something was keyed into the position-to field, PTNAME. If the Enter key is pressed after the user has keyed data into the position-to field, I'll use that data to position the file with a SETLL operation; execute the CLRSFL routine; load the subfile based on the position-to entry; and, finally, clear the position-to field (PTNAME) before displaying the subfile again.

```
     * Do loop to process the subfile until F3 or F12 is pressed
     *
     C                        dou        (cfkey = exit) or (cfkey = cancel)
     *
     C                        write      fkey1
     C                        exfmt      sf1ctl
     *
     * Process position to information entered by the user, then clear
     * and rebuild the subfile. Lastly, clear the position to field
     *
     C                        select
     C                        when       (cfkey = enter) and (ptname  *blanks)
     C        ptname          setll      sfl0011f
     C                        exsr       clrsfl
     C                        exsr       sflbld
     C                        clear                   ptname
     *
     * Add more records to the subfile if user is at the bottom
     *
     C                        when       (cfkey = rollup) and (not *in32)
     C                        exsr       sflbld

     C                        endsl
     C                        enddo
```

Figure 2.11: The mainline code using the new techniques.

Notice how I use the attention indicator byte so I can explicitly process the Enter key, which is typically the most-used key. Also notice how much easier the code is to read now that ROLLUP, instead of *IN27, is used for the Roll Up key, Enter is used for the Enter key, Exit for the F3 key, etc. Again, use of the attention indicator byte from the file information data structure and a position-to field are not required in a subfile program.

I introduce these techniques now because I use them throughout the rest of the book (as well as in all my subfile applications) and believe it's valuable information as you learn to code display programs. Now, let's get back to some subfile stuff.

PAGE-AT-A-TIME SUBFILE

The page-at-a-time subfile is yet a third type of subfile. While it requires a little more coding, it provides more flexibility to the user. The theory behind the page-at-a-time subfile is that you never have more than one page of data in your subfile at one time. The primary advantage of this type of subfile is that you aren't restricted to the 9,999-record limit of the load-all and self-extending subfiles.

Because the subfile is cleared and reloaded when each page key is pressed (up or down), you can page through an infinite amount of records. I've created a second advantage by adding a position-to field. Because you reload the subfile with each page key pressed, you can now page up from the beginning of a subfile list (as long as it's not the beginning of your data file).

With the self-extending subfile, if you used the position-to field, the data keyed into the position-to field determines the top of your list. The only way to get the previous data was to use the position-to field again. With the page-at-a-time subfile, when you use the position-to field, you can page up from the top of the list to get to previous data. This is because your program will handle both paging up and paging down. This type of subfile offers the most user flexibility, but it also requires the most code and can be the most performance-intensive.

Taking a look at the DDS for our page-at-a-time subfile (SFL003DF), notice that there are only two changes from a self-extending subfile. The first is that SFLPAG and SFLSIZ are the same. This means that your subfile will never contain more than one page of data.

If you attempt to load past the amount specified in SFLSIZ, you will get an error—so don't do that. The second change is that I've added the ROLLDOWN keyword. This tells OS/400 that your RPG program will now handle all the paging. Figure 2.12 shows the subfile control record. The rest of the DDS remains the same.

45

```
A           R SF1CTL                    SFLCTL(SFL1)
A*
A                                       SFLSIZ(0015)
A                                       SFLPAG(0015)
A                                       OVERLAY
A                                       ROLLUP
A                                       ROLLDOWN
A N32                                   SFLDSP
A N31                                   SFLDSPCTL
A   31                                  SFLCLR
A   90                                  SFLEND(*MORE)
A           RRN1          4S 0H         SFLRCDNBR
A                                    6  2'Last Name'
A                                       DSPATR(HI)
A                                    6 26'First Name'
A                                       DSPATR(HI)
A                                    6 50'MI'
A                                       DSPATR(HI)
A                                    6 55'Nick Name'
A                                       DSPATR(HI)
A                                    1  2'SFL002RG'
A                                    1 71DATE
A                                       EDTCDE(Y)
A                                    2 71TIME
A                                    1 24'Subfile Program with Position To'
A                                       DSPATR(HI)
A                                    4  2'Position to Last Name . . .'
A           PTNAME        20   B     4 30
```

Figure 2.12: Subfile control record for the page-at-a-time subfile (SFL003DF).

```
Dinfo          ds
D cfkey               369   369

Dsvlnam        S                  like(dblnam)
Dsvfnam        S                  like(dbfnam)

Dexit          C                  const(X'33')
Dcancel        C                  const(X'3C')
Denter         C                  const(X'F1')
Drollup        C                  const(X'F5')
Drolldn        C                  const(X'F4')
Dsflpag        C                  const(15)
Dsflpag_plus_1 C                  const(16)
```

Figure 2.13: D specs for page-at-a-time subfiles (SFL003RG).

While the RPG program is now a little more complex, as shown in Figures 2.12 through 2.14, it's still not too horribly complicated. In the D specs, I have added a couple of stand-alone fields, SVLNAM and SVFNAM. I will use these fields to store the first name and last name of the first subfile record. Because these fields make up the key to the database I'm using, I'll use them when the user wants to page up through the data (see Figure 2.13).

The mainline code has also changed. Let's look at the WHEN clause for a moment. When the user presses the Page Up key and the subfile has been displayed (indicator 32 is off), the GOBACK subroutine is executed. This subroutine is used for nothing other than setting the pointer correctly in the data file used for loading the subfile. I use the first record in my subfile to set lower limits (SETLL) in my data file, SFL001LF. I perform a DO loop that will read previous records in the SFL001LF up to one greater than the SFLPAG parameter. If I hit the beginning of the data file before my loop is finished, I set lower limits with *LOVAL to position the pointer to the top of the file and get out of the loop. By the time the loop has completed, my data file pointer will either be positioned at the top of the file or at some point in the file, as determined by what is contained in SAVKEY and SFLPAG_PLUS_1.

After the GOBACK subroutine is executed, I clear the subfile and load a new page based on where I left off in the GOBACK subroutine. The user can now page up or down from anywhere in the subfile, with the only limits being the beginning and end of the data file. This removes the 9,999-record limit, which may be helpful in many cases.

During the SFLBLD routine, when the subfile relative record number (RRN1) is equal to 1, I move DBLNAM to SVLNAM and DBFNAM to SVFNAM. That sets those fields for later use. You'll also notice that I added a ROLLDN constant. My program will now handle both paging down and paging up through the subfile. The last D spec you see, which is also new, will be used during the page-up process. The main routine of this program resembles what you've seen before, with the exception of the page-up processing caused by adding the ROLLDN keyword in the DDS.

Figure 2.14 shows the mainline routine.

```
 *
 *****************************************************************
 *  Main Routine
 *****************************************************************
 *
 * Clear then build the initial subfile
 *
C                     exsr      clrsfl
C                     exsr      sflbld
 *
 * Do loop to process the subfile until F3 or F12 is pressed
 *
C                     dou       (cfkey = exit) or (cfkey = cancel)
 *
C                     write     fkey1
C                     exfmt     sf1ctl
 *
 * Process position to information entered by the user, then clear
 * and rebuild the subfile. Lastly, clear the position to field
 *
C                     select
C                     when      (cfkey = enter) and (ptname  *blanks)
C     ptname          setll     sfl0011f
C                     exsr      clrsfl
C                     exsr      sflbld
C                     clear                   ptname
 *
 * Clear and rebuild the subfile when user pages down (rolls up)
 *
C                     when      (cfkey = rollup) and (not *in90)
C                     exsr      clrsfl
C                     exsr      sflbld
 *
 * Position data file to one page before current subfile data, then
 * clear and rebuild the subfile to show that previous page
 *
C                     when      (cfkey = rolldn) and (not *in32)
C                     exsr      goback
C                     exsr      clrsfl
C                     exsr      sflbld

C                     endsl
C                     enddo

C                     eval      *inlr = *on
```

Figure 2.14: Mainline routine for the page-at-a-time subfile (SFL003RG).

The code for the build and clear routines stays the same as in previous programs, but we have added a new routine for paging back. This code is pretty simple. I first SETLL on the data file, SFL001LF, using the first and last names of the first subfile record (remember my use of SVLNAM and SVFNAM?). Then I read backwards in the file using the READP operation for one greater than the subfile page size, or until I hit the top of the file. At that point, my data file pointer is either at the top of the file or at the record that occupied the top of the previous subfile page. I then call the SFLBLD routine to build and display the previous page. Figure 2.15 shows the code.

```
      *
      ***************************************************************
      *  GOBACK - page backward one page
      ***************************************************************
      *
C     goback       begsr
      *
      * Position data file to first record of subfile
      *
C     savkey       setll        sfl001lf
      *
      * Re-position pointer in file for rolling backward. If beginning
      * of file hit before done, set pointer to first record of data file.
      *
C                  do           sflpag_plus_1
C                  readp        sfl001lf
C                  if           %eof
C     *loval       setll        sfl001lf
C                  leave
C                  endif
C                  enddo
      *
C                  endsr
```

Figure 2.15: Paging back in a page-at-a-time subfile (SFL003RG).

PAGING ALTERNATIVES

Up to this point, you've learned how to page through the subfile using the paging keys, page down (roll up), and page up (roll down). You've probably also noticed that each time you press the page key, you get a whole new page of data. This doesn't have to happen. You do have some flexibility when deciding how you

page through the data and which keys to use. Two subfile keywords, SFLENTER
and SFLROLVAL, give you this flexibility.

SFLENTER

Employ the SFLENTER keyword if you want to use the ENTER key to page down
through the data. Figure 2.16 shows how to code this keyword. It's used in the
subfile control format and performs some pretty cool stuff. By using this keyword, you allow the Enter and page-down keys to function in the same way (that
is, rolling up through a page of the subfile). That's right—not only don't you lose
any capabilities, but you gain the Enter key as another way to page down. The required parameter determines which key will now be used as the Enter key for this
screen. In my example, I use CF10, which means that the user will now press F10,
as the Enter key, to pass control back to the program. All this takes place without
any modifications to the RPG program. So go ahead and give it a shot. If you've
come from a S/36 shop where the Enter key was used to page through data
(subfiles don't exist on the S/36) or you just like the idea of pressing Enter to
page through the subfile, the SFLENTER keyword might be for you.

```
     A                                              SFLENTER(CF10)
```

*Figure 2.16: The SFLENTER keyword in the subfile control format allows you to use the En-
ter key as the roll-up key.*

SFLROLVAL

There are some cases when you may want to roll less than one page of data. The
SFLROLVAL keyword allows you to do just that. By specifying this field-level
keyword in the subfile control format, you allow the user to tell the system how
many records to roll. Figure 2.17 shows how to code this keyword. The ROLVAL
field is defined as input/output, which means the user can key into that field. The
user can key a number less than the value of SFLPAG, press the page-up or
page-down key, and the subfile will page that number of records. The value used
for paging will remain the same until the user changes it. If a number greater than
SFLPAG is keyed, the value in SFLPAG is used. If a negative number or zero is

entered, an error message will be displayed. SFLROLVAL is ignored for page-at-a-time subfiles (SFLSIZ equals SFLPAG). I suggest you give it a shot with either load-all or self-extending subfiles.

| A | ROLVAL 4S 0B 6 2 | SFLROLVAL |

Figure 2.17: The SFLROLVAL keyword allows the user to determine how many records, less than one page, to roll through.

How to Choose

You now have an understanding of the three subfile types. You've seen the subtle differences in coding and now may be wondering when to use which type. That's a good question. There are no rules carved in stone stating when to use each type of subfile, but there are some guidelines you can follow.

The load-all subfile is best used when the number of records in the data file from which you're loading is predictable and small. I say predictable *and* small because just one of those attributes is not good enough for a load-all subfile. You may have a data file with a predictable number of records, but that number is 10,000. That isn't a good candidate for a load-all subfile. On the other hand, you may have a data file with a relatively small number of records (50, for example), but if the number of records is going to increase and you're not sure by how many, you may want to avoid a load-all subfile. A prime candidate for a load-all subfile is a state inquiry program. In this case, you should be fairly certain how many records are contained in the file.

You'll need to determine which files and data criteria are good candidates for load-all processing. Over time, as the data matures, you could get yourself in trouble with load-all subfiles. Think about how long you want the user to wait to see the data. If the user has to wait more than a second or two, he may not be happy. You should also be aware of how many times a day the program will be run and by how many users.

51

The load-all subfile can be quite efficient and effective if coded properly. But it can impact performance and frustrate users if it's not. When coding a load-all program, you should set the SFLSIZ to the number of records you expect to be in the file. In the case of the state inquiry, you would set the SFLSIZ somewhere around 50. This is the number of records you expect to load every time this program is run. You wouldn't want to set the SFLSIZ of the state inquiry to 10. The program would still work and the user would still see all the data, but each time the subfile is forced to self-extend, the new records are not contiguous in memory with the originally loaded records. This will slow the program's processing.

Your best bet is to use the load-all process when you're fairly certain about the amount of data that will be loaded. Then you can set your SFLSIZ appropriately. The benefits of the load-all subfile are that it's CPU friendly and very easy to code because OS/400 handles so much of the work for you. If you start getting into situations where your load-all subfile is doing a lot of self-extension or you're adding logic to stop your load-all subfile from loading too much by conditioning the DO loop or the WRITE statement, it might be time to change from a load-all to a self-extending subfile.

When you're not sure of the number of records, you predict data growth, or you know how many records are in the file but there are too many to use a load-all subfile, the self-extending subfile might be your answer. The performance of a self-extending subfile is always consistent because you only load one page at a time. This type of program is a little more CPU intensive because it goes out to the disk every time new records are loaded to the subfile and the new records are not in contiguous memory with previously written records in the subfile. However, once the records are written, scrolling back and forth through them is performed by OS/400, as with a load-all subfile. When I'm not certain about the number of records or the potential growth rate of the data, I use this type of subfile.

If the number of potential records exceeds 9,999, I use the page-at-a-time subfile. By loading one page at a time, you're not limited by the number of records. This type of subfile is the most CPU intensive because the scrolling is all handled by the program. As a result, each time the user scrolls through the data, the program has to go out to disk to get that data. However, if there are hundreds, thousands, or even millions of potential records in your data file, this type of subfile (with position-to capabilities) is the way to go. I also use page-at-a-time subfiles when I want to add user flexibility to my application. As a programmer, you have more control over the subfile with page-at-a-time processing, and as you'll see in a later chapter, this can be beneficial.

You now have at your disposal a subfile type for every occasion. Whether the data has very few records, many records, potential growth, or certain stagnation, you can rest easy knowing you have a proper subfile sword to wield.

SUMMARY AND CODE EXAMPLES

There are three types of subfile program: load-all, self-extending, and page-at-a-time.

- SFLSIZ must be greater than SFLPAG by at least one when you're using load-all and self-extending subfiles.

- SFLSIZ and SFLPAG must be equal and set to whatever will fit on one page for page-at-a-time subfiles.

- Load-all and self-expanding subfiles have a 9,999-record maximum.

- A page-at-a-time subfile can only hold one page of data. Because of that, you would use this method to display data files with more that 9,999 records.

- The paging of data is completely handled by OS/400 in the load-all technique. No programming is necessary.

- Paging down is shared between OS/400 and your program in a self-extending subfile. Paging up is still handled by OS/400.

- Your program in a page-at-a-time subfile handles all the paging. You get no help from OS/400.

SFL002DF: Display File for Self-Extending Master File Listing

```
A                                        DSPSIZ(24 80 *DS3)
A                                        PRINT
A                                        ERRSFL
A                                        CA03
A                                        CA12
A*
A           R SFL1                       SFL
A*
A             DBLNAM    R     O   5  2REFFLD(PFR/DBLNAM *LIBL/SFL001PF)
A             DBFNAM    R     O   5 26REFFLD(PFR/DBFNAM *LIBL/SFL001PF)
A             DBMINI    R     O   5 50REFFLD(PFR/DBMINI *LIBL/SFL001PF)
A             DBNNAM    R     O   5 55REFFLD(PFR/DBNNAM *LIBL/SFL001PF)
A*
A           R SF1CTL                     SFLCTL(SFL1)
A*
A                                        SFLSIZ(0018)
A                                        SFLPAG(0017)
A                                        OVERLAY
A                                        ROLLUP(27)
A N32                                    SFLDSP
A N31                                    SFLDSPCTL
A   31                                   SFLCLR
A   90                                   SFLEND(*MORE)
A             RRN1          4S OH        SFLRCDNBR
A                                     4  2'Last Name'
A                                        DSPATR(HI)
A                                     4 26'First Name'
A                                        DSPATR(HI)
A                                     4 50'MI'
A                                        DSPATR(HI)
A                                     4 55'Nick Name'
A                                        DSPATR(HI)
A                                     1  2'SFL002RG'
A                                     1 71DATE
A                                        EDTCDE(Y)
A                                     2 71TIME
A                                     1 25'Self-Extending Subfile Program'
A                                        DSPATR(HI)
A*
A           R FKEY1
A*
A                                    23  2'F3=Exit'
A                                        COLOR(BLU)
A                                    23 12'F12=Cancel'
A                                        COLOR(BLU)
```

SFL002RG: RPG Program for Self-Extending Master File Listing

```
 *
 *   To compile:
 *
 *              CRTRPGPGM PGM(XXX/SFL002RG) SRCFILE(XXX/QRPGLESRC)
 *
 *========================================================================
Fsfl002df  cf   e              workstn
F                                        sfile(sfl1:rrn1)
Fsfl001lf  if   e          k disk

Dsflpag          C                       const(17)

Dlstrrn          S              4  0 inz(0)
 *
 ***********************************************************************
 *   Main Routine
 ***********************************************************************
 *
 * Clear then build the initial subfile
 *
C                   exsr      clrsfl
C                   exsr      sflbld
 *
 * Do loop to process the subfile until F3 or F12 is pressed
 *
C                   dou       (*inkc = *on) or (*inkl = *on)
 *
C                   write     fkey1
C                   exfmt     sfl1ctl
 *
C                   select
 *
 * Add more records to the subfile if user is at the bottom
 *
C                   when      *in27
C                   exsr      sflbld

C                   endsl
C                   enddo

C                   eval      *inlr = *on
 *
 ***********************************************************************
 *   CLRSFL - Clear the subfile
 ***********************************************************************
 *
C   clrsfl          begsr
 *
 * Clear relative record numbers and subfile
 *
```

SFL002RG: RPG Program for Self-Extending Master File Listing (continued)

```
C                     eval      rrn1 = *zero
    C                      eval      lstrrn = *zero
    C                      eval      *in31 = *on
    C                      write     sf1ctl
    C                      eval      *in31 = *off
    C                      eval      *in32 = *off

    C                      endsr
     *
     ****************************************************************
     *   SFLBLD - Build the List
     ****************************************************************
     *
    C     sflbld          begsr
     *
     * Make RRN1 = to the last relative record number of the subfile
     * so that the load process will correctly add records to the bottom
     *
    C                      eval      rrn1 = lstrrn
     *
     * Load the subfile with one page of data or until end-of-file
     *
    C                      do        sflpag
    C                      read      sfl001lf                              90
    C                      if        *in90
    C                      leave
    C                      endif
    C                      eval      rrn1 = rrn1 + 1
    C                      write     sfl1
    C                      enddo
     *
    C                      if        rrn1 = *zero
    C                      eval      *in32 = *on
    C                      endif
     *
    C                      eval      lstrrn = rrn1
     *
    C                      endsr
```

SFL002DF1: Display File with Position-to and Attention-Indicator Byte

```
A                                      DSPSIZ(24 80 *DS3)
A                                      PRINT
A                                      ERRSFL
A                                      CA03
A                                      CA12
A*
A           R SFL1                     SFL
A*
A             DBLNAM    R     O  7  2REFFLD(PFR/DBLNAM *LIBL/SFL001PF)
A             DBFNAM    R     O  7 26REFFLD(PFR/DBFNAM *LIBL/SFL001PF)
A             DBMINI    R     O  7 50REFFLD(PFR/DBMINI *LIBL/SFL001PF)
A             DBNNAM    R     O  7 55REFFLD(PFR/DBNNAM *LIBL/SFL001PF)
A*
A           R SF1CTL                   SFLCTL(SFL1)
A*
A                                      SFLSIZ(0016)
A                                      SFLPAG(0015)
A                                      OVERLAY
A                                      ROLLUP
A N32                                  SFLDSP
A N31                                  SFLDSPCTL
A   31                                 SFLCLR
A   90                                 SFLEND(*MORE)
A             RRN1          4S OH      SFLRCDNBR
A                                   6  2'Last Name'
A                                      DSPATR(HI)
A                                   6 26'First Name'
A                                      DSPATR(HI)
A                                   6 50'MI'
A                                      DSPATR(HI)
A                                   6 55'Nick Name'
A                                      DSPATR(HI)
A                                   1  2'SFL002RG'
A                                   1 71DATE
A                                      EDTCDE(Y)
A                                   2 71TIME
A                                   1 24'Subfile Program with Position To'
A                                      DSPATR(HI)
A                                   4  2'Position to Last Name . . .'
A             PTNAME       20  B  4 30
A*
A           R FKEY1
A*
A                                  23  2'F3=Exit'
A                                      COLOR(BLU)
A                                  23 12'F12=Cancel'
A                                      COLOR(BLU)
```

SFL002RG1: RPG Program with Position-to and Attention-Indicator Byte

```
     *
     *  To compile:
     *
     *            CRTRPGPGM PGM(XXX/SFL002RG) SRCFILE(XXX/QRPGLESRC)
     *
     *=======================================================================
Fsfl002df  cf   e              workstn
F                                      sfile(sfl1:rrn1)
F                                      infds(info)
Fsfl0011f  if   e           k disk

Dinfo            ds
D cfkey                  369     369

Dexit            C                     const(X'33')
Dcancel          C                     const(X'3C')
Denter           C                     const(X'F1')
Drollup          C                     const(X'F5')
Dsflpag          C                     const(15)

Dlstrrn          S              4  0 inz(0)
     *
     ******************************************************************
     *  Main Routine
     ******************************************************************
     *
     * Clear then build the initial subfile
     *
C                exsr      clrsfl
C                exsr      sflbld
     *
     * Do loop to process the subfile until F3 or F12 is pressed
     *
C                dou       (cfkey = exit) or (cfkey = cancel)
     *
C                write     fkey1
C                exfmt     sf1ctl
     *
     * Process position to information entered by the user, then clear
     * and rebuild the subfile. Lastly, clear the position to field
     *
C                select
C                when      (cfkey = enter) and (ptname  *blanks)
C       ptname   setll     sfl0011f
C                exsr      clrsfl
C                exsr      sflbld
C                clear                  ptname
     *
     * Add more records to the subfile if user is at the bottom
```

SFL002RG1: RPG Program with Position-to and Attention-Indicator Byte (continued)

```
*
C                   when      (cfkey = rollup) and (not *in32)
C                   exsr      sflbld

C                   endsl
C                   enddo

C                   eval      *inlr = *on
*
*******************************************************************
*   CLRSFL - Clear the subfile
*******************************************************************
*
C     clrsfl        begsr
*
* Clear relative record numbers and subfile
*
C                   eval      rrn1 = *zero
C                   eval      lstrrn = *zero
C                   eval      *in31 = *on
C                   write     sflctl
C                   eval      *in31 = *off
C                   eval      *in32 = *off

C                   endsr
*
*******************************************************************
*   SFLBLD - Build the List
*******************************************************************
*
C     sflbld        begsr
*
* Make RRN1 = to the last relative record number of the subfile
* so that the load process will correctly add records to the bottom
*
C                   eval      rrn1 = lstrrn
*
* Load the subfile with one page of data or until end-of-file
*
C                   do        sflpag
C                   read      sfl0011f                          90
C                   if        *in90
C                   leave
C                   endif
C                   eval      rrn1 = rrn1 + 1
C                   write     sfl1
C                   enddo
*
C                   if        rrn1 = *zero
C                   eval      *in32 = *on
C                   endif
```

59

SFL002RG1: RPG Program with Position-to and Attention-Indicator Byte (continued)

```
    *
    C                       eval      lstrrn = rrn1
    *
    C                       endsr
```

SFL003DF: Display File for Page-at-a-Time Master File Listing

```
    A                                          DSPSIZ(24 80 *DS3)
    A                                          PRINT
    A                                          ERRSFL
    A                                          CA03
    A                                          CA12
    A*
    A          R SFL1                          SFL
    A*
    A            DBLNAM    R     O  7  2REFFLD(PFR/DBLNAM *LIBL/SFL001PF)
    A            DBFNAM    R     O  7 26REFFLD(PFR/DBFNAM *LIBL/SFL001PF)
    A            DBMINI    R     O  7 50REFFLD(PFR/DBMINI *LIBL/SFL001PF)
    A            DBNNAM    R     O  7 55REFFLD(PFR/DBNNAM *LIBL/SFL001PF)
    A*
    A          R SF1CTL                        SFLCTL(SFL1)
    A*
    A                                          SFLSIZ(0015)
    A                                          SFLPAG(0015)
    A                                          OVERLAY
    A                                          ROLLUP
    A                                          ROLLDOWN
    A N32                                      SFLDSP
    A N31                                      SFLDSPCTL
    A  31                                      SFLCLR
    A  90                                      SFLEND(*MORE)
    A            RRN1          4S 0H            SFLRCDNBR
    A                                       6  2'Last Name'
    A                                          DSPATR(HI)
    A                                       6 26'First Name'
    A                                          DSPATR(HI)
    A                                       6 50'MI'
    A                                          DSPATR(HI)
    A                                       6 55'Nick Name'
    A                                          DSPATR(HI)
    A                                       1  2'SFL003RG'
    A                                       1 71DATE
    A                                          EDTCDE(Y)
    A                                       2 71TIME
    A                                       1 24'Subfile Program with Position To'
    A                                          DSPATR(HI)
    A                                       4  2'Position to Last Name . . .'
    A            PTNAME       20    B  4 30
```

SFL003DF: Display File for Page-at-a-Time Master File Listing (continued)

```
A*
A              R FKEY1
A*
A                                23  2'F3=Exit'
A                                    COLOR(BLU)
A                                23 12'F12=Cancel'
A                                    COLOR(BLU)
```

SFL003RG: RPG Program for Page-at-a-Time Master File Listing

```
     *
     *   To compile:
     *
     *           CRTRPGPGM PGM(XXX/SFL003RG) SRCFILE(XXX/QRPGLESRC)
     *
     *=================================================================
Fsfl003df  cf   e           workstn
F                                    sfile(sfl1:rrn1)
F                                    infds(info)
Fsfl0011f  if   e         k disk

Dinfo           ds
D cfkey                  369     369

Dsvlnam         S                    like(dblnam)
Dsvfnam         S                    like(dbfnam)

Dexit           C                    const(X'33')
Dcancel         C                    const(X'3C')
Denter          C                    const(X'F1')
Drollup         C                    const(X'F5')
Drolldn         C                    const(X'F4')
Dsflpag         C                    const(15)
Dsflpag_plus_1  C                    const(16)
     *
     ****************************************************************
     *   Main Routine
     ****************************************************************
     *
     * Clear then build the initial subfile
     *
C                   exsr      clrsfl
C                   exsr      sflbld
     *
     * Do loop to process the subfile until F3 or F12 is pressed
     *
C                   dou       (cfkey = exit) or (cfkey = cancel)
```

SFL003RG: RPG Program for Page-at-a-Time Master File Listing (continued)

```
 *
C                   write     fkey1
C                   exfmt     sflctl
 *
 * Process position to information entered by the user, then clear
 * and rebuild the subfile. Lastly, clear the position to field
 *
C                   select
C                   when      (cfkey = enter) and (ptname  *blanks)
C     ptname        setll     sfl001lf
C                   exsr      clrsfl
C                   exsr      sflbld
C                   clear                   ptname
 *
 * Clear and rebuild the subfile when user pages down (rolls up)
 *
C                   when      (cfkey = rollup) and (not *in90)
C                   exsr      clrsfl
C                   exsr      sflbld
 *
 * Position data file to one page before current subfile data, then
 * clear and rebuild the subfile to show that previous page
 *
C                   when      (cfkey = rolldn) and (not *in32)
C                   exsr      goback
C                   exsr      clrsfl
C                   exsr      sflbld

C                   endsl
C                   enddo

C                   eval      *inlr = *on
 *
 ************************************************************************
 *   CLRSFL - Clear the subfile
 ************************************************************************
 *
C     clrsfl        begsr
 *
 * Clear relative record numbers and subfile
 *
C                   eval      rrn1 = *zero
C                   eval      *in31 = *on
C                   write     sflctl
C                   eval      *in31 = *off
C                   eval      *in32 = *off

C                   endsr
 *
```

SFL003RG: RPG Program for Page-at-a-Time Master File Listing (continued)

```
*****************************************************************
*   SFLBLD - Build the List
*****************************************************************
*
C     sflbld         begsr
*
* Load the subfile with one page of data or until end-of-file
*
C                    do        sflpag
C                    read      sfl0011f                          90

C                    if        *in90
C                    leave
C                    endif

C                    eval      rrn1 = rrn1 + 1
C                    write     sfl1
*
* save first record data
*
C                    if        rrn1 = 1
C                    eval      svlnam = dblnam
C                    eval      svfnam = dbfnam
C                    endif

C                    enddo
*
* If no records added to subfile, do not display it
*
C                    if        rrn1 = *zero
C                    eval      *in32 = *on
C                    endif
*
C                    endsr
*
*****************************************************************
*   GOBACK - page backward one page
*****************************************************************
*
C     goback         begsr
*
* Position data file to first record of subfile
*
C     savkey         setll     sfl0011f
*
* Re-position pointer in file for rolling backward. If beginning
* of file hit before done, set pointer to first record of data file.
*
C                    do        sflpag_plus_1
C                    readp     sfl0011f
```

SFL003RG: RPG Program for Page-at-a-Time Master File Listing (continued)

```
C                       if        %eof
C         *loval        setll     sfl0011f
C ss                    leave
C                       endif
C                       enddo
 *
C                       endsr
 *
 ****************************************************************
 *   KEYLISTS
 ****************************************************************
 *
C         savkey        klist
C                       kfld                    svlnam
C                       kfld                    svfnam
```

3

MODIFYING A SUBFILE
(CHANGE IS GOOD)

Subfiles aren't just for displaying data. They're also extremely useful when it's necessary to modify data in your data files. As a matter of fact, some of the most powerful subfile programs you'll write are ones that will contain update, add, and delete capabilities.

In this chapter, I'll discuss a couple of different techniques I use to modify data files using subfiles. I will also explain why I use certain techniques and not others.

The first technique will allow me to update, add, and delete from our name file, which I'll call Name Master File Maintenance. This program can be used as a template for any name-type master file such as customer, salesman, or vendor. This program will introduce you to two new DDS keywords, a new RPG operation code, and a familiar RPG operation with a new use.

SFLNXTCHG, READC, AND
SFLRCDNBR...OH YEAH, CHAIN AND UPDATE, TOO

The Subfile Next Change (SFLNXTCHG) keyword is used to mark subfile records as changed. There are times when your program will modify the contents or attributes of a subfile record before displaying the subfile back to the user. If you want OS/400 to recognize those changes, you will use SFLNXTCHG. For instance, let's say the user types some information into a subfile record. In order to determine its validity, your program will interrogate the information. If the information is incorrect, you may want to display an error message and maybe highlight the incorrect field (you'll see how to do that later in this chapter).

Using the SFLNXTCHG keyword, you can mark a subfile record as changed so that no matter what the user does when the subfile is redisplayed on the screen, the program will recognize the record as changed and attempt to revalidate it. Without SFLNXTCHG, you could still warn the user something is wrong, but if he chooses to ignore the incorrect record, your program then has no knowledge that it needs to be re-validated.

You do not need the SFLNXTCHG keyword for OS/400 to recognize that a user has made a change to a subfile record. OS/400 will mark the subfile record as changed whenever a user changes the data in that record. However, if you want to change data in a subfile record from within your program and mark that record as changed, you'll need to use the SFLNXTCHG keyword in your subfile record format and condition it on an indicator.

The SFLRCDNBR keyword lets OS/400 know which page of data to display. If you have a subfile with 10 pages of data and you want to display record 38 of that subfile, SFLRCDNBR will allow you to display the page containing record 38. You'll learn more about how to use each of these keywords in the upcoming program.

The last thing I'll introduce in this program that's related to subfiles is the READC operation code. The READC operation will read changed records from a subfile. It will read both records that have been changed by the user and those changed in the program and marked as changed by setting on the indicator conditioning SFLNXTCHG keyword.

If you will allow me to digress, I'll tell a story about the first subfile programs I wrote. I was learning subfiles early in my career and was asked to create a subfile to list some data and allow the user to change that data. I wrote a self-extending subfile that allowed the user to change a certain field in the subfile. I had never used SFLNXTCHG or READC before and didn't know how they were used. I decided that the only way to know which records were changed was to keep hidden fields in my subfile (type H in DDS, as used in the RRN1 field you've seen before) that matched the display fields.

When I loaded my subfile, I loaded both the display fields and their duplicate hidden fields. When control passed back to my program after the EXFMT operation, I set up a DO loop to start with relative record 1 and CHAIN to the subfile. I then checked to see if the display data had changed from the hidden field data. If it had, I knew that was a changed record and would process it. My DO loop continued incrementing my relative record number and chaining to the subfile to check the data and process any changes. The subfile worked and the users were happy with it, but it wasn't processing very efficiently. The user would sometimes only make one change, but my program would still check every record. I thought there had to be a better way. Well, there was, and by reading on, you will learn about it.

The DDS for the subfile (SFL1) and subfile control (SF1CTL) record formats in SFL004DF should look much like those of a self-extending subfile—because that's what it is. When you look at the code in Figure 3.1, you'll notice that I have no ROLLDN keyword defined in the subfile control record format—OS/400 will take care of the rolling down for me. Because SFLSIZ is greater than SFLPAG, the subfile will be allowed to expand if the user wants it to. The paging down will be handled by OS/400 except when new records are added to the subfile. In that case, it will be done by the program. (For complete code listings, refer to the end of chapter.)

```
A             R SFL1                      SFL
A*
A  74                                     SFLNXTCHG
A             DBIDNM   R       H          REFFLD(PFR/DBIDNM *LIBL/SFL001PF)
A             OPTION        1A  B 10    3VALUES(' ' '2' '4' '5')
A             DBLNAM   R       O 10    7REFFLD(PFR/DBLNAM *LIBL/SFL001PF)
A             DBFNAM   R       O 10   31REFFLD(PFR/DBFNAM *LIBL/SFL001PF)
A             DBMINI   R       O 10   55REFFLD(PFR/DBMINI *LIBL/SFL001PF)
A             DBNNAM   R       O 10   60REFFLD(PFR/DBNNAM *LIBL/SFL001PF)
A             R SF1CTL                    SFLCTL(SFL1)
A*
A                                         CF06
A                                         SFLSIZ(0013)
A                                         SFLPAG(0012)
A                                         ROLLUP
A                                         OVERLAY
A  N32                                    SFLDSP
A  N31                                    SFLDSPCTL
A   31                                    SFLCLR
A   90                                    SFLEND(*MORE)
A             RRN1          4S 0H         SFLRCDNBR
A                                    9  7'Last Name'
A                                         DSPATR(HI)
A                                    9 31'First Name'
A                                         DSPATR(HI)
A                                    9 55'MI'
A                                         DSPATR(HI)
A                                    9 60'Nick Name'
A                                         DSPATR(HI)
A                                    1  2'SFL004RG'
A                                    1 71DATE
A                                         EDTCDE(Y)
A                                    2 71TIME
A                                    1 24'Subfile Program with Update      '
A                                         DSPATR(HI)
A                                    4  2'Position to Last Name . . .'
A             PTNAME       20A  B   4 30
A                                    9  2'Opt'
A                                         DSPATR(HI)
A                                    6  2'Type options, press Enter.'
A                                         COLOR(BLU)
A                                    7  4'2=Change'
A                                         COLOR(BLU)
A                                    7 19'4=Delete'
A                                         COLOR(BLU)
A                                    7 34'5=Display'
A                                         COLOR(BLU)
```

Figure 3.1: Subfile control and record formats for Name Master Maintenance (SFL004DF).

In Figure 3.1, notice SFLNXTCHG and SFLRCDNBR keywords in the code, entered in the subfile record format (SFL). SFLNXTCHG is used in the subfile record format (SFL1) and conditioned with indicator 74. This is the indicator I will manipulate in my RPG program to mark subfile records that have been changed not by the user but by my program. User changes are marked automatically by OS/400. The SFLRCDNBR keyword is used in conjunction with the relative record number field (RRN1) in the subfile control record (SFLCTL). When you implement SFLRCDNBR, OS/400 will determine on which page the current relative record number sits and cause your program to display that page. Because I want the user to return to where he left off when he makes a change to a particular subfile record, this will be important.

The other thing you will notice about the DDS is that I now have something other than output or hidden fields defined in my subfile record format. Up to this point, we have seen only output (O type) in the subfile control record format. In this program, I am defining a field as "B" for both input and output that will allow the user to select specific options. Each option will correspond to a specific action to perform in the program. The VALUES keyword tells OS/400 the valid options that can be entered. Any other options will give the user a warning error. Now, instead of simply displaying data in the subfile, the user will have the chance to do something with this data. Figure 3.2 shows the screen this DDS will produce.

```
 SFL004RG              Subfile Program with Update              12/08/99
                                                                12:46:38

    Position to Last Name . . .

    Type options, press Enter.
      2=Change        4=Delete        5=Display

    Opt   Last Name               First Name        MI   Nick Name
          Anthony                 Tony              A    Triple A
          Bert                    Al                C    Alphabet Man
          Coker                   Jim               L    Da AS/400 Guru
          Harrison                Harry             H    Happy
          Johnson                 John              J    JJ
          Naisium                 Jim               B    Sweaty
          Patterson               Gary              R    The All-Knowing One
          Saint                   Louis             A    Missouri
          Samuelson               Sam               S    The snake
          Simpson                 Othello           K    Don't call me OJ
          Stevenson               Steve             S    Mike
          Tessential              Quinn             C    Important
                                                               More...

    F3=Exit   F6=Add   F12=Cancel
```

Figure 3.2: Example of the update subfile screen.

The user has a couple of different options from which to choose. As before, he can scroll through the data or establish a position to somewhere else in the subfile. You've already seen how to handle that. If the desired data is on the page he's looking at, the user can choose a "2" to edit that record, a "5" to display it, or a "4" to delete the record. This brings me to the last new thing about this DDS, which is the second subfile. Yes, you can code multiple subfiles in a display file, although, as you already know from reading chapter 1, only 24 of your subfiles can be active at one time and only 12 can be displayed on a single screen. This second subfile, which is very basic and introduces nothing new, is of the load-all nature. I'll use this subfile to display a confirmation screen to the user before he deletes records from the data file. Figure 3.3 shows the DDS code for the second subfile.

```
A           R SFL2                     SFL
A*
A              DBIDNM   R       H        REFFLD(PFR/DBIDNM *LIBL/SFL001PF)
A              DBLNAM   R       O  7  3REFFLD(PFR/DBLNAM *LIBL/SFL001PF)
A              DBFNAM   R       O  7 29REFFLD(PFR/DBFNAM *LIBL/SFL001PF)
A*
A*
A           R SF2CTL                    SFLCTL(SFL2)
A*
A                                       SFLSIZ(0016)
A                                       SFLPAG(0015)
A                                       SFLDSP
A   41                                  SFLCLR
A  N41                                  SFLDSPCTL
A  N41                                  SFLEND(*MORE)
A                                       OVERLAY
A              RRN2           4S 0H
A                                     3  3'Press Enter to confirm your choice-
A                                        s for Delete.'
A                                        COLOR(BLU)
A                                     4  3'Press F12=Cancel to return to chan-
A                                        ge your choices.'
A                                        COLOR(BLU)
A                                     6  3'Last Name'
A                                        DSPATR(HI)
A                                     6 29'First Name'
A                                        DSPATR(HI)
A                                     1 28'Confirm Delete of Records'
A                                        DSPATR(HI)
```

Figure 3.3: Subfile control and record formats for delete confirmation (SFL004DF).

70

Now let's move on to the RPG code. Figure 3.4 shows the RPG program F specs that will work with this DDS. Notice that I have defined two subfiles in the F specs for display file SFL004DF. These two subfiles correspond to the two subfiles I defined in my DDS.

```
Fsfl004df  cf   e                workstn
F                                           sfile(sfl1:rrn1)
F                                           sfile(sfl2:rrn2)
F                                           infds(info)
```

Figure 3.4: Specification for the display file in RPG program SFL004RG.

When the user presses the Enter key in the main routine with nothing in the position-to field, the PRCSFL subroutine will be executed. This code snippet is shown in Figure 3.5. The PRCSFL subroutine will then read the changed subfile records and process them accordingly.

```
 *
 * Process screen to interrogate options selected by user
 *
C                when      (cfkey = enter) and (ptname = *blanks)
C                exsr      prcsfl
```

Figure 3.5: Calling PRCSFL when the user presses the Enter key with nothing in the position-to field (SFL004RG).

Now let's look at the PRCSFL subroutine (see Figure 3.6). The routine contains a DO loop that will read the changed records in SFL1. When a user enters one of the valid options in the options field, including a blank (which can be done with the spacebar or field exit key), the READC operation will pick that record up and run it through the select routine.

```
 ***********************************************************************
 *  PRCSFL - Process the options selected
 ***********************************************************************
 *
C    prcsfl       begsr
```

Figure 3.6: Subroutine PRCSFL, which processes the user options (SFL004RG).

```
         *
         * Clear the confirmation subfile before starting
         *
        C                    exsr      clrsf2
         *
         * Read all the subfile records that were changed by the user
         *
        C                    readc     sfl1
         *
         * Do loop to process until all changed records are read
         *
        C                    dow       not %eof

        C                    select
```

Figure 3.6: Subroutine PRCSFL, which processes the user options (SFL004RG) (continued).

Depending on which option was selected, the program will execute another sub-routine (or, in the case of Option 4, write records to another subfile). Selecting options 2 and 5 will provide the user a detail screen of data related to that subfile record. In the case of this program, the detail screen will contain the address information of the name listed on the subfile record.

It is important to remember that the user can select multiple records for processing. That is, he can select more than one record to be displayed, changed, or deleted. He can also select a mixture of the options to be processed. For example, if the user wanted to view subfile records 1, 3, and 5, delete records 9 and 10, and change address information on record 7, he could do so by placing the appropriate option next to all the appropriate subfile records and pressing the Enter key.

The subfile records will be processed in the order in which they exist in the subfile. Because this is a self-extending subfile, the user could page down and select other records for processing without losing what was entered on the previous page or pages. The SFLRCDNBR keyword in my DDS will allow me to display the page that contains the last record selected for processing by the user. Once the Enter key is pressed, all the changed records will be processed. If the user were to select options and then position to somewhere else in the subfile using the position-to field, however, he would lose what was previously selected. Selecting Option 5 will allow the user to view the information from the master record.

Figure 3.7 shows the screen that will be displayed by selecting Option 5 from the subfile list, and Figure 3.8 displays the code.

```
SFL004RG                Subfile Program with Update              12/08/99
                                                                13:03:17

  Customer Number: 0000001

  First Name . . : Kevin

  Last Name. . . : Vandever

  Middle Initial : M

  Nick Name. . . : Subfile Man

  Address Line 1 :

  Address Line 2 :

  Address Line 3 :




  F3=Exit    F12=Cancel
```

Figure 3.7: Screen for view detail request.

```
   *
   * when a 5 is entered throw the DISPLAY screen
   * until F3 or F12 is pressed on that screen
   *
   C                 when        option = display
   C                 movel(p)    *blanks       mode
   C                 exfmt       panel2
   C                 eval        option = *blank
   C                 update      sfl1
   C                 if          (cfkey = exit) or (cfkey = cancel)
   C                 leave
   C                 endif
```

Figure 3.8: Code from PRCSFL that processes a view request from the user (SFL004RG).

Figure 3.9 shows the screen that will be displayed when the user selects Option 2 (update). At first glance, it looks identical to the one for a view request, but there is one difference: the upper-left hand corner will show the word "Update" when

Option 2 is selected. The other, more significant change is that the user is allowed to change the data fields on the displayed screen when Option 2 is selected. This gives the user the ability to select subfile records and change the detailed information related to them.

```
SFL004RG              Subfile Program with Update              12/08/99
Update                                                         13:05:05

  Customer Number . : 0000012

  First Name. . . . . William

  Last Name . . . . . Williamson

  Middle Initial. . . W

  Nick Name . . . . . The web

  Address Line 1. . .

  Address Line 2. . .

  Address Line 3. . .




 F3=Exit    F12=Cancel
```

Figure 3.9: Screen for update request.

Figure 3.10 shows the code for this example.

```
    *
    * when a 2 is entered execute the update subroutine,
    * blank out the option field, and update the subfile record
    *
    C                     when      option = change
    C                     movel(p)  'Update'      mode
    C                     exsr      chgdtl
    C                     eval      option = *blank
    C                     update    sfl1
    C                     if        (cfkey = exit) or (cfkey = cancel)
    C                     leave
    C                     endif
```

Figure 3.10: Code from PRCSFL that processes an update request from the user (SFL004RG).

Now let's talk about Option 4. This option is taken when the user wants to delete records from the data file. It's important, if not courteous, to provide a confirmation screen to the user before allowing him to delete records from a data file. I do this by building a load-all subfile that will contain the records the user has selected for delete. When the READC loop is finished processing (that is, after all the records selected by the user have been interrogated) I'll check to see if I loaded any records into the delete confirmation screen by checking the relative record number (RRN2). If RRN2 is greater than zero, I'm going to display the subfile using the EXFMT operation and wait for the user's response. Figure 3.11 shows the delete confirmation subfile, and Figure 3.12 shows the code from subroutine PRCSFL.

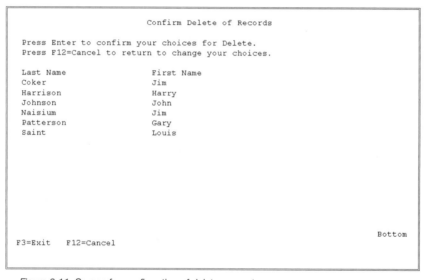

Figure 3.11: Screen for confirmation of delete request.

```
 *
 * when a 4 is entered write the record the the confirmation screen,
 * set on the SFLNXTCHG indicator to mark this record as changed,
 * and update the subfile.  I mark this record incase F12 is pressed
 * from the confirmation screen and the user wants to keep his
 * originally selected records
 *
C                         when       option = delete
```

Figure 3.12: Code from PRCSFL that processes a delete request from the user (SFL004RG).

```
C                       eval       rrn2 = rrn2 +1
C                       write      sfl2
C                       eval       *in74 = *on
C                       update     sfl1
C                       eval       *in74 = *off

C                       endsl

C                       readc      sfl1
C                       enddo
*
* If records were selected for delete (4), throw the subfile to
* screen.  If enter is pressed execute the DLTRCD subroutine to
* physically delete the records, clear, and rebuild the subfile
* from the last deleted record (you can certainly position the
* database file whereever you want)
*
C                       if         rrn2 > 0
C                       eval       lstrrn2 = rrn2
C                       eval       rrn2 = 1
C                       write      fkey2
C                       exfmt      sf2ctl
C                       if         (cfkey  exit) and (cfkey  cancel)
C                       exsr       dltrcd
C     dblnam            setll      sfl0011f
C                       exsr       clrsf1
C                       exsr       sflbld
C                       endif
C                       endif
```

Figure 3.12: Code from PRCSFL that processes a delete request from the user (continued).

Warning: Remember that the position-to in this self-extending subfile clears and rebuilds the subfile. If you use this example, be careful not to reposition the subfile with the position-to field unless you have processed all of your selections. Of course, you can change the logic to process the selected options before repositioning the subfile by executing the PRCSFL in the position-to WHEN clause of the main routine, but I chose not to do that in this case.

Notice that when I write to the delete confirmation subfile (SFL2) in the PRCSFL subroutine, I set on indicator 74 to activate the SFLNXTCHG keyword and update SFL1 with the UPDATE keyword. I then deactivate SFLNXTCHG by setting off indicator 74. What this does is mark that subfile record for change even though it has already been read by the READC operation and the user has made no other changes to that record. This is how I mark a record for change inside my program. Because I didn't clear the options field before updating the subfile, the "4" remains on the subfile record. By doing this, the user can choose to remove records he doesn't want to delete and leave the records he does, press Enter, and voila—the records he left marked magically show up on the delete confirmation screen. Figure 3.13 shows the screen displayed if the user selects F12 from the delete confirmation screen. Notice that the records the user selected for delete are still marked with 4s. I did this in case the user didn't like what he saw on the confirmation screen and wanted to "undelete," an individual entry or two. He could simply press F12 and remove the 4s from the records he didn't want to delete and press Enter to get a new confirmation screen, without having to reenter all the records he wants to delete. The SFLNXTCHG keyword makes this possible.

```
SFL004RG              Subfile Program with Update           12/08/99
                                                            13:17:26

Position to Last Name . . .

Type options, press Enter.
  2=Change       4=Delete        5=Display

Opt   Last Name               First Name         MI   Nick Name
      Anthony                 Tony               A    Triple A
      Bert                    Al                 C    Alphabet Man
  4   Coker                   Jim                L    Da AS/400 Guru
  4   Harrison                Harry              H    Happy
  4   Johnson                 John               J    JJ
  4   Naisium                 Jim                B    Sweaty
  4   Patterson               Gary               R    The All-Knowing One
  4   Saint                   Louis              A    Missouri
      Samuelson               Sam                S    The snake
      Simpson                 Othello            K    Don't call me OJ
      Stevenson               Steve              S    Mike
      Tessential              Quinn              C    Important
                                                             More...
F3=Exit   F6=Add   F12=Cancel
```

Figure 3.13: Redisplaying original choices when the user cancels from the delete confirmation screen.

Figure 3.14 shows the DLTRCD subroutine, which will be executed from subroutine PRCSFL when the user specifies delete. The program clears the original subfile (SFL1) and reloads it—minus the deleted records, of course.

```
    ********************************************************************
    *   DLTRCD - delete records
    ********************************************************************
    *
C       dltrcd        begsr
    *
    * read all the records in the confirmation subfile
    * and delete them from the data base file
    *
C                     do         lstrrn2        count
C       count         chain      sfl2
C                     if         %found
C       dbidnm        delete     pfr                         99
C                     endif
C                     enddo
C                     endsr
```

Figure 3.14: The DLTRCD subroutine deletes the records selected by the user (SFL004RG).

ADD TO THE FUN WITH ADD CAPABILITY

I have also included the ability to add records to the data file from this program. I won't detail this logic because it really has nothing to do with subfiles. I allow the user to press F6 when he wants to add a record to the data file. I then provide him with a screen similar to that of the modification screen displayed when the user selects Option 2 from the subfile. The user can enter the new information and add that data to the data file by pressing Enter. Once the add routine is finished, I clear and reload the subfile so it will include the newly added record.

YOU'RE NOW READY FOR MASTER FILE MAINTENANCE

You've just seen a very useful template for a Master File Maintenance program. The user is allowed to view, change, and delete data from a data file. I use this type of subfile program when I'm working with files that will have a limited number of additions and modifications. "What's limited?" you ask. For me, limited is something of Master File-like quality. Master files are not transactional files, meaning you won't have users pounding away at the keyboard adding data to them. My program doesn't lend itself very well for that kind of work. For one, the user has to hit F6 every time he wants to add a record. This becomes very time consuming if there are hundreds or thousands of records to add to a file, as is sometimes the case with transactional-type files such as an order entry detail file.

The previous program was kind of boring when it comes to new subfile techniques. Nothing new really happened to the subfile except that is was used to select records for further processing. What I'll show you next is a subfile technique that's not only able to keep up with the most skilled data entry professional; but also might even enhance his skills. The following subfile program will afford you the same capabilities as the previous Master File Maintenance program, only in a completely different way, and with the subfile taking a more active role. The display file (SFL005DF) and the RPG program (SFL005RG) are included in their entirety at the end of the chapter.

SFLINZ, SFLRNA, AND INPUT SUBFILES

In our previous file maintenance program, you added records by pressing F6 and filling in a data entry screen. However, depending on the number of fields you're dealing with, you may be able to input data into your data file directly from you subfile records. Implementing input subfiles is a technique that allows for maximum data entry capabilities. With this type of subfile, you're going to give the user a page of blank subfile records, which he can fill with data and, pressing the Enter or other valid function key, write to a file. Using this technique, you can build a complete file maintenance program that includes the same update and delete capabilities the previous example did. In addition, you can use it if you have a Master-type file with a limited number of fields and want to use this type of subfile program for maintenance.

The Hard Way

First, let's concentrate on input only. Remember the story of my first subfile program? Well, as a part of that project, I also had to give the user a separate screen he could use to add new data to the data file. Again, without much subfile knowledge, and not willing to do a little research first, I dug right in. I created a load-all subfile with about 50 records. In the subfile load routine in my RPG program, I cleared the subfile using the SFLCLR keyword, and then performed a DO loop 50 times and wrote empty records into the subfile. Just as before, this approach worked and the users had their 50 records to enter data. I then chained to all 50, looking for non-blank records to write to my data file.

The Correct Way

I've already explained the fact that I should have used READC to read my changed records, but there's more. I could have used a technique to write the 50 blank records to my subfile without using a DO loop in my RPG. That way involves using the subfile initialize (SFLINZ) keyword in your DDS instead of subfile clear (SFLCLR). SFLINZ works just like the SFLCLR keyword you've used before except that instead of creating an empty subfile, which is the result when you use SFLCLR, SFLINZ provides you with a subfile with the number of records specified in your SFLSIZ keyword. These fields, depending on their type, will all be initialized to zeros or blanks. Figure 3.15 shows the SFLINZ keyword.

```
     A             R SF1CTL                    SFLCTL(SFL1)
     A*
     A                                         SFLSIZ(0050)
     A                                         SFLPAG(0017)
     A                                         OVERLAY
     A N32                                     SFLDSP
     A N31                                     SFLDSPCTL
     A   31                                    SFLINZ
     A                                         SFLRNA
     A   90                                    SFLEND(*MORE)
     A             RRN1          4S 0H         SFLRCDNBR(CURSOR)
```

Figure 3.15: Example of subfile control record format with keywords used to initialize a subfile with active and inactive records (SFL005DF).

This subfile is very easy to code. The DDS is as simple as the first load-all subfile from chapter 1. The RPG is also very simple. There's no load routine to get the initialized records, only a routine to read the changed records using the

READC operation and process those changes. A keyword you can use along with the SFLINZ keyword is the subfile record not active (SFLRNA) keyword, also shown in Figure 3.15. This keyword works in conjunction with the SFLINZ keyword to make the initialized records inactive. You may want to make subfile records inactive if you plan on providing a way for the user to add data to a file. You can initialize a page of empty subfile records and make them inactive until the user actually keys something into the empty subfile record. A subfile can have inactive subfile records. In fact, the only way you can make subfile records inactive is by specifying SFLRNA with the SFLINZ keyword. Now let's look at the three ways you can make subfile records active:

1. When a record is written to the subfile record format using the RPG WRITE operation, that record is now active.

2. If the user keys data or changes the record (spacebar or field exit key) of an inactive record, that record becomes active.

3. Specifying the SFLINZ keyword without the SFLRNA keyword will render the subfile active.

By specifying SFLRNA in my DDS, I'll make my 50 initialized records inactive. Because the READC operation will only look for changes in active records, I will save CPU processing time. If I make changes in only one of my 50 initialized records, the READC operation is going to check only that one record because it's the only active record in the subfile. By using SFLRNA, I can almost get away with not using READC to process my changes. I could simply code a DO loop to start at relative record 1 and chain to each subfile record to see if data has been entered, process the data, increment the relative record number, and perform the chain again. This is because the CHAIN command will only recognize active subfile records, just as READC does.

However, the problem with using CHAIN instead of READC, even with inactive records, is that CHAIN cannot work with a mixture of inactive and active records. For example, if the user enters data on record 1, tabs through record 2, leaving it inactive, and enters data on record 3, the conditional indicator on the CHAIN operation would be set on the first time it hits an inactive record. Logic would therefore pass out of the loop. The second changed record would be skipped because a CHAIN on an inactive record behaves like a no-hit on a database file. The READC is smart enough to process all the changed records, even if there are inactive records in between them. It's therefore in your best interest to use the READC operation even if you use SFLRNA with SFLINZ. The combination ensures that your program will process all the changed records while reading the minimum amount of subfile records. Figure 3.16 shows the RPG code that processes the subfile. Except for having to clear the subfile first, it looks just like our previous program.

```
     *
     *****************************************************************
     *   PRCSFL - Process the subfile
     *****************************************************************
          C     prcsfl        begsr
     *
     C                   readc     sfl1
     *
     * Do loop to process until all changed records are read
     *
     C                   dow       not %eof
     *
     C                   select
     *
     * Add when something's in the subfile
     *
     C                   when      dblnam = *blanks
     C     *hival        setgt     sfl001pf
     C                   readp     sfl001pf
     C                   If        not %eof
     C                   eval      dbidnm = dbidnm + 1
     C                   write     pfr
     C                   endif
     C                   endsl
     *
     C                   readc     sfl1
     C                   enddo
     *
     C                   endsr
     *
```

Figure 3.16: Processing a subfile with READC when SFLRNA and SFLINZ have been specified in the DDS (SFL005RG).

SFLCSRPRG AND INPUT SUBFILES

Use of the subfile cursor progression (SFLCSRPRG) keyword can also aid the data entry professional. I use this field when I want to control which field the cursor goes to when the Tab key or Field Exit key is pressed. The normal progression of the cursor is from left to right across the screen, moving to all input-capable fields on one line before going to the first field on line 2.

Let's say the normal progression is not how the user wants to enter the data. Maybe he wants to enter all the last names first and then the first names. SFLCSRPRG lets you accomplish this. All you have to do is place the SFLCSRPRG keyword under the field you want the cursor to progress to and away you go. Figure 3.17 shows an example.

```
A              R SFL1                    SFL
A*
A                DBIDNM    R        H       REFFLD(PFR/DBIDNM *LIBL/SFL001PF)
A                DBLNAM    R        B  5   2REFFLD(PFR/DBLNAM *LIBL/SFL001PF)
A                                           SFLCSRPRG
A                                           CHECK(LC)
A                DBFNAM    R        B  5  26REFFLD(PFR/DBFNAM *LIBL/SFL001PF)
A                                           CHECK(LC)
A                DBMINI    R        B  5  50REFFLD(PFR/DBMINI *LIBL/SFL001PF)
A                                           CHECK(LC)
A                DBNNAM    R        B  5  55REFFLD(PFR/DBNNAM *LIBL/SFL001PF)
A                                           CHECK(LC)
```

Figure 3.17: This code allows the user to fill the last name of all the subfile records before moving on to the next field (SFL005DF).

The keyword isn't activated until the cursor enters the field on which you defined SFLCSRPRG. Because the last name is the first entry field in my program, the cursor would start out on first name, and the user, using the tab or Field Exit key, could either enter the first name or move to last name. Once there, the user would enter a last name, hit tab or Field Exit, and the cursor would jump down to the next record in the last-name field. Using this technique, the user could enter all the last names before entering any first names, without having to use any extra keystrokes.

If you had more fields in the subfile but wanted to fill each column first before moving on to the next field, you could place SFLCSRPRG on every field in the subfile. This would cause your cursor to move top to bottom instead of left to right for all fields. One potential problem with this is that SFLCSRPRG will only work with device controllers that can handle the enhanced data stream. If you run into problems using this keyword, your controller may not be able to handle the enhanced data stream.

SFLINZ, SFLRNA, SFLRCDNBR, AND UPDATE SUBFILES

As cool as input subfiles are, an application alone they do not make. Let's look back at our original Master File Maintenance program for a minute. Why couldn't I use this type of subfile technique with my Name Master file? Why should I have to press F6 every time I want to add a record? I've seen that I don't always have to use a function key to add records. I can now add records directly from my subfile. What about update and delete? Instead of Option 2 to update the data or Option 4 to delete a record, why can't I just type over, or blank out, the data in the subfile and update the file that way? The truth is that you can use this type of program for Master File Maintenance programs.

```
 SFL007RG              Add Data to Blank Subfile Lines          3/01/00
                                                               12:50:09

    Last Name            First Name         MI   Nick Name
    Vandever             Kevin              M    Subfile Man
    Vannerberg           Kern               X    kevin
    Williamson           William            W    The web
    Zachery              Zak                Z    The snoozer











                                                              More...

    F3=Exit    F12=Cancel
```

Figure 3.18: Example of the alternate update/add subfile technique (SFL007RG).

The program below is another version of our Name Master File Maintenance program from before, and also an extension of our input subfile program. Figure 3.18 shows what the new maintenance screen will look like.

In this program, I provide the user with a load-all subfile that allows all the data fields to be changed. There are no options to be taken to display, change, or delete the data. To add records, you simply page to the end of the subfile and enter data in the empty subfile records. There is no F6 key to press. To change data records, simply key over the data in the subfile record, and the data will be updated in the data file the next time the Enter key is pressed. To delete records, Field Exit through the data fields of a subfile record to make them blank, and that record will be deleted from the data file. Check out the code at the end of the chapter.

Tying It All Together

Let's look first at the DDS (Figure 3.19). Notice that I define all my fields as type B just as I did in the input subfile (refer to Figure 3.18 again). Remember, the "B", which means input/output. I also have added a hidden field to hold the identification number field. The hidden field is the key to the physical file that I'll use to delete records. If the user blanks out a subfile record, I can still preserve the key data to the file in my hidden field. My program can then CHAIN to the physical file using the hidden field and delete that record from the file. In addition to hidden fields being used to preserve data on input/output subfile records, as you've just seen, they are also valuable when you want to maintain some information about a specific subfile record but don't want to display that data on the on the screen.

```
A          DBLNAM    R        B  5  2REFFLD(PFR/DBLNAM *LIBL/SFL001PF)
A                                    SFLCSRPRG
A          DBIDNM    R        H       REFFLD(PFR/DBIDNM *LIBL/SFL001PF)

A                                     CHECK(LC)
A          DBFNAM    R        B  5 26REFFLD(PFR/DBFNAM *LIBL/SFL001PF)
A                                    CHECK(LC)
A          DBMINI    R        B  5 50REFFLD(PFR/DBMINI *LIBL/SFL001PF)
```

Figure 3.19: Load-all subfile with input/output-capable fields (SFL007DF).

```
A                                      CHECK(LC)
A              DBNNAM    R        B   5 55REFFLD(PFR/DBNNAM *LIBL/SFL001PF)
A                                      CHECK(LC)
A*
A              R SF1CTL                SFLCTL(SFL1)
A*
A                                      SFLSIZ(0050)
A                                      SFLPAG(0017)
A                                      OVERLAY
A N32                                  SFLDSP
A N31                                  SFLDSPCTL
A   31                                 SFLINZ
A                                      SFLRNA
```

Figure 3.19: Load-all subfile with input/output-capable fields (continued).

Another thing to note is that because I want blank lines to follow the current data in the file this will be a load-all subfile program. Because I'm going to allow entry fields for adding data, I'm going to use SFLINZ instead of SFLCLR. Assuming that I've made SFLSIZ large enough, this will give me the desired lines at the end of my subfile. To offset making SFLSIZ too large, I'll use SFLRNA to make the blank subfile records inactive. They'll only be made active, and therefore dealt with by the CPU, by one of the three ways mentioned earlier in this chapter.

Now for the RPG. I turn on indicator 31 to initialize 50 inactive records and load all the data from my data file. Because the records are inactive, I can use the WRITE operation to load data into them. If the subfile records were active, I would have to CHAIN to the subfile and UPDATE it with the information from the data file. Did you get that?

Normally, you use the WRITE operation to write records to the subfile. If you had initialized 50 records, as I did, and made them active, you would have to CHAIN to the active, but empty, subfile record and UPDATE it with the data. Because I initialized the subfile and made the records inactive (SFLRNA), I'm still able to use the WRITE operation to get data into the subfile. Got it? Sorry—just want to make sure you understand the difference. Figure 3.20 shows this segment of the code.

```
C        sflbld        begsr
*
*  Clear subfile - RRN1 has to > 0 to initialize records
*
C                      eval       *in31 = *on
C                      eval       rrn1 = 1
C                      write      sflctl
C                      eval       rrn1 = 0
C                      eval       *in31 = *off
*
*  Load data to subfile
*
C        *loval        setll      sfl0011f
C                      read       sfl0011f

C                      dow        (not %eof) and (rrn1 <= 50)
C                      eval       rrn1 = rrn1 + 1
C                      eval       dbidnm = in_dbidnm
C                      eval       dblnam = in_dblnam
C                      eval       dbfnam = in_dbfnam
C                      eval       dbmini = in_dbmini
C                      eval       dbnnam = in_dbnnam
C                      write      sfl1
C                      read       sfl0011f
C                      enddo
```

Figure 3.20: Loading data into the subfile (SFL007RG).

Once I'm finished loading the subfile and allowing it to be displayed by setting the appropriate indicator, I display it to the user. If the user pages down through the subfile, he will eventually come to the end of the data and the beginning of the blank lines. To modify a record, he simply keys over the data in the subfile record. To delete a record, he blanks out the data on the subfile record (I've made it so he only has to blank out the last name). To add a record, he keys data into one of the blank lines.

Once the Enter key is pressed, the program processes the changed records, in the PRCSFL subroutine, by using a READC loop, the hidden field, and the data entered in the subfile to analyze what to do with the record. If the subfile (or last name in this case) is empty but there's something in the hidden field, that record is a candidate for delete because it holds the hidden key. If there's data in the subfile but nothing in the hidden field, that's an add. If READC detects a changed record with data in the record and something in the hidden field, that record is a modification to an existing record. Figure 3.21 shows the PRCSFL subroutine that does all this fine work. Notice that there's a little more to this version as opposed to the input-subfile version.

```
****************************************************************
*   PRCSFL - Process the subfile
****************************************************************
*
C     prcsfl        begsr
*
C                   readc       sfl1
*
* Do loop to process until all changed records are read
*
C                   dow         not %eof
*
C                   select
*
* Add when hidden field is empty but something's in the subfile
*
C                   when        (dbidnm = 0) and (dblnam > *blanks)
C     *hival        setgt       sfl001pf
C                   readp       sfl001pf
C                   eval        up_dblnam = dblnam
C                   eval        up_dbfnam = dbfnam
C                   eval        up_dbmini = dbmini
C                   eval        up_dbnnam = dbnnam
C                   eval        up_dbidnm = up_dbidnm + 1
C                   write       up_pfr
*
* Update when hidden field is not empty and neither is last name
*
C                   when        (dbidnm  0) and (dblnam > *blanks)
C     dbidnm        chain       sfl001pf
C                   eval        up_dblnam = dblnam
C                   eval        up_dbfnam = dbfnam
C                   eval        up_dbmini = dbmini
C                   eval        up_dbnnam = dbnnam
C                   if          %found
C                   update      up_pfr
C                   endif
*
* Delete when hidden field is not empty but last name is empty
```

Figure 3.21: This routine processes all the options selected by the user.

```
      *
      C                    when       (dbidnm  0) and (dblnam = *blanks)
      C        dbidnm      chain      sfl001pf
      C                    if         %found
      C                    delete     up_pfr
      C                    endif
      *
      C                    endsl
      C                    readc      sfl1
      C                    enddo
      *
      C                    exsr       sflbld
      *
      C                    endsr
```

Figure 3.21: This routine processes all the options selected by the user (continued).

More on Update

I'm not validating any information on the subfile records. I'm simply allowing the user to key data, and then I'm doing something with that data. Now I want to change my program to not allow the user to add data if the last-name field is blank. I will show you how, in addition to modifying the contents of a subfile, to modify a subfile record's attributes. Figure 3.22 shows the DDS source I will add.

```
      A             DBLNAM    R       B  5  2REFFLD(PFR/DBLNAM *LIBL/SFL001PF)
      A                                     SFLCSRPRG
      A                                     CHECK(LC)
      A  42                                 DSPATR(RI)
      A  42                                 DSPATR(PC)
```

Figure 2.22: Display attributes for the last-name field.

I added two display attribute (DSPATR) keywords, both of which are conditioned on indicator 42. The first DSPATR line says that when indicator 42 is on, set the last name, DBLNAM, to reverse image (RI). The second DSPATR says to position the cursor (PC) to this field when indicator 42 is on. Now let's look at the RPG program to see how to set those attributes.

Figure 2.23 shows the new WHEN clause to handle that.

```
C                         when      dblnam = *blanks
C                         eval      *in42 = *on
C                         eval      *in74 = *on
C                         update    sfl1
C                         eval      *in74 = *off
C                         eval      *in42 = *off
```

Figure 2.23: Logic to change the attributes of a subfile record.

I'm going to reverse-image and position the cursor to any record the READC operation picked up as changed but in which no last name was entered. This probably means the user keyed some information into the subfile record but forgot to key the last name. So, I check to see if the last name is blank using a WHEN clause within the READC DO loop. If it's blank, I set on indicator 42, which is the indicators used to condition the DSPATR keywords in my subfile record format, and indicator 74, which is the SFLNXTCHG indicator. I then UPDATE the subfile record.

Because indicators 42 and 74 are on, any keywords conditioned within the subfile record format with those indicators will take effect. I then set the indicators off for the next READC iteration. Now when the subfile is displayed, the incorrect (blank last name) field will be displayed in reverse image so it's noticeable to the user, and the cursor will be positioned in that field so the user can easily change the data. If more than one record is in error, the cursor will position to the first record in error, but all the fields in error will display in reverse image.

The reason I set the SFLNXTCHG indicator (74) is just in case the user ignores the incorrect data. If that happens, READC will still pick up the field as changed, regardless of what the user does, the next time the subfile is processed. The WHEN clause in Figure 2.23 will be run again and the field will again be displayed in error.

Another Option

If you feel—or have been told by the user—that this program will be used more to add records than to modify or delete records, you'll want a fast method to get to the first empty record in the subfile. The best way to do that is to use the

SFLRCDNBR keyword as before, but with a slight twist. As you may remember, the SFLRCDNBR keyword is used to display the page of the current relative record number. If the relative record number is 16 and record 16 is on the second page of the subfile, the second page will be displayed when the EXFMT operation is used in your program.

The twist to accomplishing this is to add the parameter (CURSOR) to the SFLRCDFMT keyword, as I've done in the DDS shown in Figure 3.24. What this does is display the page where the current relative record number exists and places the cursor on the exact line that matches the relative record number. So in your load-all routine, if you add 1 to your relative record number instead of initializing it to 1after all the data has been loaded from the data file, the program will display the first page with empty subfile records and place the cursor at the first empty subfile line.

```
A             R SF1CTL                    SFLCTL(SFL1)
A*
A                                         SFLSIZ(0050)
A                                         SFLPAG(0017)
A                                         OVERLAY
A N32                                     SFLDSP
A N31                                     SFLDSPCTL
A   31                                    SFLINZ
A                                         SFLRNA
A   90                                    SFLEND(*MORE)
A             RRN1          4S 0H         SFLRCDNBR(CURSOR)
```

Figure 3.24: Using SFLRCDNBR(CURSOR) to display the first page of empty subfile records.

Look before You Leap

Before using this technique to modify or delete records from a data file, there are a couple of things you need to take into consideration. First, when deleting records in this fashion, you're providing no confirmation to the user. A record could be inadvertently cleared and subsequently deleted without the user ever knowing it. Also, updating and record locking becomes a bit more crucial using this technique. Each time a record is displayed for update in my first maintenance program, it's retrieved from the data file. The record is easily locked while the user remains on the update screen.

In the third example (the input subfile being the second), all the data is loaded at the beginning of the program. The user can change any record as he scrolls through the data. In the meantime, the data may have changed between the time it was added to your subfile, when you finally modify it in your subfile, and the user pressed the Enter key to update the data file. If other users are able to get into this program at the same time, they may not always have the most current changes. They also may make changes, thus wiping out the other changes. You can certainly allocate the files to one use of the program and solve the problem. But the fact remains that data integrity must be compared with the speed of entry each time you design a file maintenance subfile program.

SUMMARY AND CODE EXAMPLES

- Use the CHAIN operation to access a subfile record by relative record number

- Use UPDATE to update a specific subfile record after a CHAIN or READC has accessed that record

- READC reads only changed records in your subfile.

- SFLNXTCHG allows you to mark records as changed in your program, without user intervention, so the READC operation will pick them up.

- SFLRCDNBR allows you to display a specific page of a subfile based on the relative record number

- SFLINZ allows you to create a subfile full of initialized records, negating the need for a DO loop in your RPG program to accomplish the same task.

- SFLRNA works in conjunction with SFLINZ to make the initialized records inactive and save processing time.

- SFLCSRPGR allows you to change the way data is entered on the subfile. Instead of left-to-right data entry, you may want to allow top-to-bottom data entry. This keyword only works if the device controller can handle the enhanced data stream.

- Using a full-fledged input and update subfile requires some thought about data integrity versus speed of entry. Make sure you engage in the analysis stage before using this kind of subfile for Master File maintenance.

SFL004DF: Display File for Master File Maintenance

```
A*
A*
A                                       DSPSIZ(24 80 *DS3)
A                                       PRINT
A                                       ERRSFL
A                                       CA03
A                                       CA12
A*
A          R SFL1                       SFL
A*
A    74                                 SFLNXTCHG
A            DBIDNM    R       H         REFFLD(PFR/DBIDNM *LIBL/SFL001PF)
A            OPTION        1A  B 10     3VALUES(' ' '2' '4' '5')
A            DBLNAM    R     O 10        7REFFLD(PFR/DBLNAM *LIBL/SFL001PF)
A            DBFNAM    R     O 10       31REFFLD(PFR/DBFNAM *LIBL/SFL001PF)
A            DBMINI    R     O 10       55REFFLD(PFR/DBMINI *LIBL/SFL001PF)
A            DBNNAM    R     O 10       60REFFLD(PFR/DBNNAM *LIBL/SFL001PF)
A          R SF1CTL                     SFLCTL(SFL1)
A*
A                                       CF06
A                                       SFLSIZ(0013)
A                                       SFLPAG(0012)
A                                       ROLLUP
A                                       OVERLAY
A N32                                   SFLDSP
A N31                                   SFLDSPCTL
A    31                                 SFLCLR
A    90                                 SFLEND(*MORE)
A            RRN1          4S OH        SFLRCDNBR
A                             9  7'Last Name'
A                                       DSPATR(HI)
A                             9 31'First Name'
A                                       DSPATR(HI)
A                             9 55'MI'
A                                       DSPATR(HI)
```

$\longrightarrow$

93

SFL004DF: Display File for Master File Maintenance (continued)

```
A                                 9 60'Nick Name'
A                                   DSPATR(HI)
A                                 1  2'SFL004RG'
A                                 1 71DATE
A                                   EDTCDE(Y)
A                                 2 71TIME
A                                 1 24'Subfile Program with Update      '
A                                   DSPATR(HI)
A                                 4  2'Position to Last Name . . .'
A          PTNAME      20A  B  4 30
A                                 9  2'Opt'
A                                   DSPATR(HI)
A                                 6  2'Type options, press Enter.'
A                                   COLOR(BLU)
A                                 7  4'2=Change'
A                                   COLOR(BLU)
A                                 7 19'4=Delete'
A                                   COLOR(BLU)
A                                 7 34'5=Display'
A                                   COLOR(BLU)
A*
A          R PANEL1
A                                 1  2'SFL004RG'
A          MODE         6  O  2  2DSPATR(HI)
A                                 1 24'Subfile Program with Update      '
A                                   DSPATR(HI)
A                                 1 71DATE
A                                   EDTCDE(Y)
A                                 2 71TIME
A          DBIDNM    R      O  4 23REFFLD(PFR/DBIDNM *LIBL/SFL001PF)
A                                   DSPATR(HI)
A          DBFNAM    R      B  6 23REFFLD(PFR/DBFNAM *LIBL/SFL001PF)
A                                   CHECK(LC)
A          DBLNAM    R      B  8 23REFFLD(PFR/DBLNAM *LIBL/SFL001PF)
A                                   CHECK(LC)
A          DBMINI    R      B 10 23REFFLD(PFR/DBMINI *LIBL/SFL001PF)
A                                   CHECK(LC)
A          DBNNAM    R      B 12 23REFFLD(PFR/DBNNAM *LIBL/SFL001PF)
A                                   CHECK(LC)
A          DBADD1    R      B 14 23REFFLD(PFR/DBADD1 *LIBL/SFL001PF)
A                                   CHECK(LC)
A          DBADD2    R      B 16 23REFFLD(PFR/DBADD2 *LIBL/SFL001PF)
A                                   CHECK(LC)
A          DBADD3    R      B 18 23REFFLD(PFR/DBADD3 *LIBL/SFL001PF)
A                                   CHECK(LC)
A                                23  2'F3=Exit'
A                                   COLOR(BLU)
A                                23 12'F12=Cancel'
A                                   COLOR(BLU)
A                                 4  3'Customer Number . :'
```

SFL004DF: Display File for Master File Maintenance (continued)

```
A                                    6  3'First Name. . . . .'
A                                    8  3'Last Name . . . . .'
A                                   10  3'Middle Initial. . .'
A                                   12  3'Nick Name . . . . .'
A                                   14  3'Address Line 1. . .'
A                                   16  3'Address Line 2. . .'
A                                   18  3'Address Line 3. . .'
A          R PANEL2
A*
A                                    1  2'SFL004RG'
A            MODE        6   O  2  2DSPATR(HI)
A                                    1 24'Subfile Program with Update     '
A                                       DSPATR(HI)
A                                    1 71DATE
A                                       EDTCDE(Y)
A                                    2 71TIME
A            DBIDNM    R       O  4 20REFFLD(PFR/DBIDNM *LIBL/SFL001PF)
A                                       DSPATR(HI)
A            DBFNAM    R       O  6 20REFFLD(PFR/DBFNAM *LIBL/SFL001PF)
A                                       DSPATR(HI)
A            DBLNAM    R       O  8 20REFFLD(PFR/DBLNAM *LIBL/SFL001PF)
A                                       DSPATR(HI)
A            DBMINI    R       O 10 20REFFLD(PFR/DBMINI *LIBL/SFL001PF)
A                                       DSPATR(HI)
A            DBNNAM    R       O 12 20REFFLD(PFR/DBNNAM *LIBL/SFL001PF)
A                                       DSPATR(HI)
A            DBADD1    R       O 14 20REFFLD(PFR/DBADD1 *LIBL/SFL001PF)
A                                       DSPATR(HI)
A            DBADD2    R       O 16 20REFFLD(PFR/DBADD2 *LIBL/SFL001PF)
A                                       DSPATR(HI)
A            DBADD3    R       O 18 20REFFLD(PFR/DBADD3 *LIBL/SFL001PF)
A                                       DSPATR(HI)
A                                   23  2'F3=Exit'
A                                       COLOR(BLU)
A                                   23 12'F12=Cancel'
A                                       COLOR(BLU)
A                                    4  3'Customer Number:'
A                                    6  3'First Name . . :'
A                                    8  3'Last Name. . . :'
A                                   10  3'Middle Initial :'
A                                   12  3'Nick Name. . . :'
A                                   14  3'Address Line 1 :'
A                                   16  3'Address Line 2 :'
A                                   18  3'Address Line 3 :'
A*
A          R SFL2                      SFL
A*
A            DBIDNM    R       H       REFFLD(PFR/DBIDNM *LIBL/SFL001PF)
A            DBLNAM    R       O  7  3REFFLD(PFR/DBLNAM *LIBL/SFL001PF)
A            DBFNAM    R       O  7 29REFFLD(PFR/DBFNAM *LIBL/SFL001PF)
```

SFL004DF: Display File for Master File Maintenance (continued)

```
A*
A*
A          R SF2CTL                    SFLCTL(SFL2)
A*
A                                      SFLSIZ(0016)
A                                      SFLPAG(0015)
A                                      SFLDSP
A   41                                 SFLCLR
A N41                                  SFLDSPCTL
A N41                                  SFLEND(*MORE)
A                                      OVERLAY
A          RRN2         4S 0H
A                                    3  3'Press Enter to confirm your choice-
A                                       s for Delete.'
A                                       COLOR(BLU)
A                                    4  3'Press F12=Cancel to return to chan-
A                                       ge your choices.'
A                                       COLOR(BLU)
A                                    6  3'Last Name'
A                                       DSPATR(HI)
A                                    6 29'First Name'
A                                       DSPATR(HI)
A                                    1 28'Confirm Delete of Records'
A                                       DSPATR(HI)
A*
A          R FKEY1
A*
A                                   23  2'F3=Exit'
A                                       COLOR(BLU)
A                                      +3'F6=Add'
A                                       COLOR(BLU)
A                                      +3'F12=Cancel'
A                                       COLOR(BLU)
A*
A          R FKEY2
A*
A                                   23  2'F3=Exit'
A                                       COLOR(BLU)
A                                      +3'F12=Cancel'
A                                       COLOR(BLU)
A          R FKEY3
A*
A                                   23  2'F12=Cancel'
A                                       COLOR(BLU)
```

SFL004RG: RPG Program for Master File Maintenance

```
     *
     *   To compile:
     *
     *            CRTRPGPGM PGM(XXX/SFL004RG) SRCFILE(XXX/QRPGLESRC)
     *
     *======================================================================
Fsfl004df  cf   e              workstn
F                                      sfile(sfl1:rrn1)
F                                      sfile(sfl2:rrn2)
F                                      infds(info)
Fsfl001lf  if   e         k disk       rename(pfr:lfr)
Fsfl001pf  uf a e         k disk

Dinfo            ds
D cfkey                369   369

Dexit            C                     const(X'33')
Dcancel          C                     const(X'3C')
Dadd             C                     const(X'36')
Denter           C                     const(X'F1')
Drollup          C                     const(X'F5')
Dsflpag          C                     const(12)
Ddisplay         C                     const('5')
Dchange          C                     const('2')
Ddelete          C                     const('4')

Dlstrrn          S              4  0 inz(0)
Dlstrrn2         S              4  0 inz(0)
Dcount           S              4  0 inz(0)
Dnew_id          S                     like(dbidnm)
     *
     **********************************************************************
     *  Main Routine
     **********************************************************************
     *
     * Clear then build the initial subfile
     *
C                exsr      clrsf1
C                exsr      sflbld
     *
     * Do loop to process the subfile until F3 is pressed.  If F12
     * is pressed from other screens, I still want to stay in this loop.
     *
C                dou       cfkey = exit
     *
C                write     fkey1
C                exfmt     sfl1ctl
     *
     * Process position to information entered by the user, then clear
     * and rebuild the subfile. Lastly, clear the position to field
```

97

SFL004RG: RPG Program for Master File Maintenance (continued)

```
      *
C                       select
C                       when      (cfkey = enter) and (ptname  *blanks)
C      ptname           setll     sfl0011f
C                       exsr      clrsf1
C                       exsr      sflbld
C                       clear                   ptname
      *
      * Process screen to interrogate options selected by user
      *
C                       when      (cfkey = enter) and (ptname = *blanks)
C                       exsr      prcsfl
      *
      * User presses F6, throw the add screen, clear, and rebuild subfile
      *
C                       when      cfkey = add
C                       movel(p)  'Add  '        mode
C                       exsr      addrcd
C      *loval           setll     sfl0011f
C                       exsr      clrsf1
C                       exsr      sflbld
      *
      * Add more records to subfile if user pages from bottom of subfile
      *
C                       when      (cfkey = rollup) and (not *in32)
C                       exsr      sflbld

C                       when      cfkey = cancel
C                       leave

C                       endsl
C                       enddo

C                       eval      *inlr = *on
      *
      ******************************************************************
      *  CLRSF1 - Clear the subfile
      ******************************************************************
      *
C      clrsf1           begsr
      *
      * Clear relative record numbers and subfile
      *
C                       eval      rrn1 = *zero
C                       eval      lstrrn = *zero
C                       eval      *in31 = *on
C                       write     sf1ctl
C                       eval      *in31 = *off
C                       eval      *in32 = *off
```

SFL004RG: RPG Program for Master File Maintenance (continued)

```
C                       endsr
*
******************************************************************
*   CLRSF2 - Clear the subfile
******************************************************************
*
C       clrsf2          begsr
*
* Clear relative record numbers and subfile for confirmation screen
*
C                       eval      rrn2 = *zero
C                       eval      lstrrn2 = *zero
C                       eval      *in41 = *on
C                       write     sf2ctl
C                       eval      *in41 = *off

C                       endsr
*
******************************************************************
*   SFLBLD - Build the List
******************************************************************
*
C       sflbld          begsr
*
* Make RRN1 = to the last relative record number of the subfile
* so that the load process will correctly add records to the bottom
*
C                       eval      rrn1 = lstrrn
*
* Load the subfile with one page of data or until end-of-file
*
C                       do        sflpag
C                       read      sfl001lf                         90
C                       if        *in90
C                       leave
C                       endif
C                       eval      rrn1 = rrn1 + 1
C                       eval      option = *blank
C                       write     sfl1
C                       enddo
*
* If no records are loaded to subfile, don't display it
*
C                       if        rrn1 = *zero
C                       eval      *in32 = *on
C                       endif
*
C                       eval      lstrrn = rrn1
*
C                       endsr
*
```

SFL004RG: RPG Program for Master File Maintenance (continued)

```
    ******************************************************************
    *   PRCSFL - Process the options selected
    ******************************************************************
    *
C     prcsfl        begsr
    *
    * Clear the confirmation subfile before starting
    *
C                   exsr        clrsf2
    *
    * Read all the subfile records that were changed by the user
    *
C                   readc       sfl1
    *
    * Do loop to process until all changed records are read
    *
C                   dow         not %eof

C                   select
    *
    * when a 5 is entered throw the DISPLAY screen
    * until F3 or F12 is pressed on that screen
    *
C                   when        option = display
C                   movel(p)    *blanks      mode
C                   exfmt       panel2
C                   eval        option = *blank
C                   update      sfl1
C                   if          (cfkey = exit) or (cfkey = cancel)
C                   leave
C                   endif
    *
    * when a 2 is entered execute the update subroutine,
    * blank out the option field, and update the subfile record
    *
C                   when        option = change
C                   movel(p)    'Update'     mode
C                   exsr        chgdtl
C                   eval        option = *blank
C                   update      sfl1
C                   if          (cfkey = exit) or (cfkey = cancel)
C                   leave
C                   endif
    *
    * when a 4 is entered write the record the the confirmation screen,
    * set on the SFLNXTCHG indicator to mark this record as changed,
    * and update the subfile.  I mark this record incase F12 is pressed
    * from the confirmation screen and the user wants to keep his
    * originally selected records
    *
C                   when        option = delete
```

SFL004RG: RPG Program for Master File Maintenance (continued)

```
C                    eval      rrn2 = rrn2 +1
C                    write     sfl2
C                    eval      *in74 = *on
C                    update    sfl1
C                    eval      *in74 = *off

C                    endsl

C                    readc     sfl1
C                    enddo
 *
 * If records were selected for delete (4), throw the subfile to
 * screen.  If enter is pressed execute the DLTRCD subroutine to
 * physically delete the records, clear, and rebuild the subfile
 * from the last deleted record (you can certainly position the
 * database file where ever you want)
 *
C                    if        rrn2 > 0
C                    eval      lstrrn2 = rrn2
C                    eval      rrn2 = 1
C                    write     fkey2
C                    exfmt     sf2ctl
C                    if        (cfkey  exit) and (cfkey  cancel)
C                    exsr      dltrcd
C        dblnam      setll     sfl0011f
C                    exsr      clrsf1
C                    exsr      sflbld
C                    endif
C                    endif

C                    endsr
 *
 ********************************************************************
 *  CHGDTL - allow user to change data
 ********************************************************************
 *
C        chgdtl      begsr
 *
 * chain to data file using selected subfile record
 *
C        dbidnm      chain     sfl001pf
 *
 * If the record is found (it better be), throw the change screen.
 * If F3 or F12 is pressed, do not update the data file
 *
C                    if        %found
C                    exfmt     panel1

C                    if        (cfkey  exit) and (cfkey  cancel)
C                    update    pfr
C                    endif
```

SFL004RG: RPG Program for Master File Maintenance (continued)

```
C                    endif

C                    endsr
 *
 *****************************************************************
 *   ADDRCD - allow user to add data
 *****************************************************************
 *
C     addrcd         begsr
 *
 * set to last record in the the file to get the last ID number
 *
C     *hival         setgt      sfl001pf
C                    readp      sfl001pf
 *
 * set a new unique ID and throw the screen
 *
C                    if         not %eof
C                    eval       new_id = dbidnm + 1
C                    clear                 pfr
C                    eval       dbidnm = new_id
C                    exfmt      panel1
 *
 * add a new record if the pressed key was not F3 or F12
 *
C                    if         (cfkey  exit) and (cfkey  cancel)
C                    write      pfr
C                    endif

C                    endif

C                    endsr
 *
 *****************************************************************
 *   DLTRCD - delete records
 *****************************************************************
 *
C     dltrcd         begsr
 *
 * read all the records in the confirmation subfile
 * and delete them from the data base file
 *
C                    do         lstrrn2          count
C     count          chain      sfl2
C                    if         %found
C     dbidnm         delete     pfr                          99
C                    endif
C                    enddo

C                    endsr
```

SFL005DF: Display File for Input Subfile Program

```
A*===================================================================
A*
A*  To compile:
A*
A*            CRTDSPF FILE(XXX/SFL005DF) SRCFILE(XXX/QDDSSRC)
A*
A*===================================================================
A*
A*
A                                     DSPSIZ(24 80 *DS3)
A                                     PRINT
A                                     ERRSFL
A                                     CA03
A                                     CA12
A*
A           R SFL1                    SFL
A*
A             DBIDNM    R       H     REFFLD(PFR/DBIDNM *LIBL/SFL001PF)
A             DBLNAM    R       B  5  2REFFLD(PFR/DBLNAM *LIBL/SFL001PF)
A                                     SFLCSRPRG
A                                     CHECK(LC)
A             DBFNAM    R       B  5 26REFFLD(PFR/DBFNAM *LIBL/SFL001PF)
A                                     CHECK(LC)
A             DBMINI    R       B  5 50REFFLD(PFR/DBMINI *LIBL/SFL001PF)
A                                     CHECK(LC)
A             DBNNAM    R       B  5 55REFFLD(PFR/DBNNAM *LIBL/SFL001PF)
A                                     CHECK(LC)
A*
A*
A           R SF1CTL                  SFLCTL(SFL1)
A*
A                                     SFLSIZ(0050)
A                                     SFLPAG(0017)
A                                     OVERLAY
A N32                                 SFLDSP
A N31                                 SFLDSPCTL
A  31                                 SFLINZ
A                                     SFLRNA
A  90                                 SFLEND(*MORE)
A             RRN1         4S 0H      SFLRCDNBR
A                                   1  2'SFL005RG'
A                                   1 25'Add Data to Blank Subfile Lines'
A                                     DSPATR(HI)
A                                   1 71DATE
A                                     EDTCDE(Y)
A                                   2 71TIME
A                                   4  2'Last Name'
A                                     DSPATR(HI)
A                                   4 26'First Name'
```

SFL005DF: Display File for Input Subfile Program (continued)

```
A                                    DSPATR(HI)
A                            4 50'MI'
A                                    DSPATR(HI)
A                            4 55'Nick Name'
A                                    DSPATR(HI)
A*
A           R FKEY1
A*
A                           23  2'F3=Exit'
A                                    COLOR(BLU)
A                           23 12'F12=Cancel'
A                                    COLOR(BLU)
```

SFL005RG: RPG Program for Input Subfile

```
*
*  To compile:
*
*              CRTRPGPGM PGM(XXX/SFL005RG) SRCFILE(XXX/QRPGLESRC)
*
*========================================================================
Fsfl005df  cf   e            workstn
F                                    sfile(sfl1:rrn1)
Fsfl001pf  if a e            k disk
*
***********************************************************************
*  Main Routine
***********************************************************************
*
*  Initialize subfile - RRN1 has to > 0 to initialize records
*
C                 eval      *in31 = *on
C                 eval      rrn1 = 1
C                 write     sfl1ctl
C                 eval      *in31 = *off
C                 eval      *in90 = *on
*
*  Do loop to process the subfile until F3 or F12 is pressed
*
C                 dou       *inkc or *inkl
*
C                 write     fkey1
C                 exfmt     sfl1ctl
*
*  Process changes if enter key pressed
*
C                 if        (not *inkc) and (not *inkl)
```

SFL005RG: RPG Program for Input Subfile (continued)

```
C                   exsr      prcsfl
C                   endif
 *
C                   enddo
 *
C                   eval      *inlr = *on
 *
 *******************************************************************
 *   PRCSFL - Process the subfile
 *******************************************************************
 *
C     prcsfl        begsr
 *
C                   readc     sfl1
 *
 * Do loop to process until all changed records are read
 *
C                   dow       not %eof
 *
C                   select
 *
 * Add when something's in the subfile
 *
C                   when      dblnam = *blanks
C                   eval      *in42 = *on
C                   eval      *in74 = *on
C                   update    sfl1
C                   eval      *in74 = *off
 *
C                   when      dblnam > *blanks
C     *hival        setgt     sfl001pf
C                   readp     sfl001pf
C                   eval      dbidnm = dbidnm + 1
C                   write     pfr
C                   endsl
 *
C                   readc     sfl1
C                   enddo
 *
C                   endsr
 *
```

SFL007DF: Display File for Alternative Master File Maintenance

```
 *=========================================================================
 *
 *  To compile:
 *
 *               CRTDSPF FILE(XXX/SFL005DFSFL007DF) SRCFILE(XXX/QDDSSRC)
 *
 *=========================================================================
A*
A                                        DSPSIZ(24 80 *DS3)
A                                        PRINT
A                                        ERRSFL
A                                        CA03
A                                        CA12
A*
A          R SFL1                        SFL
A*
A            DBIDNM    R       H         REFFLD(PFR/DBIDNM *LIBL/SFL001PF)
A            DBLNAM    R       B  5  2REFFLD(PFR/DBLNAM *LIBL/SFL001PF)
A                                        SFLCSRPRG
A                                        CHECK(LC)
A            DBFNAM    R       B  5 26REFFLD(PFR/DBFNAM *LIBL/SFL001PF)
A                                        CHECK(LC)
A            DBMINI    R       B  5 50REFFLD(PFR/DBMINI *LIBL/SFL001PF)
A                                        CHECK(LC)
A            DBNNAM    R       B  5 55REFFLD(PFR/DBNNAM *LIBL/SFL001PF)
A                                        CHECK(LC)
A*
A          R SF1CTL                      SFLCTL(SFL1)
A*
A                                        SFLSIZ(0050)
A                                        SFLPAG(0017)
A                                        OVERLAY
A N32                                    SFLDSP
A N31                                    SFLDSPCTL
A   31                                   SFLINZ
A                                        SFLRNA
A   90                                   SFLEND(*MORE)
A            RRN1              4S 0H      SFLRCDNBR(CURSOR)
A                                      4  2'Last Name'
A                                        DSPATR(HI)
A                                      4 26'First Name'
A                                        DSPATR(HI)
A                                      4 50'MI'
A                                        DSPATR(HI)
A                                      4 55'Nick Name'
A                                        DSPATR(HI)
A                                      1  2'SFL007RG'
A                                      1 27'Simple Subfile Program'
A                                        DSPATR(HI)
A                                      1 71DATE
```

SFL007DF: Display File for Alternative Master File Maintenance (continued)

```
A                                     EDTCDE(Y)
A                               2 71TIME
A*
A          R FKEY1
A*
A                              23  2'F3=Exit'
A                                     COLOR(BLU)
A                              23 12'F12=Cancel'
A                                     COLOR(BLU)
```

SFL007RG: RPG Program for Alternative Master File Maintenance

```
 *
 *   To compile:
 *
 *              CRTRPGPGM PGM(XXX/SFL007RG) SRCFILE(XXX/QRPGLESRC)
 *
 *=======================================================================
Fsfl007df  cf   e              workstn
F                                        sfile(sfl1:rrn1)
Fsfl0011f  if   e         k disk         prefix(in_)
Fsfl001pf  uf a e         k disk         prefix(up_)
F                                        rename(pfr:up_pfr)
 *
 *******************************************************************
 *   Main Routine
 *******************************************************************
 *
 *  Build the subfile
 *
C                   exsr      sflbld
 *
 *  Do loop to process the subfile until F3 or F12 is pressed
 *
C                   dou       *inkc or *inkl
 *
C                   write     fkey1
C                   exfmt     sfl1ctl
 *
 *  Process changes if enter key pressed
 *
C                   if        (not *inkc) and (not *inkl)
C                   exsr      prcsfl
C                   endif
 *
C                   enddo
 *
```

⟶

107

SFL007RG: RPG Program for Alternative Master File Maintenance (continued)

```
C                      eval       *inlr = *on
  *
  **********************************************************************
  *   SFLBLD - Build the List
  **********************************************************************
  *
C       sflbld         begsr
  *
  *   Clear subfile - RRN1 has to > 0 to initialize records
  *
C                      eval       *in31 = *on
C                      eval       rrn1 = 1
C                      write      sf1ctl
C                      eval       rrn1 = 0
C                      eval       *in31 = *off
  *
  * Load data to subfile
  *
C       *loval         setll      sfl0011f
C                      read       sfl0011f

C                      dow        (not %eof) and (rrn1 <= 50)
C                      eval       rrn1 = rrn1 + 1
C                      eval       dbidnm = in_dbidnm
C                      eval       dblnam = in_dblnam
C                      eval       dbfnam = in_dbfnam
C                      eval       dbmini = in_dbmini
C                      eval       dbnnam = in_dbnnam
C                      write      sfl1
C                      read       sfl0011f
C                      enddo
  *
  * If no records were loaded, do not display the subfile - else
  * increment the relative record by one to place the cursor on
  * the first empty subfile record - SFLRCDNBR(CURSOR)
  *
C                      if         rrn1 = *zero
C                      eval       *in32 = *on
C                      else
C                      eval       rrn1 = rrn1 + 1
C                      endif
  *
  * set on indicator 90 to display more and bottom
  *
C                      eval       *in90 = *on
  *
C                      endsr
  *
  **********************************************************************
  *   PRCSFL - Process the subfile
  **********************************************************************
```

SFL007RG: RPG Program for Alternative Master File Maintenance (continued)

```
     *
C       prcsfl       begsr
     *
C                    readc      sfl1
     *
 * Do loop to process until all changed records are read
     *
C                    dow        not %eof
     *
C                    select
     *
 * Add when hidden field is empty but something's in the subfile
     *
C                    when       (dbidnm = 0) and (dblnam > *blanks)
C      *hival        setgt      sfl001pf
C                    readp      sfl001pf
C                    eval       up_dblnam = dblnam
C                    eval       up_dbfnam = dbfnam
C                    eval       up_dbmini = dbmini
C                    eval       up_dbnnam = dbnnam
C                    eval       up_dbidnm = up_dbidnm + 1
C                    write      up_pfr
     *
 * Update when hidden field is not empty and neither is last name
     *
C                    when       (dbidnm  0) and (dblnam > *blanks)
C      dbidnm        chain      sfl001pf
C                    eval       up_dblnam = dblnam
C                    eval       up_dbfnam = dbfnam
C                    eval       up_dbmini = dbmini
C                    eval       up_dbnnam = dbnnam
C                    if         %found
C                    update     up_pfr
C                    endif
     *
 * Delete when hidden field is not empty but last name is empty
     *
C                    when       (dbidnm  0) and (dblnam = *blanks)
C      dbidnm        chain      sfl001pf
C                    if         %found
C                    delete     up_pfr
C                    endif
     *
C                    endsl
C                    readc      sfl1
C                    enddo
     *
C                    exsr       sflbld
     *
C                    endsr
     *
```

4

WINDOW SUBFILES: WHO NEEDS A PC TO HAVE SCROLLABLE WINDOWS?

This chapter discusses windows and windowed subfiles. To show you how easy windowed subfiles are to implement, let's revisit our Name Master file program from the previous chapter. Remember our delete confirmation screen? This was the screen used to list the subfile records selected for delete by the user. Figure 4.1 shows the screen as it was designed in the previous chapter.

What if the user wants to be able to see part of the data from the original screen while he's looking at the confirmation screen? Or maybe he wants to see if there are records from the original subfile that he wants to delete, but doesn't want to press F12 from the confirmation screen to do so. Figure 4.2 shows the newly designed confirmation screen as a windowed subfile. The transformation was extremely easy to create and required very little change to my RPG program.

```
                        Confirm Delete of Records

   Press Enter to confirm your choices for Delete.
   Press F12=Cancel to return to change your choices.


   Last Name               First Name
   Coker                   Jim
   Tessential              Quinn
   Vandever                Kevin
   Vannerberg              Kern







                                                                Bottom

   F3=Exit     F12=Cancel
```

Figure 4.1: Original design of delete confirmation screen.

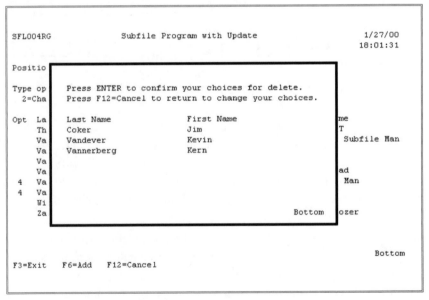

Figure 4.2: Delete confirmation screen as a window.

SO LITTLE CHANGED, SO MUCH ACCOMPLISHED

Figure 4.3 shows the DDS for the new windowed subfile. I changed my record format name from SFL1 to WINDOW1. I didn't have to, but I think this better reflects that it's a windowed subfile. Because it's still in the subfile record format, I'll give it the SFL keyword.

```
A           R WINDOW1                    SFL
A*
A             DBIDNM    R        H        REFFLD(PFR/DBIDNM *LIBL/SFL001PF)
A             DBLNAM    R        O  6   2REFFLD(PFR/DBLNAM *LIBL/SFL001PF)
A             DBFNAM    R        O  6  26REFFLD(PFR/DBFNAM *LIBL/SFL001PF)
A*
A           R SF2CTL                     SFLCTL(WINDOW1)
A*
A                                        SFLDSP
A N41                                    SFLDSPCTL
A  41                                    SFLCLR
A N41                                    SFLEND(*MORE)
A                                        SFLSIZ(0009)
A                                        SFLPAG(0008)
A                                        WINDOW(4 10 16 52)
A             RRN2            4S 0H
A                                     5  2'Last Name'
A                                        DSPATR(HI)
A                                     5 26'First Name'
A                                        DSPATR(HI)
A                                     2  2'Press ENTER to confirm your choice-
A                                        s for delete.'
A                                        COLOR(BLU)
A                                     3  2'Press F12=Cancel to return to chan-
A                                        ge your choices.'
A                                        COLOR(BLU)
```

Figure 4.3: The DDS for a window subfile (SFL006DF).

It's interesting to note that if you use Screen Design Aid (SDA) to code your display formats, which I occasionally do, SDA will prompt you, when you select Option 1 to add a new format, to provide the type of record format it is. Instead of selecting SFL as you would with a normal subfile record format, you would select Window Subfile (WDWSFL). SDA will then prompt you for the subfile control record format that controls this subfile, and you'll enter the name as normal (I still used SF2CTL in my example).

This is important to know because if you're using SDA and enter WDWSFL as the type of record format, SDA will provide you with both the subfile and the window keywords to use. Selecting type SFL in SDA won't provide you the opportunity to define window keywords. You'll have to do so directly in the code. Also, even though you define the record format as WDWSFL, it will show up as SFL in your DDS specifications. I bring this up because many programmers use SDA, and I thought it might be beneficial to mention how SDA works with subfiles and windows, especially as it relates to the WDWSFL-to-SFL keyword quirk.

The other change you'll notice in the subfile record format is that the starting positions are different. The new starting positions are related to the window and not the entire screen. Regardless of where you position your window, the starting points for the fields will be in column 2 of that window. This allows you to display the window based on cursor position, as well as hard-coded starting positions.

Looking at the subfile control record format, notice that only two things have changed. First, I added the WINDOW keyword. The WINDOW keyword describes the length, width, and position of the window. In this case, my window starts in row 4, column 10, and is 16 lines long and 52 characters wide.

The second change is to the OVERLAY keyword, which allows me to overlay the previous data without clearing the screen. That's it for the DDS. All I had to change in the RPG program was the name of the subfile record format. Instead of writing to SFL1, I now write to WINDOW1. Now, when the user selects records to be deleted, he will see the new windowed subfile as his confirmation screen. Figure 4.4 shows the changed RPG code: first, the definition of WINDOW1 in the file specification; next, the writing of WINDOW1 when the user specifies a delete; and, finally, the reading of the records in the window from format WINDOW1 to determine if the user deleted any records.

```
Fsfl006df  cf   e           workstn
F                                       sfile(sfl1:rrn1)
F                                       sfile(window1:rrn2)
F                                       infds(info)
```

Figure 4.4: Modifications to the RPG program to use the new window subfile (SFL006RG).

114

```
      ****************************************************************
      *   PRCSFL - Process the options selected
      ****************************************************************
      *
      C       prcsfl        begsr
      *
      * when a 4 is entered write the record the the confirmation screen,
      * set on the SFLNXTCHG indicator to mark this record as changed,
      * and update the subfile.  I mark this record incase F12 is pressed
      * from the confirmation screen and the user wants to keep his
      * originally selected records
      *
      C                     when          option = delete
      C                     eval          rrn2 = rrn2 +1
      C                     write         window1
      C                     eval          *in74 = *on
      C                     update        sfl1
      C                     eval          *in74 = *off
      C
      C                     endsl
      ****************************************************************
      *   DLTRCD - delete records
      ****************************************************************
      *
      C       dltrcd        begsr
      *
      * read all the records in the confirmation subfile
      * and delete them from the database file
      *
      C                     do            lstrrn2          count
      C       count         chain         window1
      C                     if            %found
      C       dbidnm        delete        pfr                            99
      C                     endif
      C                     enddo
      C
      C                     endsr
```

Figure 4.4: Modifications to the RPG program to use the new window subfile (SFL006RG) (continued).

I've just given you an extremely simple example of a windowed subfile. And really, it's pretty simple to implement a windowed subfile, no matter how I do it. OS/400 does so much of the work for me. The RPG program (you can find the complete code at the end of this chapter) has barely changed from the master file maintenance program in the last chapter. You can see the power of DDS to control the display features of a screen. RPG is only along for the ride.

SFLEND AND THE BAR SCENE

If I want to add a little pizzazz to the screen, I can add a scroll bar to either or both of my subfiles in this program. Let's add a scroll bar to the confirmation window I just showed you. See Figure 4.5.

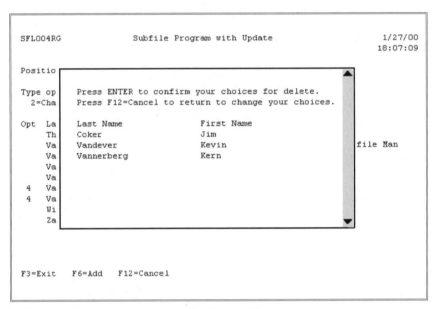

```
SFL004RG               Subfile Program with Update              1/27/00
                                                                18:07:09

  Positio ┌──────────────────────────────────────────────────┐▲
          │                                                    │
  Type op │  Press ENTER to confirm your choices for delete.   │
    2=Cha │  Press F12=Cancel to return to change your choices.│
          │                                                    │
  Opt  La │  Last Name              First Name                 │
       Th │  Coker                  Jim                        │
       Va │  Vandever               Kevin                      │file Man
       Va │  Vannerberg             Kern                       │
       Va │                                                    │
       Va │                                                    │
    4  Va │                                                    │
    4  Va │                                                    │
       Wi │                                                    │
       Za │                                                    │▼
          └──────────────────────────────────────────────────┘

  F3=Exit   F6=Add   F12=Cancel
```

Figure 4.5: Example of a window subfile with a scroll bar.

In chapter 1, I talked about the SFLEND keyword and mentioned that it had other valid parameters that would be discussed later. Well, it's later. In the subfile control record format, SF2CTL, I'll change my SFLEND keyword parameter from *MORE to *SCRBAR, recompile my DDS and program, and—voila! (See the code in Figure 4.6.) Notice that the only change is the addition of *SCRBAR to the SFLEND keyword.

```
A            R WINDOW1                    SFL
A*
A            DBIDNM    R       H      REFFLD(PFR/DBIDNM *LIBL/SFL001PF)
A            DBLNAM    R       O  6  2REFFLD(PFR/DBLNAM *LIBL/SFL001PF)
A            DBFNAM    R       O  6 26REFFLD(PFR/DBFNAM *LIBL/SFL001PF)
```

Figure 4.6: SFL record format with coding for a scroll bar (SFL006DF with SFLEND modification).

```
A*
A           R SF2CTL                    SFLCTL(WINDOW1)
A*
A                                       SFLDSP
A N41                                   SFLDSPCTL
A   41                                  SFLCLR
A N41                                   SFLEND(*SCRBAR *MORE)
A                                       SFLSIZ(0009)
A                                       SFLPAG(0008)
A                                       WINDOW(4 10 16 52)
```

Figure 4.6: SFL record format with coding for a scroll bar (SFL006DF with SFLEND modification) (continued).

This scroll bar can be used like a scroll bar on a PC; that is, it can be controlled with a pointing device such as a mouse. It doesn't remove the capability to scroll using the keyboard, but merely provides another option to the user. It's extremely easy to implement. Because not all workstation controllers support pointer devices and scroll bars, you may want to add both the *SCRBAR and *MORE parameters to the SFLEND keyword. That way, if the scroll bar isn't supported, the user will still see "More" and "Bottom" on the lower right of his subfile, as he's accustomed to. No additional programming had to be done to display and control the scroll bar, and the RPG didn't change at all.

The RPG programs SFL005RG, SFL006RG, and SFL007RG on your CD are all basically the same. The only reason there are three separate programs is because I created a new display file with each new feature and changed a record format name or two. As a result, I created separate RPG source members to reflect each change.

BUT WAIT! THERE'S MORE

I've already shown you a couple of techniques related to windowed subfiles, but I haven't really explained all there is to know about how to implement them. There's more to a windowed subfile than the WINDOW keyword and a new parameter in the SFLEND keyword. Before we go on, I'll define some terms and introduce some new DDS keywords related to windows.

117

WINDOWS 101

Windows are very powerful tools to use for displaying subfiles because they do more than just present information in a smaller format. They provide system-resource save and restore functions, cursor control, and message handling, all without much effort by the programmer. With a couple of keyword entries, OS/400 will handle much of the work for you.

A window is an area of information that overlays part of your display screen. You may view and update information in the window, as well as view information on the portion of the screen the window isn't covering. When a window is displayed, it's the only part of the screen that's active. As a result, you can't do anything with the screen that the window is covering until the window is removed. You can display up to 12 windows at a time, but no matter how many are displayed, only one can be active at a time.

The *window definition record* is the record format that contains the WINDOW keyword. In the case of my program example, it's the subfile control record format, SF2CTL, for the confirmation screen. You can also have a *window reference* record format. While the window reference format contains the WINDOW keyword, the keyword refers to another format for the actual window attributes. I didn't use it in my example, but it comes in handy when you have multiple windows that all have the same attributes. You can define the attributes in one record format and refer to that format using the WINDOW keyword with the format name as a parameter.

The window border is the area that surrounds the window. In my example, I used the defaults, which means I didn't have to explicitly define them in my DDS. The border doesn't have to be visible. The active window is the one that has had the last input or output operation performed against it. When you use visible borders, the active window will appear to be the top-most window. When writing multiple window applications, be aware that removing a window from the display and overlaying a window are two different actions. When a window is removed from a display, it's no longer accessible to the user. When a window is overlaid by another window, it might not be visible to the user and it is no longer active. It is, however, still accessible to the user and can be made active again when the over-laying window is removed.

THE KEYWORDS

There are five DDS keywords programmers have at their disposal to create windows and window subfiles. With them, you make OS/400 do a lot for you and create some very effective and efficient window applications.

WINDOW (window) – This is the one required keyword used to define a window in your application. It's used to define the window, change the contents of a window, or make an inactive window active again. You can define how the program acts when the cursor is outside the window borders, tell where messages are to be displayed, or simply point to another record format to get your attributes.

WDWBORDER (window border) – This keyword is used to define the color, display attributes, and characters of a window border.

WDWTITLE (window title) – This keyword is used to embed the title of the window inside the border. Embedded in the top or bottom of the border, it allows you to define the text, color, and attributes for the title of the window. Note, though, that not all workstation controllers support text in the bottom of the border. Also, some do not allow left and right justification of title text.

RMVWDW (remove window) – This keyword is used to remove previous windows when a new window is displayed or an existing window is made active when it's redisplayed.

USRRSTDSP (user restore display) – This keyword stops OS/400 from performing automatic save and restore functions on the underlying display when windows are displayed and removed. In most cases, you probably want to allow OS/400 to do its thing because it requires no effort on the part of the programmer. There are times, however, when performance is more of an issue and you may want to disable this activity. Preventing the automatic save and restore of the underlying display may improve your response time. Another use of the USRRSTDSP keyword is when you want an overlaid window to pop-up and become active. You can also use it to make two windows seem like they're both active—something I will show you in a later chapter.

WINDOWS 201

In the windows world, OS/400 automatically performs save and restore operations in your application. Before a window is displayed, OS/400 saves the whole display, including any windows not being removed. When windows are removed, OS/400 restores the display minus the removed windows. If a new window is added to the display, the active record is saved when the new window record is written, and the entire display remains as background data. The new window becomes the active record. The saved record doesn't have to be a window. OS/400 handles non-window records in the same way if the display files are created (CRTDSPF) with the restore display parameter (RSTDSP) set to *YES.

If the window record being written to the display is a previously existing window, more recent windows are removed without being saved. The target window is then restored by OS/400, the new record is written, and that window becomes active.

If a non-window record is written to the display, all bets are off. Any existing windows are removed without being saved, the new record is written to the display as it existed prior to any windows, and that display becomes active.

OS/400 provides these services without any consideration required from you, the programmer. It's best if you know the rules, but you don't really have to. You don't really have to think about what's going on beneath the application code. You know OS/400 is taking care of you as you display and remove your windows. There are times, however, when you might want to bypass some of the processing provided by OS/400.

Most of the time, this decision will be made based on whether your windows are displayed over communication lines or locally. Response time is critical when your users are attached remotely. The save and restore operations performed by OS/400 can adversely affect response times for remote users, depending on how fast your communication rate is. High-speed communication lines and local area networks (LAN) provide almost local-like response and therefore probably need no tweaking. Anything less, such as 9600-baud rate lines, may require you to perform some tweaking to improve response times.

MORE ON USRRSTDSP AND TWEAKING

The USRRSTDSP keyword contains a lot of power. You can use it to bypass the system save and restore processing performed by OS/400 and, instead, program your application to rebuild the display only when necessary. This technique can improve system performance and reduce response times for your users. They will love you for it. In addition to solving response time issues for remote users, you can implement USRRSTDSP when you display only one window at a time and each window exists in a different display file. It may also be unnecessary for OS/400 to perform all that saving and restoring when you display a series of windows, but note that the user will never return to the earlier windows. You can also have some fun with USRRSTDSP when you want more than one window to seem active at one time. I'll show you that in a later chapter.

The following are times when two saves are performed on the same display:

- When your application displays only one window at a time.

- When your display file is created with the Restore Display parameter turned on: RSTDSP(*YES).

- When the first window record to overlay the display is located in a separate file.

The first SAVE operation is performed when the display file is suspended. The second SAVE operation is performed because a window is being displayed. USRRSTDSP eliminates the second, unnecessary SAVE operation.

What does IBM say? The following excerpt from *Application Display Programming V4R1,* section 2.4.13.2, explains it well. To bypass system save and restore processing, IBM suggests that you perform the following steps:

1. Create your own procedure to rebuild the display after a window is removed. Be sure to include any data the user enters and that must be redisplayed.

2. Specify the record-level USRRSTDSP keyword on the window following the first window you don't want the system to save. The USRRSTDSP keyword keeps the system from performing save and restore operations. The USRRSTDSP keyword is allowed only on records containing the WINDOW keyword; it's ignored on the window reference record.

Once the USRRSTDSP keyword is specified, it remains in effect, even if the option indicator is set off, until you read or write to either the initial, windowless display or the window that is two windows before the window on which the USRRSTDSP keyword was specified. Assume that six windows are on the display and the USRRSTDSP keyword was specified on the fourth. To turn off USRRSTDSP and have the system resume saving the display, you must write to the second window. As shown in the diagram below, the system has saved only the first two windows:

```
 _____
|                                                       |
|      _____                   |
|     | 1. Saved                     |                   |
|     |       _____ |__                 |
|     |     | 2. Saved               |  |                |
|     |     |       _____|  |__              |
|     |     |     | 3. Not saved        |   |            |
|     |     |     |       _____|   |__          |
|     |__|  |     |     | 4. USRRSTDSP; not saved |      |
|        |  |     |     |       _____|   |__   |
|        |__|  |  |     |     | 5. Not saved          |  |
|           |  |  |     |     |       _____|__|
|           |__|  |     |     | | 6. Not saved          | |
|              |  |     |     |                         | |
|              |__|  |  |     |                         | |
|                 |  |  |     |                         | |
|                 |__|  |     |                         | |
|                    |  |     |                         | |
|                    |__|     |_____| |
|_____|
```

The USRRSTDSP keyword interacts with other keywords and window-related functions. Before using the keyword, you should understand the following points (assume that the USRRSTDSP keyword is in effect):

- If a window record is written to a window that was saved (window 1 or 2 in the above example), the saved display is restored, the current record is written to the target window, and the target window becomes active. At this point, the USRRSTDSP keyword is no longer in effect.

- If a window definition record is written to a window that was not saved (window 3, 4, or 5 in the above example), it becomes a new window. It's merged with the previous display image and written to the display. No windows are removed.

- If a window record is read from a window that was not saved (window 3, 4, or 5 in the above example), an error message is returned to the application.

- If the initial display has been saved and the application writes to a window record specifying the RMVWDW keyword, any existing windows are removed. The new window is displayed on top of the initial display. The new window is active, and USRRSTDSP is no longer in effect.

- If the initial display isn't saved and the application writes to a window record that specifies the RMVWDW keyword, all existing windows are removed. The new window is displayed on top of the initial display. The new window is active, and USRRSTDSP is still in effect.

- If a non-window record is written to the display and USRRSTDSP is specified on the first window, then the window is not removed, and the non-window record may overlay all or part of the window.

Empowered with all this new knowledge, let's take a look at another example of a windowed subfile. In the following example, I won't use USRRSTDSP, even though I'm coding under one of the conditions IBM recommends. I will allow

OS/400 to control the saving and restoring of the display for the purpose of this example—and because it does it so well. If you're anxious to put USRRSTDSP to use, I will use it later in this book. Also, while I'm telling you what I'm not going to do, I will mention that the following example does not employ the RMVWDW keyword. I hold no disdain for this particular keyword, but I also have no use for it in this example. For you own sake, though, please feel free to add a window to this display and check out the RMVWDW keyword on your own.

WHAT PROMPTED YOU TO DISPLAY?

In my experience, window subfiles are most widely used as prompting tools. If a user is keying data and that data exists somewhere in a Master file, why should he have to rekey the data when he can look it up? Providing the user with a pop-up window to display and allow selection not only saves time, but also helps avoid possible keying errors.

At the end of the chapter, I have provided the complete listings for program (PNL001RG) and DDS (PNL001DF) that allow a user to key some data. In this program, the user is going to be able to press the F4 key to prompt for name information from our Name Master file. When the user presses F4, a window will pop up and list names. The user will be able to select a name and bring it back to his original display to fill in his data entry screen. PNL001RG and PNL001DF are merely a simulated data entry program and an associated display file. I say "simulated" because they're really not doing anything. I coded only the beginnings to show you how the prompting and returning of data work. I didn't provide a full-fledged maintenance program—you already have that.

The window we'll be discussing isn't part of PNL001DF and PNL001RG. It's a separate program and display file. When the user presses F4, he's calling a new program to get his data. This technique is useful because it's likely that many applications will require a name-prompting tool. If you make that tool a part of every program that needs it, you're setting yourself up for a program maintenance nightmare by duplicating code in so many places. Ever heard the term code reuse? Well, by coding the prompting program separately, you set it up to be used by other programs, without the duplication of code.

RTNCSRLOC AND PROMPTING

Figure 4.7 shows the addition of the CF04 to the DDS, which makes F4 a valid function key. In this example, the user will press F4 when he wants to prompt for a name.

```
A*
A                                       DSPSIZ(24 80 *DS3)
A                                       PRINT
A                                       ERRSFL
A                                       CA03
A                                       CA12
A                                       CF04
```

Figure 4.7: The addition of function key 4 to allow prompting (PNL001DF).

Figure 4.8 introduces you to a new keyword, return cursor location (RNTCSRLOC), which we added to the PANEL1 format. This keyword isn't subfile specific, but deserves mentioning. It's used to return the record format and field name that contain the cursor when control is returned to your program. This keyword has several parameters and many uses, but mentioning them is outside what I want to accomplish here. For this program, I'm really only interested in the field name. I want my RPG program to know which field the user was on when he pressed F4. The parameters &FLD and &RCD are defined in the record format as hidden 10-byte alpha fields. I'm not going to use this information in my example, but as we get into the RPG, this information will allow you to understand the flexibility afforded by this keyword.

```
A          R PANEL1
A                                       RTNCSRLOC(&RCD &FLD)
A                              1  2'PNL001RG'
A                              1 24'Program to prompt a window  '
A                                       DSPATR(HI)
A                              1 71DATE
A                                       EDTCDE(Y)
A                              2 71TIME
A            FLD          10A H
A            RCD          10A H
```

Figure 4.8: Example of the RTNCSRLOC keyword with hidden fields defined for field and record (PNL001DF).

As I stated earlier, this isn't a full-fledged data entry program. I'm merely providing you with a sample to show how you might activate a window subfile in another program. The code in Figure 4.9 shows a typical function key interrogation routine. If F4 (represented by the prompt constant) is pressed, the GETDTA subroutine is executed.

```
C                     if      cfkey = prompt
C                     exsr    getdta
C                     endif
```

Figure 4.9: If the F4 key is pressed, prompt for a name (PNL001RG).

Figure 4.10 shows the GETDTA subroutine. When F4 is pressed, the program will call program SFL008RG (the windowed subfile) and pass one parameter. Nothing is sent to SFL008RG. The DBIDNM parameter is used only to hold the customer number of the name selected by the user. If there's something in DBIDNM upon returning from SFL008RG, it's used to chain to the data file and retrieve the appropriate information for the screen.

```
C       getdta        begsr
  *
C                     call    'SFL008RG'
C                     parm                    dbidnm
  *
C                     if      dbidnm > 0
C       dbidnm        chain   sfl001pf
C                     if      not %found
C                     eval    dblnam = error
C                     endif
C                     endif
  *
C                     endsr
```

Figure 4.10: The prompt window is actually a separate program called from the GETDTA routine (PNL001RG).

In this example, there's only one prompting program to be called, SFL008RG. No matter which field your cursor is on, the name window will display when F4 is pressed. But what if you have other data that you wish to prompt for? How do you tell which prompting program to call? Well, if I wanted to, I could use the field name returned to my program by the RTNCSRLOC keyword. Depending on the field name returned, I could call a different prompting window, as shown in Figure 4.11.

This code shows how I could have coded the program if I wanted to call a different prompting program, depending on which field the user placed the cursor before pressing the F4 key. In the first WHEN clause, I could check for the field DBFNAM, which is the FIRST NAME field, and call my original GETDTA subroutine. A second WHEN clause could be used to determine if F4 was pressed on the first address field, DBADD1. If this clause is satisfied, another subroutine might get executed to call a different windowed subfile program. This type of structure can continue for as many fields as you want to prompt.

```
C                     if        cfkey = prompt
C                     select
C                     When      FLD = DBFNAM
C                     exsr      getdta

C                     When      FLD = DBADD1
C                     exsr      XYZ

C                     endsl
C                     endif
```

Figure 4.11: Method to tell your program which prompting program to call based on where the cursor resides (PNL001RG).

SELECTION LISTS—A COOL WAY TO RETURN DATA

Now let's take a look at the actual windowed subfile for this example. After all, that's why you're reading this chapter, isn't it?

SFL008DF is the DDS for my windowed subfile that will be called from PNL001RG. In this DDS, I'll use some additional window keywords mentioned earlier in this chapter and break out a few of the subfile keywords introduced to you in chapter 1. Instead of providing the user with a simple load-all subfile from which to choose his data, I am going to add a twist. That twist is in the form of a selection list.

A selection list subfile is perfect for prompting and returning data. What differentiates a selection list subfile from a regular subfile is its ability to restrict the user to one choice or allow many choices. With a selection list, you can also allow simple cursor maneuvering and data selection without adding an input field. You'll understand more on the latter point as you continue. To make this subfile a selection list, I employ two of the subfile selection list keywords introduced to you in chapter 1.

DESIGNING THE SELECTION LIST

You've seen most of the DDS for this example before. It's a load-all subfile as determined by SFLSIZ and SFLPAG not being equal. You'll also notice that there is no ROLLUP or ROLLDOWN keyword—another indication that this is a load-all subfile. Figure 4.12 shows the subfile window record format in which I define a one-byte hidden field, CTLFLD, and assign it as the selection list choice control field with the SFLCHCCTL keyword.

```
A          R WINDOW1                 SFL
A*
A            CTLFLD        1Y 0H      SFLCHCCTL
A            DBIDNM    R       H      REFFLD(PFR/DBIDNM *LIBL/SFL001PF)
A            FULLNM       40   0  6  2
```

Figure 4.12: A window subfile where OS/400 will enforce the logic rules for the user (SFL008DF).

Coding it this way allows OS/400 to ensure the selection list rules, which are determined later in my control record format, are enforced. I also define another hidden field, DBIDNM. This is my customer number, and although it won't be displayed, it's what I'll pass back to the calling program when the user makes a selection.

The last field is a 40-byte alpha field called FULLNM. This field will house the first and last name from the data file. The reason I decided to concatenate the two fields is because of a restriction with selection lists, which dictates that you can have only one output field when a selection list is used. Because I want both names to be displayed in the window, I concatenate them into one field. Clever, huh?

Now look at the code in Figure 4.13 and my window keywords. This code is in the definition of the subfile control record format, WINDOW1. You've already seen the WINDOW keyword, but it's a little different here.

```
A                                    WINDOW(*DFT 14 44 *NOMSGLIN)
A                                    WDWBORDER((*COLOR PNK))
A                                    WDWTITLE((*TEXT 'Name Selection') (-
A                                    *COLOR WHT))
A                                    WDWTITLE((*TEXT 'F12=Cancel') (*COL-
A                                    OR BLU) *BOTTOM)
```

Figure 4.13: The window keywords that define where the window will display and how it will look (SFL008DF).

Instead of hard-coded coordinates for starting positions, I use the parameter *DFT. This will allow my window to display in relation to where the cursor is located on the display. If the cursor is at the top of the screen when F4 is pressed, the window will display underneath the cursor. If the cursor is at the bottom, the window will display above it. I define the window as 14 lines long and 44 characters wide and tell it that I don't need a message line.

The next windows keyword you see is the WDWBORDER keyword. This allows you to define the borders of your window. I used the default borders in my last example, so I didn't have to explicitly define it. You can define the characters, color, and attributes of your window. In this example, I'm going use the default characters and attributes, but I'm also going to change the color to pink. (It's my wife's favorite color, okay?) Because it's so simple, this is one keyword I like to define in SDA.

The next keyword can't be defined using SDA, so don't waste your time. The WDWTITLE keyword allows you to insert text into your border. The text can be placed on the top or bottom and can be on the left, center, or right. Some workstation controllers don't support bottom border titles or non-centered top border titles. You can code for them, and if your controller doesn't support them, they'll be ignored. My first border title is type *TEXT, centered on the top and colored white. Because centered and *TOP are the defaults for this keyword, I didn't explicitly define them.

The second WDWBORDER keyword allows me to add text to the bottom of my border. Because I can't add a separate record format to display the valid function keys, as I can with a regular subfile, I need another way to accomplish this. A bottom window border is that way. I am going to add the *TEXT data "F12=Cancel", color it blue, and place it on the bottom border of the window. Because left-justified placement is the default for bottom window borders, I don't have to explicitly define it.

Before I go on, I may have lost some of you when I quickly brushed over the fact that I can't have a function key record format. Each record format in which I add the WINDOW keyword becomes a window. If I create a record format to display function keys without the WINDOW keyword, it will be written to the original display. If I add the WINDOW keyword or reference a format with the WINDOW keyword, it becomes its own window. The only way to show the user the function keys at the bottom of the window is to do so in the border.

Figure 4.14 illustrates the two keywords that are important to this selection list. These are also part of the definition of the subfile control record format, WINDOW1.

Figure 4.14: These keywords are used to provide a single choice list for the user (SFL008DF).

The first important keyword is the subfile single choice (SFLSNGCHC) keyword, which tells OS/400 that only one choice can be selected and returned from the list. The user can scroll through and try to select many entries, but only the last entry selected is the one returned when Enter is pressed. The Restrict Cursor (*RSTCSR) parameter restricts the cursor to the list so the user can use the arrow

130

keys to scroll down the current page without leaving the list. When the cursor reaches the bottom of the list, it automatically goes back to the top of the list.

The subfile cursor relative record number (SFLCSRRRN) keyword and its parameter return the subfile relative record number so the cursor is on when control is returned back to the RPG program. The &RRN1 parameter is defined as a hidden field of five zoned decimal. Your program will use the relative record number to send the correct information back to the calling program.

Earlier in this chapter, I showed you how to display a window over a record format in the same display file by using the OVERLAY keyword. Well, in this example, you're going to display a window over a record format in a different display file. OVERLAY will not work in this case.

To display your window without erasing the current display, you'll use the AS-SUME keyword. The ASSUME keyword is used to tell OS/400 to assume that the record is already written when the display file is open. As a result, OS/400 won't attempt to erase the current display before displaying the window. Ironically, you can't use the ASSUME keyword and WINDOW keywords in the same record format. Because of this, I create the record shown in Figure 4.15 called ASSUME with the ASSUME keyword and one non-display field.

```
A               R ASSUME
A*
A                                       ASSUME
```

Figure 4.15: The ASSUME keyword allows the user to display one program's window over another program's display without erasing the current display (SFL008DF).

I never have to reference this record in my RPG, but I can write the window without erasing the current display by placing it in my DDS. (It's now our little secret how to fool OS/400.)

Figure 4.16 shows what the window looks like when the user presses F4 from
PNL001RG.

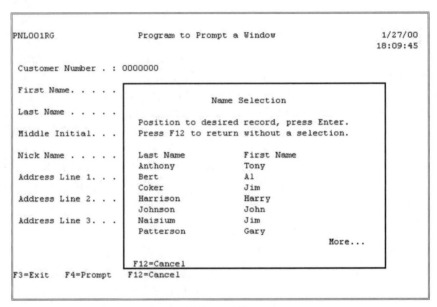

```
PNL001RG              Program to Prompt a Window              1/27/00
                                                             18:09:45

  Customer Number . : 0000000

  First Name. . . . .  ┌─────────────────────────────────────────────┐
                       │              Name Selection                 │
  Last Name . . . . .  │                                             │
                       │  Position to desired record, press Enter.   │
  Middle Initial. . .  │  Press F12 to return without a selection.   │
                       │                                             │
  Nick Name . . . . .  │  Last Name          First Name              │
                       │  Anthony            Tony                     │
  Address Line 1. . .  │  Bert               Al                      │
                       │  Coker              Jim                     │
  Address Line 2. . .  │  Harrison           Harry                   │
                       │  Johnson            John                    │
  Address Line 3. . .  │  Naisium            Jim                     │
                       │  Patterson          Gary                    │
                       │                                More...       │
                       │                                             │
                       │  F12=Cancel                                 │
  F3=Exit   F4=Prompt  │  F12=Cancel                                 │
                       └─────────────────────────────────────────────┘
```

Figure 4.16: Example of a selection window subfile.

PROGRAMMING THE SELECTION LIST

As usual, the DDS does most of the work. However, there are a couple of things
to talk about in the RPG. The RPG doesn't care if you're using a regular subfile
or a selection list subfile. As a matter of fact, the only hint you get that this is a
selection list—and it's a slight hint at that—is found in the code in Figure 4.17.

```
     *
     * Load the subfile
     *
     C     *loval        setll     sfl0011f
     C                   dou       %eof
```

Figure 4.17: Because selection list subfiles can only contain one field, I concatenate the
first and last names into the FULLNM field (SFL008RG).

```
C                    read      sfl0011f
C                    if        not %eof
C                    eval      rrn1 = rrn1 + 1
C                    eval      FULLNM = DBLNAM + DBFNAM
C                    write     window1
C                    endif
C                    enddo
```

Figure 4.17: Because selection list subfiles can only contain one field, I concatenate the first and last names into the FULLNM field (SFL008RG) (continued).

You can see where I concatenate the first and last names into FULLNM. This doesn't guarantee that this is a selection list, but it's the closest thing to a clue. Other than that, the load-all routine works like all the others you've seen in this book. In the main routine, I clear the subfile, load the subfile, and then display it. I don't even bother with a DOW or DOU loop because control only needs to be passed back to the program once before returning to the calling program. The user will either select a record and press Enter, or press F12 to cancel. In either case, the program only needs one pass through it. If the user scrolls through the subfile, that scrolling will be handled by OS/400—but you already knew that, didn't you?

Figure 4.18 shows what happens when control is passed back to the program. If F3 and F12 are not pressed, the program CHAINs to the WINDOW1 subfile record format with the relative record number returned by the RTNCSRLOC keyword. By chaining to the subfile, I can get the customer number (DBIDNM) of the selected record and pass it back to the calling program. If F3 or F12 is pressed, the ELSE clause is executed, which zeros out the customer number before returning to the calling program. Looking back at PNL001RG, you'll see that it checks for DBIDNM > 0 before it does anything.

```
*
* If enter was hit, return the selected record
*
C                    if        (not *inkc) and (not *inkl)
C        rrn1        chain     window1
```

Figure 4.18: This logic gets the information from the subfile record that was selected by the user in order to pass it back to the calling program (SFL008RG).

```
C                        else
C                        eval      dbidnm = 0
C                        endif
   *
C                        eval      *inlr = *on
```

Figure 4.18: This logic gets the information from the subfile record that was selected by the user in order to pass it back to the calling program (SFL008RG) (continued).

There you have it. Not much to the RPG in this example. All the new stuff was in the DDS. However, you have learned that, with very little code, you can provide your users with a very effective way to display and return data from a pop-up window.

SUMMARY AND CODE EXAMPLES

- Windowed subfiles are relatively easy to create because all the work is done in the DDS.

- Without changing the RPG, you can make it control a windowed subfile that was converted from a regular subfile.

- Selection list subfiles offer additional selection-control criteria and cursor movement within the subfile.

- OS/400 handles all the save and restore processing when windows are written to the display.

- You can disable the save and restore processing by using the USRRSTDSP keyword.

- The ASSUME keyword cannot be used in the same format as the WINDOW keyword, but it's paramount if you want to display a window from a called program over a display without first erasing that display.

PNL001DF: Display File for a Single Record Display Screen

```
A*
A*
A                                          DSPSIZ(24 80 *DS3)
A                                          PRINT
A                                          ERRSFL
A                                          CA03
A                                          CA12
A                                          CF04
A*
A          R PANEL1
A*
A                                    1  2'PNL001RG'
A            MODE        6A   O      2  2DSPATR(HI)
A                                    1 24'Subfile Program with Update      '
A                                       DSPATR(HI)
A                                    1 71DATE
A                                       EDTCDE(Y)
A                                    2 71TIME
A            DBIDNM      R    O      4 23REFFLD(PFR/DBIDNM *LIBL/SFL001PF)
A            DBFNAM      R    B      6 23REFFLD(PFR/DBFNAM *LIBL/SFL001PF)
A            DBLNAM      R    B      8 23REFFLD(PFR/DBLNAM *LIBL/SFL001PF)
A            DBMINI      R    B     10 23REFFLD(PFR/DBMINI *LIBL/SFL001PF)
A            DBNNAM      R    B     12 23REFFLD(PFR/DBNNAM *LIBL/SFL001PF)
A            DBADD1      R    B     14 23REFFLD(PFR/DBADD1 *LIBL/SFL001PF)
A            DBADD2      R    B     16 23REFFLD(PFR/DBADD2 *LIBL/SFL001PF)
A            DBADD3      R    B     18 23REFFLD(PFR/DBADD3 *LIBL/SFL001PF)
A                                   23  2'F3=Exit'
A                                       COLOR(BLU)
A                                   23 12'F4=Prompt'
A                                       COLOR(BLU)
A                                   23 24'F12=Cancel'
A                                       COLOR(BLU)
A                                    4  3'Customer Number . :'
A                                    6  3'First Name. . . . .'
A                                    8  3'Last Name . . . . .'
A                                   10  3'Middle Initial. . .'
A                                   12  3'Nick Name . . . . .'
A                                   14  3'Address Line 1. . .'
A                                   16  3'Address Line 2. . .'
A                                   18  3'Address Line 3. . .'
```

PNL001RG: RPG Program for a Single Record Display Screen

```
*
*  To compile:
*
*           CRTRPGPGM PGM(XXX/PNL001RG) SRCFILE(XXX/QRPGLESRC)
*
```

→

PNL001RG: RPG Program for a Single Record Display Screen (continued)

```
*===================================================================
Fpnl001df  cf   e              workstn
F                                     infds(info)
Fsfl001pf  if   e         k disk

Dinfo           ds
D cfkey               369     369

Dexit          C                const(X'33')
Dcancel        C                const(X'3C')
Dprompt        C                const(X'34')
Denter         C                const(X'F1')
Derror         C                const('No name found')
 *
 ******************************************************************
 *  Main Routine
 ******************************************************************
 *
C               dou      (cfkey = exit) or (cfkey = cancel)
 *
C               exfmt    panel1
 *
C               if       cfkey = prompt
C               exsr     getdta
C               endif
 *
C               enddo
 *
C               eval     *inlr = *on
 *
 ******************************************************************
 *  GETDTA - prompt for data
 ******************************************************************
 *
C     getdta    begsr
 *
C               call     'SFL008RG'
C               parm                      dbidnm
 *
C               if       dbidnm > 0
C     dbidnm    chain    sfl001pf
C               if       not %found
C               eval     dblnam = error
C               endif
C               endif
 *
C               endsr
```

SFL006DF: Display File with Delete Confirmation Window

```
A*
A                                     DSPSIZ(24 80 *DS3)
A                                     PRINT
A                                     ERRSFL
A                                     CA03
A                                     CA12
A*
A          R SFL1                     SFL
A*
A   74                                SFLNXTCHG
A            DBIDNM  R       H        REFFLD(PFR/DBIDNM *LIBL/SFL001PF)
A            OPTION      1A  B 10  3VALUES(' ' '2' '4' '5')
A            DBLNAM  R       O 10  7REFFLD(PFR/DBLNAM *LIBL/SFL001PF)
A            DBFNAM  R       O 10 31REFFLD(PFR/DBFNAM *LIBL/SFL001PF)
A            DBMINI  R       O 10 55REFFLD(PFR/DBMINI *LIBL/SFL001PF)
A            DBNNAM  R       O 10 60REFFLD(PFR/DBNNAM *LIBL/SFL001PF)
A          R SF1CTL                   SFLCTL(SFL1)
A*
A                                     CF06
A                                     SFLSIZ(0013)
A                                     SFLPAG(0012)
A                                     ROLLUP
A                                     OVERLAY
A N32                                 SFLDSP
A N31                                 SFLDSPCTL
A   31                                SFLCLR
A   90                                SFLEND(*MORE)
A            RRN1        4S OH        SFLRCDNBR
A                                 9  7'Last Name'
A                                     DSPATR(HI)
A                                 9 31'First Name'
A                                     DSPATR(HI)
A                                 9 55'MI'
A                                     DSPATR(HI)
A                                 9 60'Nick Name'
A                                     DSPATR(HI)
A                                 1  2'SFL006RG'
A                                 1 71DATE
A                                     EDTCDE(Y)
A                                 2 71TIME
A                                 1 24'Subfile Program with Update     '
A                                     DSPATR(HI)
A                                 4  2'Position to Last Name . . .'
A            PTNAME     20A  B  4 30
A                                 9  2'Opt'
A                                     DSPATR(HI)
A                                 6  2'Type options, press Enter.'
A                                     COLOR(BLU)
A                                 7  4'2=Change'
A                                     COLOR(BLU)
```

SFL006DF: Display File with Delete Confirmation Window (continued)

```
A                                      7 19'4=Delete'
A                                         COLOR(BLU)
A                                      7 34'5=Display'
A                                         COLOR(BLU)
A*
A           R PANEL1
A                                      1  2'SFL004RG'
A             MODE       6   0  2 2DSPATR(HI)
A                                      1 24'Subfile Program with Update      '
A                                        DSPATR(HI)
A                                      1 71DATE
A                                        EDTCDE(Y)
A                                      2 71TIME
A             DBIDNM     R      0  4 23REFFLD(PFR/DBIDNM *LIBL/SFL001PF)
A                                        DSPATR(HI)
A             DBFNAM     R      B  6 23REFFLD(PFR/DBFNAM *LIBL/SFL001PF)
A                                        CHECK(LC)
A             DBLNAM     R      B  8 23REFFLD(PFR/DBLNAM *LIBL/SFL001PF)
A                                        CHECK(LC)
A             DBMINI     R      B 10 23REFFLD(PFR/DBMINI *LIBL/SFL001PF)
A                                        CHECK(LC)
A             DBNNAM     R      B 12 23REFFLD(PFR/DBNNAM *LIBL/SFL001PF)
A                                        CHECK(LC)
A             DBADD1     R      B 14 23REFFLD(PFR/DBADD1 *LIBL/SFL001PF)
A                                        CHECK(LC)
A             DBADD2     R      B 16 23REFFLD(PFR/DBADD2 *LIBL/SFL001PF)
A                                        CHECK(LC)
A             DBADD3     R      B 18 23REFFLD(PFR/DBADD3 *LIBL/SFL001PF)
A                                        CHECK(LC)
A                                     23  2'F3=Exit'
A                                        COLOR(BLU)
A                                     23 12'F12=Cancel'
A                                        COLOR(BLU)
A                                      4  3'Customer Number . :'
A                                      6  3'First Name. . . . .'
A                                      8  3'Last Name . . . . .'
A                                     10  3'Middle Initial. . .'
A                                     12  3'Nick Name . . . . .'
A                                     14  3'Address Line 1. . .'
A                                     16  3'Address Line 2. . .'
A                                     18  3'Address Line 3. . .'
A           R PANEL2
A*
A                                      1  2'SFL004RG'
A             MODE       6   0  2 2DSPATR(HI)
A                                      1 24'Subfile Program with Update      '
A                                        DSPATR(HI)
A                                      1 71DATE
A                                        EDTCDE(Y)
A                                      2 71TIME
A             DBIDNM     R      0  4 20REFFLD(PFR/DBIDNM *LIBL/SFL001PF)
```

SFL006DF: Display File with Delete Confirmation Window (continued)

```
A                                        DSPATR(HI)
A          DBFNAM    R       O  6 20REFFLD(PFR/DBFNAM *LIBL/SFL001PF)
A                                        DSPATR(HI)
A          DBLNAM    R       O  8 20REFFLD(PFR/DBLNAM *LIBL/SFL001PF)
A                                        DSPATR(HI)
A          DBMINI    R       O 10 20REFFLD(PFR/DBMINI *LIBL/SFL001PF)
A                                        DSPATR(HI)
A          DBNNAM    R       O 12 20REFFLD(PFR/DBNNAM *LIBL/SFL001PF)
A                                        DSPATR(HI)
A          DBADD1    R       O 14 20REFFLD(PFR/DBADD1 *LIBL/SFL001PF)
A                                        DSPATR(HI)
A          DBADD2    R       O 16 20REFFLD(PFR/DBADD2 *LIBL/SFL001PF)
A                                        DSPATR(HI)
A          DBADD3    R       O 18 20REFFLD(PFR/DBADD3 *LIBL/SFL001PF)
A                                        DSPATR(HI)
A                                 23  2'F3=Exit'
A                                        COLOR(BLU)
A                                 23 12'F12=Cancel'
A                                        COLOR(BLU)
A                                  4  3'Customer Number:'
A                                  6  3'First Name . . :'
A                                  8  3'Last Name. . . :'
A                                 10  3'Middle Initial :'
A                                 12  3'Nick Name. . . :'
A                                 14  3'Address Line 1 :'
A                                 16  3'Address Line 2 :'
A                                 18  3'Address Line 3 :'
A*
A*
A          R WINDOW1                     SFL
A*
A          DBIDNM    R       H           REFFLD(PFR/DBIDNM *LIBL/SFL001PF)
A          DBLNAM    R       O  6  2REFFLD(PFR/DBLNAM *LIBL/SFL001PF)
A          DBFNAM    R       O  6 26REFFLD(PFR/DBFNAM *LIBL/SFL001PF)
A*
A          R SF2CTL                      SFLCTL(WINDOW1)
A*
A                                        SFLDSP
A N41                                    SFLDSPCTL
A   41                                   SFLCLR
A N41                                    SFLEND(*MORE)
A                                        SFLSIZ(0009)
A                                        SFLPAG(0008)
A                                        WINDOW(4 10 16 52)
A          RRN2      4S 0H
A                                  5  2'Last Name'
A                                        DSPATR(HI)
A                                  5 26'First Name'
A                                        DSPATR(HI)
A                                  2  2'Press ENTER to confirm your choice-
A                                        s for delete.'
```

SFL006DF: Display File with Delete Confirmation Window (continued)

```
A                                        COLOR(BLU)
A                                     3  2'Press F12=Cancel to return to chan-
A                                        ge your choices.'
A                                        COLOR(BLU)
A*
A            R FKEY1
A*
A                                    23  2'F3=Exit'
A                                        COLOR(BLU)
A                                        +3'F6=Add'
A                                        COLOR(BLU)
A                                        +3'F12=Cancel'
A                                        COLOR(BLU)
A*
A            R FKEY2
A*
A                                    23  2'F3=Exit'
A                                        COLOR(BLU)
A                                        +3'F12=Cancel'
A                                        COLOR(BLU)
```

SFL006RG: RPG Program with Delete Confirmation Window

```
 *
 *   To compile:
 *
 *           CRTRPGPGM PGM(XXX/SFL006RG) SRCFILE(XXX/QRPGLESRC)
 *
 *=======================================================================
Fsfl006df  cf   e                  workstn
F                                       sfile(sfl1:rrn1)
F                                       sfile(window1:rrn2)
F                                       infds(info)
Fsfl001lf  if   e          k disk   rename(pfr:lfr)
Fsfl001pf  uf a e          k disk

Dinfo            ds
D cfkey                   369     369

Dexit            C                 const(X'33')
Dcancel          C                 const(X'3C')
Dadd             C                 const(X'36')
Denter           C                 const(X'F1')
Drollup          C                 const(X'F5')
Dsflpag          C                 const(12)
Ddisplay         C                 const('5')
Dchange          C                 const('2')
Ddelete          C                 const('4')
```

SFL006RG: RPG Program with Delete Confirmation Window (continued)

```
Dlstrrn          S              4  0 inz(0)
Dlstrrn2         S              4  0 inz(0)
Dcount           S              4  0 inz(0)
Dnew_id          S                 like(dbidnm)
 *
 ****************************************************************
 *  Main Routine
 ****************************************************************
 *
 * Clear then build the initial subfile
 *
C                     exsr      clrsf1
C                     exsr      sflbld
 *
 * Do loop to process the subfile until F3 is pressed.  If F12
 * is pressed from other screens, I still want to stay in this loop.
 *
C                     dou       cfkey = exit
 *
C                     write     fkey1
C                     exfmt     sf1ctl
 *
 * Process position to information entered by the user, then clear
 * and rebuild the subfile. Lastly, clear the position to field
 *
C                     select
C                     when      (cfkey = enter) and (ptname  *blanks)
C     ptname          setll     sfl0011f
C                     exsr      clrsf1
C                     exsr      sflbld
C                     clear                 ptname
 *
 * Process screen to interrogate options selected by user
 *
C                     when      (cfkey = enter) and (ptname = *blanks)
C                     exsr      prcsfl
 *
 * User presses F6, throw the add screen, clear, and rebuild subfile
 *
C                     when      cfkey = add
C                     movel(p)  'Add  '      mode
C                     exsr      addrcd
C     *loval          setll     sfl0011f
C                     exsr      clrsf1
C                     exsr      sflbld
 *
 * Add more records to subfile if user pages from bottom of subfile
 *
C                     when      (cfkey = rollup) and (not *in32)
```

141

SFL006RG: RPG Program with Delete Confirmation Window (continued)

```
C                     exsr       sflbld

C                     when       cfkey = cancel
C                     leave

C                     endsl
C                     enddo

C                     eval       *inlr = *on
 *
 *****************************************************************
 *   CLRSF1 - Clear the subfile
 *****************************************************************
 *
C     clrsf1          begsr
 *
 * Clear relative record numbers and subfile
 *
C                     eval       rrn1 = *zero
C                     eval       lstrrn = *zero
C                     eval       *in31 = *on
C                     write      sf1ctl
C                     eval       *in31 = *off
C                     eval       *in32 = *off

C                     endsr
 *
 *****************************************************************
 *   CLRSF2 - Clear the subfile
 *****************************************************************
 *
C     clrsf2          begsr
 *
 * Clear relative record numbers and subfile for confirmation screen
 *
C                     eval       rrn2 = *zero
C                     eval       lstrrn2 = *zero
C                     eval       *in41 = *on
C                     write      sf2ctl
C                     eval       *in41 = *off

C                     endsr
 *
 *****************************************************************
 *   SFLBLD - Build the List
 *****************************************************************
 *
C     sflbld          begsr
 *
 * Make RRN1 = to the last relative record number of the subfile
```

SFL006RG: RPG Program with Delete Confirmation Window (continued)

```
* so that the load process will correctly add records to the bottom
*
C                 eval      rrn1 = lstrrn
*
* Load the subfile with one page of data or until end-of-file
*
C                 do        sflpag
C                 read      sfl0011f                              90
C                 if        *in90
C                 leave
C                 endif
C                 eval      rrn1 = rrn1 + 1
C                 eval      option = *blank
C                 write     sfl1
C                 enddo
*
* If no records are loaded to subfile, don't display it
*
C                 if        rrn1 = *zero
C                 eval      *in32 = *on
C                 endif
*
C                 eval      lstrrn = rrn1
*
C                 endsr
*
*******************************************************************
*    PRCSFL - Process the options selected
*******************************************************************
*
C    prcsfl       begsr
*
* Clear the confirmation subfile before starting
*
C                 exsr      clrsf2
*
* Read all the subfile records that were changed by the user
*
C                 readc     sfl1
*
* Do loop to process until all changed records are read
*
C                 dow       not %eof
*
C                 select
*
* when a 5 is entered throw the DISPLAY screen
* until F3 or F12 is pressed on that screen
*
C                 when      option = display
```

SFL006RG: RPG Program with Delete Confirmation Window (continued)

```
C                    movel(p)  *blanks        mode
C                    exfmt     panel2
C                    eval      option = *blank
C                    update    sfl1
C                    if        (cfkey = exit) or (cfkey = cancel)
C                    leave
C                    endif
 *
 * when a 2 is entered execute the update subroutine,
 * blank out the option field, and update the subfile record
 *
C                    when      option = change
C                    movel(p)  'Update'        mode
C                    exsr      chgdtl
C                    eval      option = *blank
C                    update    sfl1
C                    if        (cfkey = exit) or (cfkey = cancel)
C                    leave
C                    endif
 *
 * when a 4 is entered write the record the the confirmation screen,
 * set on the SFLNXTCHG indicator to mark this record as changed,
 * and update the subfile.  I mark this record incase F12 is pressed
 * from the confirmation screen and the user wants to keep his
 * originally selected records
 *
C                    when      option = delete
C                    eval      rrn2 = rrn2 +1
C                    write     window1
C                    eval      *in74 = *on
C                    update    sfl1
C                    eval      *in74 = *off

C                    endsl

C                    readc     sfl1
C                    enddo
 *
 * If records were selected for delete (4), throw the subfile to
 * screen.  If enter is pressed execute the DLTRCD subroutine to
 * physically delete the records, clear, and rebuild the subfile
 * from the last deleted record (you can certainly position the
 * database file where ever you want)
 *
C                    if        rrn2 > 0
C                    eval      lstrrn2 = rrn2
C                    eval      rrn2 = 1
C                    write     fkey2
C                    exfmt     sf2ctl
C                    if        (cfkey  exit) and (cfkey  cancel)
```

SFL006RG: RPG Program with Delete Confirmation Window (continued)

```
C                     exsr      dltrcd
C        dblnam       setll     sfl001lf
C                     exsr      clrsf1
C                     exsr      sflbld
C                     endif
C                     endif

C                     endsr
*
********************************************************************
*   CHGDTL - allow user to change data
********************************************************************
*
C        chgdtl       begsr
*
* chain to data file using selected subfile record
*
C        dbidnm       chain     sfl001pf
*
* If the record is found (it better be), throw the change screen.
* If F3 or F12 is pressed, do not update the data file
*
C                     if        %found
C                     exfmt     panel1

C                     if        (cfkey  exit) and (cfkey  cancel)
C                     update    pfr
C                     endif

C                     endif

C                     endsr
*
********************************************************************
*   ADDRCD - allow user to add data
********************************************************************
*
C        addrcd       begsr
*
* set to last record in the the file to get the last ID number
*
C        *hival       setgt     sfl001pf
C                     readp     sfl001pf
*
* set a new unique ID and throw the screen
*
C                     if        not %eof
C                     eval      new_id = dbidnm + 1
C                     clear                   pfr
C                     eval      dbidnm = new_id
```

SFL006RG: RPG Program with Delete Confirmation Window (continued)

```
C                    exfmt    panel1
 *
 * add a new record if the pressed key was not F3 or F12
 *
C                    if       (cfkey  exit) and (cfkey  cancel)
C                    write    pfr
C                    endif

C                    endif

C                    endsr
 *
 ******************************************************************
 *   DLTRCD - delete records
 ******************************************************************
 *
C     dltrcd         begsr
 *
 * read all the records in the confirmation subfile
 * and delete them from the data base file
 *
C                    do       lstrrn2        count
C     count          chain    window1
C                    if       %found
C     dbidnm         delete   pfr                                  99
C                    endif
C                    enddo

C                    endsr
```

SFL008DF: Display File for Selection List Window

```
A*
A                                    DSPSIZ(24 80 *DS3)
A                                    PRINT
A                                    ERRSFL
A                                    CA03
A                                    CA12
A*
A*
A*
A          R WINDOW1                 SFL
A*
A            CTLFLD       1Y 0H      SFLCHCCTL
A            DBIDNM     R     H      REFFLD(PFR/DBIDNM *LIBL/SFL001PF)
A            FULLNM       40  0  6  2
A*
A*
```

SFL008DF: Display File for Selection List Window (continued)

```
A*
A           R SF1CTL                    SFLCTL(WINDOW1)
A*
A                                       SFLDSP
A N31                                   SFLDSPCTL
A   31                                  SFLCLR
A N31                                   SFLEND(*MORE)
A                                       SFLSIZ(0050)
A                                       SFLPAG(0007)
A                                       WINDOW(*DFT 14 44 *NOMSGLIN)
A                                       WDWBORDER((*COLOR PNK))
A                                       WDWTITLE((*TEXT 'Name Selection') (-
A                                       *COLOR WHT))
A                                       WDWTITLE((*TEXT 'F12=Cancel') (*COL-
A                                       OR BLU) *BOTTOM)
A                                       SFLSNGCHC(*RSTCSR)
A                                       SFLCSRRRN(&RRN1)
A           RRN1          5S 0H
A                                    5  2'Last Name'
A                                       DSPATR(HI)
A                                    5 22'First Name'
A                                       DSPATR(HI)
A                                    3  2'Press F12 to return without a sele-
A                                       ction.'
A                                       COLOR(BLU)
A                                    2  2'Position to desired record, press -
A                                       Enter.'
A                                       COLOR(BLU)
A           R ASSUME
A*
A                                       ASSUME
A                                    1  3' '
```

SFL008RG: RPG Program for Selection List Window

```
*
*   To compile:
*
*           CRTRPGPGM PGM(XXX/SFL008RG) SRCFILE(XXX/QRPGLESRC)
*
*========================================================================
Fsfl008df  cf   e           workstn
F                                     sfile(window1:rrn1)
Fsfl001lf  if   e           k disk
*
*******************************************************************
*   Main Routine
*******************************************************************
```

147

SFL008RG: RPG Program for Selection List Window (continued)

```
C      *entry      plist
C                  parm                    dbidnm
 *
 * Clear then build the initial subfile
 *
C                  exsr     clrsf1
C                  exsr     sflbld
 *
C                  exfmt    sf1ctl
 *
 * If enter was hit, return the selected record
 *
C                  if       (not *inkc) and (not *inkl)
C      rrn1        chain    window1
C                  else
C                  eval     dbidnm = 0
C                  endif
 *
C                  eval     *inlr = *on
 *
 *******************************************************************
 *   CLRSF1 - Clear the subfile
 *******************************************************************
 *
C      clrsf1      begsr
 *
 * Clear relative record numbers and subfile
 *
C                  eval     rrn1 = *zero
C                  eval     *in31 = *on
C                  write    sf1ctl
C                  eval     *in31 = *off
C                  eval     *in32 = *off
 *
C                  endsr
 *
 *******************************************************************
 *   SFLBLD - Build the List
 *******************************************************************
 *
C      sflbld      begsr
 *
 * Load the subfile
 *
C      *loval      setll    sfl0011f
C                  dou      %eof
C                  read     sfl0011f
C                  if       not %eof
C                  eval     rrn1 = rrn1 + 1
C                  eval     FULLNM = DBLNAM + DBFNAM
```

148

SFL008RG: RPG Program for Selection List Window (continued)

```
C                   write     window1
C                   endif
C                   enddo
 *
 * If no records are loaded to subfile, don't display it
 *
C                   if        rrn1 = *zero
C                   eval      *in32 = *on
C                   else
C                   eval      rrn1 = 1
C                   endif
 *
C                   endsr
```

5

MESSAGE SUBFILES: WHAT'S THAT + NEXT TO MY MESSAGE?

Message subfiles are special subfiles that are designed to hold—you guessed it!—messages. Message subfiles have some unique properties that make them very useful, loading themselves automatically from messages on a given program message queue (we'll talk about program message queues in a bit).

Message subfiles also allow users to view the second-level help text associated with a message—without any additional programming effort. Message subfiles make it possible to set up a consistent set of information, warning, or error messages in a message file for a given program or application, and display those messages to the user with the greatest of ease. Well, at least with some ease. If it all sounds a little too good to be true, that's because it is. With just a little direction from your RPG and DDS, message subfiles pretty much take care of themselves. Programmers in England might say, "They're independent little buggers." In America, they say, "Cool."

MESSAGE SUBFILE GROUND RULES

In general, here's how you use a message subfile:

1. Set up a message file (*MSGF) containing the messages you want to use in your application. You can use an existing message file or create your own. You shouldn't usually modify system-supplied message files, such as QCPFMSG. Message files are created with the CRTMSGF command. New messages can be added via the ADDMSGD command or the WRKMSGF command.

2. Define a message subfile in your display file.

3. Code your application program to send program messages to the program message queue. The best way to accomplish this in RPG is to use the Send Program Message (QMHSNDPM) application program interface (API). You can also use the SNDPGMMSG command, although the best place to use that command is in a CL program.

4. After displaying the message subfile, clear the messages from the program message queue using the Remove Program Message (QMHRMVPM) API. You can also use the RMVMSG command from a CL program. Never fear—I'll show you how to display message subfiles using CL.

There are a couple of things that you should know before we move on.

Program Message Queues

First, for every call stack entry—which can be an OPM program or an ILE procedure—there exists a corresponding program message queue with the same name (see Table 5.1). This is important to know, especially when you start dealing with ILE and multiple call stack entries.

Table 5.1: Call Stack Entries and Associated Program Message Queues.

Call stack entry	Program message queue
1) QCMD	QCMD
2) OPMPGM1	OPMPGM1
3) ILEPROC1	ILEPROC1
4) ILEPROC2	ILEPROC2

Program Status Data Structure—Procedure Name

Second, the program status data structure in RPG IV has fields that contain the program name and the procedure name. The source code in Figure 5.1 shows an example. This will save you from having to hard code the program name in your Send and Remove APIs, as well as free you from some extra coding in your program (as if message subfiles aren't already doing enough for you already). I'll show you what I mean as we get into the code. As usual, the complete code listings are included at the end of the chapter.

```
* RPG IV program status data structure
D PSDS            SDS
D  SDS_PROC           *PROC                        Procedure name
D  SDS_PGM              334    343                 Pgm proc is in
```

Figure 5.1: The program status data structure is useful for retrieving a program message queue name.

Message Handling APIs

Third, don't worry if you're not familiar with APIs. I'll go through all you need to know in order to use the two message-handling APIs mentioned earlier. APIs are simply callable programs (or in some cases procedures) that are supplied to you by a software vendor (IBM in this case) that allow you to perform low-level or complex functions. Programmers often shy away from APIs because of their sometimes-complicated interfaces, but if you're willing to brave new worlds and give them a try, I think you'll find a wealth of programming power just waiting to be tapped.

More on Program Message Queues

I created my own message file, but you can certainly use the system-supplied messages and insert your own text. For instance, if users are accustomed to seeing message ID CPF9898 from the system-supplied message file, QCPFMSG, as being something serious, you could still use that message ID and substitute it with your own message. This doesn't mean you change the CPF9898 message in the actual message file. Rather, you simply override the message text in your program. If there are substitution parameters associated with a specific message, you can also fill in those parameters using the program message APIs. If message files aren't your bag, you can also send text messages to the program message queue and use no message file at all.

That about covers it. Now let's look at some code!

THE SAME BUT DIFFERENT

In my example, I've set up two messages, SFL0001 and SFL0002, in a message file called SFLMSGF. SFL016DF is a display file that demonstrates the use of message subfiles. It consists of three record formats: SCREEN1, MSGSFL, and MSGCTL. SCREEN1, the primary screen, allows the user to enter data. As you'll see in the RPG program (SFL016RG), this data isn't going anywhere; its purpose is purely to demonstrate how to use a message subfile. MSGSFL is the message subfile record format, and MSGCTL is the control format for MSGSFL. Because they operate in tandem to control the workings of the subfile, these formats work much like the SF1CTL and SFL1 formats you've seen throughout this book.

There are, however, some differences between regular subfiles and message subfiles. With regular subfiles, you have to handle the loading and clearing in your program. In your RPG program, you'll typically set on the indicator used to condition the SFLCLR keyword in your DDS, write to the subfile control format (SF1CTL, in most examples in this book), and set off the indicator to get ready to load and display. With message subfiles, you don't explicitly clear the subfile in your program. Instead, you link the subfile to a program message queue, and remove messages from that message queue. This, in essence, clears the subfile.

This same theory holds true for loading the subfile. When displaying subfile records in a regular subfile, you must first execute some sort of load routine. This routine usually consists of a DO loop that reads records from a database file and writes them to the subfile record format. Message subfiles will have none of that. By linking the message subfile to a specific program message queue and sending messages to that queue, the message subfile will automatically load itself with records from the program message queue.

Message subfiles require the use of several special DDS keywords. Let's look at the message subfile record in SFL016DF to see how they're arranged (see Figure 5.2).

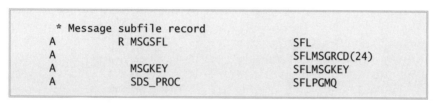

```
    * Message subfile record
A          R MSGSFL                SFL
A                                  SFLMSGRCD(24)
A            MSGKEY                SFLMSGKEY
A            SDS_PROC              SFLPGMQ
```

Figure 5.2: Message subfile record format keywords in SFL016DF.

In the message subfile record format (MSGSFL), the following keywords are required:

SFLMSGRCD is used to set the starting line on the display for the message subfile. In most cases, it's set to 24 (the bottom line of the display), although you could display more than one message at a time. In that case, you would set this parameter accordingly.

SFLMSGKEY controls the message key of the first message to be displayed in the message subfile. Every message on a message queue has a unique message key assigned as the message arrives on the message queue. In certain cases, you may wish to maintain old messages on the queue and only display messages from a certain point forward in the message subfile. Setting the message key allows you to control which messages are displayed.

SFLPGMQ determines which program message queue messages are pulled from. In my example, it's being populated with the name of the main procedure from the program status data structure in the RPG program. This technique allows you to easily copy the message subfile record formats into a new display file, with no changes being required to the display file. Of course, the SDS_PROC field must be declared in the program status data structure in the controlling program. This keyword also defines the output fields for you. No explicit code is necessary for you to define your subfile fields.

Figure 5.3 shows the message subfile control record format (MSGCTL).

```
A               R MSGCTL                    SFLCTL(MSGSFL)
A                                           SFLSIZ(2)
A                                           SFLPAG(1)
A                                           SFLDSP
A                                           SFLDSPCTL
A                                           SFLINZ
A N99                                       SFLEND
A               SDS_PROC                    SFLPGMQ
```

Figure 5.3: Message subfile control record format keywords in SFL016DF.

SFLCTL, SFLSIZ, SFLPAG, SFLDSP, SFLEND, and SFLDSPCTL behave normally in a message subfile, except that SFLDSP and SFLDSPCTL must be used without conditioning indicators. Also, SFLPAG must be at least one less than SFLSIZ in a message subfile; they cannot be equal.

Message subfiles are considered load-all subfiles. Notice that I don't use the *MORE parameter on my message subfile. The reason for this is that using the *MORE parameter causes "More…" and "Bottom" to display one line under the last line on the display. Because I'm using line 24, which is the last possible line on the display, I would get an error if I tried to use the *MORE parameter. The "+" works for me, but if you're dying to use *MORE with your message subfiles, try starting on line 23, SFLMSGRCD(23), and keeping SFLPAG as 1. Then you won't get an error.

Let's look at the differences in how two of the keywords behave when they're in a message subfile.

SFLINZ, in the case of a message subfile, causes the system to automatically load the subfile with messages from the specified message queue. This is different than its use in regular subfiles. Remember, in regular subfiles, SFLINZ loads the subfile with the number of records indicated by SFLSIZ and sets the fields to their default values.

SFLPGMQ is used to control from which program message queue messages are pulled. It's being populated with the name of the main procedure from the program status data structure in the RPG program. It might seem redundant redundant to use this keyword in both formats, but it really, really isn't. Specifying this keyword in the subfile record format allows you to link the subfile to a specific program message queue, which allows you to clear and possibly load the subfile by controlling the program message queue. However, it's the SFLPGMQ keyword entry in the subfile control format that allows you to automatically load the subfile. If you don't specify it in the subfile control format, you'll need to code the load routine in your program. Always use this keyword in subfile control format. This is one case where redundancy causes efficiency.

The RPG

The RPG is basically used to control SCREEN1. It doesn't have any direct contact with the message subfile. The RPG program will send messages to, and remove messages from, the program message queue and help the message subfile link to the program message queue by retrieving the message queue name from the program data structure and sharing it the display file. As you will soon see, however, it doesn't directly load, clear, or display the subfile.

Remember Figure 5.1? Take a look at it again. The program status data structure provides information about the program just as a file information data structure provides information about a specific file. In my example, I want to retrieve the procedure name associated with this program, which I can get by specifying the keyword *PROC. I'll the define SDS_PROC to associate with the *PROC keyword. Notice that this is the same name I used in my DDS. By doing this, I can pass the name of the procedure, and subsequently the program message queue name, to the display file and allow it to link the program message queue to the message subfile. I also specified the program name, which can be retrieved from positions 334 through 343. I'm not going to use that field in my example, but I thought I would show you it's there for your convenience should you choose to use it.

157

Figure 5.4 shows the fields I'll use as parameters to call the message handling APIs. I'll talk about those fields in more detail when I get to the API call statements. These are the D specs from RPG program SFL016RG.

```
D   msgId          s              7A
D   msgLoc         s             20A   inz('SFLMSGF    *LIBL     ')
D   msgRplDta      s              1A   inz(' ')
D   msgRplDtaLen   s              4B 0 inz(0)
D   msgType        s             10A   inz('*DIAG')
D   msgQueue       s            276A   inz('*')
D   msgCallStack   s              4B 0 inz(0)
D   msgKey         s              4A   inz(' ')
D   msgErr         s              4B 0 inz(0)
D   msgrmv         s             10A   inz('*ALL')
```

Figure 5.4: D specs that will be used to call the message APIs in SFL016RG.

```
C                   dou       (cfkey = exit) or (cfkey = cancel)
C                   write     msgctl
C                   exfmt     screen1
C                   eval      msgKey = *blanks
C                   exsr      rcvmsg

C                   select
C                   when      cfkey = enter
C                   if        first_name  'Kevin'
C                   movel(p)  'SFL0001'      msgId
C                   exsr      sndmsg
C                   endif

C                   if        last_name  'Vandever'
C                   movel(p)  'SFL0002'      msgId
C                   exsr      sndmsg
C                   endif
C
C                   endsl

C                   enddo
C  *
C                   eval      *inlr = *on
```

Figure 5.5: Mainline of program SFL016RG.

The mainline of the RPG (Figure 5.5) is simply a DOU loop that processes SCREEN1. I perform a WRITE to the message subfile control format, MSGCTL, before SCREEN1 is written to allow the user to enter some data. This WRITE causes the message subfile to be loaded with any messages that exist in the program message queue and then written to the screen. The first time through, I haven't sent any messages to the program message queue. As a result, the message subfile is empty. The initial screen allows the user to enter a first and last name. When the Enter key is pressed, the RPG program interrogates the names and determines whether a message should be sent. In my example, if the user doesn't enter "Kevin" as the first name, message ID "SFL0001" is moved to the MSGID field and the SNDMSG subroutine is executed. If "Vandever" isn't entered as the last name, MSGID is evaluated to "SFL0002" and SNDMSG is executed again (we'll cover this subroutine in more detail later).

Each time the SNDMSG subroutine is executed, a message is written to the program message queue and displayed to the screen when the write operation is performed. Because I want the messages removed after they've been displayed, the first thing I do upon returning from SCREEN1 is execute the RMVMSG subroutine. This clears the program message queue, and subsequently the message subfile, for the next interrogation of data. Figure 5.6 shows what happens when the user enters the first name correctly but misspells the last name. Once the user corrects the last name and presses Enter, the message disappears.

```
                      Message Subfile Example

       Type a First and Last Name and Press Enter to test the Message Subfile.

              Enter First Name . . Kevin

              Enter Last Name. . . Vandenhoff












          F3=Exit    F12=Cancel

       Last name must be Vandever
```

Figure 5.6: Single error message for a misspelled last name.

Figure 5.7 shows the reward for spelling the name correctly—no error messages.

If the user spelled both names incorrectly, two messages would be written to the program message queue. Now, when the message subfile is displayed on the screen, you'll see the first message with a + symbol on the far right-hand side signifying more records. If you place your cursor on the subfile record and press the Page Down key to get the next record, you'll see the second error message.

```
                         Message Subfile Example

     Type a First and Last Name and Press Enter to test the Message Subfile.


          Enter First Name . . Kevin

          Enter Last Name. . . Vandever












     F3=Exit    F12=Cancel
```

Figure 5.7: No error messages.

Figures 5.8 and 5.9 show what happens when you page through the messages.

```
                        Message Subfile Example

    Type a First and Last Name and Press Enter to test the Message Subfile.


        Enter First Name . . Kevinnnn

        Enter Last Name. . . Vandeverrrr








  F3=Exit    F12=Cancel

First name must be Kevin                                                +
```

Figure 5.8: Display of first of two error messages.

```
                        Message Subfile Example

    Type a First and Last Name and Press Enter to test the Message Subfile.


        Enter First Name . . Kevinnnn

        Enter Last Name. . . Vandeverrrr








  F3=Exit    F12=Cancel

Last name must be Vandever
```

Figure 5.9: Display of second of two error messages.

If you're using a message file and have added second-level help for your messages, you can see those second-level messages by placing the cursor on the message subfile record and pressing the Help key. Figure 5.10 shows the results of pressing Help on the second message in the subfile.

```
                        Additional Message Information

 Message ID . . . . . . :    SFL0002
 Date sent  . . . . . . :    01/27/00       Time sent  . . . . . . :    18:23:59

 Message . . . . :   Last name must be Vandever

 Because Kevin Vandever has such a huge ego, he only wants his name in the
   employee master file.  Someone needs to slap this guy upside his head.




                                                                      Bottom
 Press Enter to continue.

 F1=Help    F3=Exit    F6=Print     F9=Display message details
 F10=Display messages in job log    F12=Cancel   F21=Select assistance level
```

Figure 5.10: Display of second-level help for an error message.

You can search all day for the extra code I left out of this program to allow this feature, but you won't find it. That's because it's taken care of for you by OS/400. I think you should take a moment now to thank OS/400 and message subfiles for making your life so much easier.

QMHSNDPM

Let's take a look at what is essentially my subfile load routine. The SNDMSG subroutine is executed whenever I need to send a message to the program message queue. To accomplish this task, I use the QMHSNDPM message handling API, as shown in Figure 5.11.

```
c       sndmsg        begsr

c                     call        'QMHSNDPM'
c                     parm                    msgId
c                     parm                    msgLoc
c                     parm                    msgRplDta
c                     parm                    msgRplDtaLen
c                     parm                    msgType
c                     parm                    msgQueue
c                     parm                    msgCallStack
c                     parm                    msgKey
c                     parm                    msgErr

c                     endsr
```

Figure 5.11: This is the API used to send a message to the program's message queue in SFL016RG.

You don't have to use this API to send program messages. Rather, you could write a CL program that uses the SNDPGMMSG command and call that program instead. Or you could use the QCMDEXC API to run the Send Program Message (SNDPGMMSG) command from your RPG. To me, when working with RPG, the cleanest and most efficient method is to use the message APIs directly instead of using QCMDEXC to run the SNDPGMMSG command. However, when coding in CL, it's much easier to work directly with the SNDPGMMSG command and skip the use of the APIs.

Now let's talk about the parameters. As you can see, there are nine required parameters associated with the QMHSNDPM API. There are also four optional parameters, but that's all I am going to say about them. The following is a list of the parameters I use in my program, with a brief explanation:

MSGID contains the seven-byte message identification. This field is associated with the message identifier in the message file. If you are not using a message file, this field will be blank.

MSGLOC qualifies the message file associated with the message ID in the first parameter. The first 10 positions of this field will contain the name of the message file, and the last 10 will contain the library. The keywords *LIBL and

*CURLIB may also be used instead of a library. If the MSGID parameter is blank, this parameter should also be blank.

MSGRPLDTA is a variable-length character field or pointer used in a few different ways. If a message identifier is specified, this parameter specifies the data that's inserted in the predefined message's substitution variables. You've seen that before. It's when a message and a program name or statement number appears embedded in the message. If your messages contain substitution variables, this is the parameter you'll use to fill those parameters with helpful information. If blanks are used for the message identifier, this parameter specifies the complete text of an immediate message. In my example, I want to use the message text exactly as it reads in the message file. To do so, I define this parameter as a 1-byte character field and initialize it to blank—more specifically, I don't use it.

MSGRPLDTALEN is the parameter used to tell the API the length of the previous parameter. In my example, I'm not using it, so I set it to 0. But if you were sending 70-byte messages using the MSGRPLDTA parameter, the parameter would be set to 70.

MSGTYPE is the parameter I use to define the type of message to send. In my example, I'm sending diagnostic messages (*DIAG), but you could also send informational, completion, escape, notify, inquiry, request, and status messages.

MSGQUEUE is the program message queue call stack to which I send the messages. I used the reserved value of "*" because I'm sending to the current call stack entry—the one in which this procedure is running. This parameter is 276 bytes long because of ILE. You could have many nested procedures in your application, and this parameter allows you to explicitly qualify them by name, separated by a ":". The last 20 bytes are reserved for the module and program name of the nested procedures. My program, procedure, and module are known by the same name, and because I'm sending to the current call stack, I only need the "*".

MSGCALLSTACK tells the API on what level in the call stack to look for the entry named in the previous parameter. In my case, because I'm using the current call stack, I set this parameter to 0. If you wanted to send a message to an entry in the previous call stack, you would set this parameter to 1.

MSGKEY is the key to messages being sent. Because I want all messages to be sent, displayed, and removed, I set this to blanks.

MSGERR is the name of the data structure that returns error information. I don't remember ever getting any errors in my life, so I set this to blanks and don't use it.

That's how I use the parameters in the QHMSNDPM API in my example. If you're planning on implementing a true RPGIV/ILE application, I suggest you check out IBM's message handling API documentation (I hesitate to provide a URL because the information moves so much) to obtain a complete understanding of this API and how it's used in the ILE.

QMHRMVPM

You've seen how I send messages, which also builds my subfile. Now let's take a look at how to remove messages, which also clears my subfile. I use the QMHRMVPM API for this task, as shown in Figure 5.12.

```
c         rcvmsg        begsr

c                       call      'QMHRMVPM'
c                       parm                    msgQueue
c                       parm                    msgCallStack
c                       parm                    msgKey
c                       parm                    msgRmv
c                       parm                    msgErr

c                       endsr
```

Figure 5.12: This is the API used to receive a message from the program's message queue in SFL016RG.

This API contains five required and four optional parameters. I'm not going to touch on the optional parameters in my example, but as I mentioned earlier, if you plan to implement a true RPG IV/ILE application, complete with subprocedures, service programs, and multiple activation groups, I suggest you read up on this API

I've already talked about the first four parameters because they're also used in the QMHSNDPM API, but I'll happily mention them again. You need the message queue, which I set to "*" to signify the current call stack; the call stack level, which I set to 0 again because I'm removing messages at the current call stack level; the message key, which I set to blanks because I want to remove all message keys; and the name of the message error structure, which I don't use in my example. The only new parameter of the bunch is the MSGRMV parameter. The MSGRMV parameter, which is actually the fourth parameter, is used to tell which messages to remove. Because I want to remove all messages each time I call this API, I set this parameter to *ALL.

Still Not Sold?

What do you think of that? A simple RPG program that contains no subfile code but completely controls the contents of a subfile by sending and removing messages. I can see it. Some of you may still not be comfortable with the message handling APIs. You like the simplicity of the SNDPGMMSG and RMVMSG commands. That's okay. I understand, and I am here to please. You don't have to use them. As I said before, you can code a CL program that uses the commands to handle your program message queue and call that CL from your RPG program. You can also use the QCMDEXC API to run the commands from your RPG program. Another possible solution, depending on your application, is to control your screen and program message queue from a CL program.

CL TO THE RESCUE

In case you're not aware of it, you can use a CL program to open a file. Read carefully: I said *a* file – as in "one." If your application calls for you to open only one file, CL is a possible solution. There aren't many times when a display file is controlled in a CL program. Typically, a display file is used to display data from a database file.

Well, with your newfound knowledge, you now understand that a CL program can't open both the display file and the database file. That disqualifies the CL program. However, there are times when you can use a CL program to control a display file. A good example is a menu. A menu doesn't usually use a database file, unless you store your menu option information in a database file—which is a great technique, by the way. If you're displaying a menu or an entry screen and don't need a database or printer file to open, and want to use messages to communicate information to the user, employ a CL program. And what do you know? In my example, I'm only opening one file—the display file. So let's convert it to the CL program SFL016CL, as shown in Figure 5.13.

```
             PGM

             DCLF       FILE(SFL016DF) RCDFMT(*ALL)
             CHGVAR     VAR(&SDS_PROC) VALUE('SFL016CL')
    START:   SNDF       DEV(*FILE) RCDFMT(MSGCTL)
             SNDRCVF    DEV(*FILE) RCDFMT(SCREEN1)
             RMVMSG     MSGQ(*PGMQ) CLEAR(*ALL)

             IF         COND(&IN03 = '1' *OR &IN12 = '1') THEN(GOTO +
                          CMDLBL(END))

             IF         COND(&FIRST_NAME *NE 'Kevin') THEN(DO)
             SNDPGMMSG  MSGID(SFL0001) MSGF(SFLMSGF) TOPGMQ(*SAME)
             ENDDO

             IF         COND(&LAST_NAME *NE 'Vandever') THEN(DO)
             SNDPGMMSG  MSGID(SFL0002) MSGF(SFLMSGF) TOPGMQ(*SAME)
             ENDDO

             GOTO       CMDLBL(START)

    END:     ENDPGM
```

Figure 5.13: Control the display file and program message file from a CL program (SFL016CL).

How simple is that? About 16 lines of executable code. The first thing I do is declare the file and all its formats using the DCLF command. Notice that I used the same display file as before. Next comes the only real trick to this technique. I used the program data structure in the RPG program to provide the program message queue name. I don't have that luxury in CL, so I'm going to have to physically move the appropriate procedure name (which has the same name as the program message queue) to the SDS_PROC field defined in my DDS. Then I use the SNDF command to load the message subfile and display it. The SNDF command is equivalent to the RPG WRITE operation code.

Once I write the message subfile, I write the SCREEN1 format and read from it using the SNDRCVF command. This command is comparable to the RPG EXFMT command. Now I perform the same data interrogation I did in my RPG program, but instead of using the APIs to remove and send messages, I use the CL commands. Okay, I admit it, the commands are much easier to use. Give this technique a whirl and prompt (F4) on the RMVMSG and SNDPGMMSG commands. You'll notice parameters that coincide with the API parameters. If nothing else, learning the APIs will help you better understand the CL commands.

A Powerful Combination. Using the program message queue to communicate information to the user provides you a lot of flexibility. Add the wizardry of message subfiles, and you're on your way toward creating a killer application—and you haven't even started coding the business logic yet.

CODE EXAMPLES

The following code examples are used in this chapter.

SFL016DF: Display File for Error Message Subfile

```
A                                       DSPSIZ(24 80 *DS3)
A                                       CA03(03)
A                                       CA12(12)
A          R SCREEN1
A*
A                                       OVERLAY
A                                     1 29'Message Subfile Example'
A                                       DSPATR(HI)
A                                     4  5'Type a First and Last Name and Pre-
A                                         ss Enter to test the Message Subfil-
A                                         e.'
A                                       COLOR(BLU)
A                                     7  9'Enter First Name . .'
A            FIRST_NAME    20   B    7 30CHECK(LC)
```

SFL016DF: Display File for Error Message Subfile (continued)

```
A                                9  9'Enter Last Name. . .'
A              LAST_NAME    20  B  9 30CHECK(LC)
A                               22  3'F3=Exit'
A                                  COLOR(BLU)
A                               22 13'F12=Cancel'
A                                  COLOR(BLU)
 * Message subfile record
 *     SFLMSGRCD controls which line the message subfile starts on.
 *     SFLMSGKEY controls the message key of the message that is to
 *        be the first one displayed.
 *     SFLPGMQ controls which program message queue messages are pulled from
 *        It is being populated with the name of the main procedure from the
 *        program status data structure in the RPG program.
A              R MSGSFL                   SFL
A                                         SFLMSGRCD(24)
A                MSGKEY                    SFLMSGKEY
A                SDS_PROC                  SFLPGMQ
 *
 * Message subfile control record
 *     SFLPAG > SFLSIZ to allow the system to control page up and down
 *        in the subfile.  The subfile will be automatically extended
 *        based on the number of entries in the program message queue.
 *     SFLDSP and SFLDSPCTL cause the subfile and control record to be
 *        displayed when the control format is thrown
 *     SFLINZ, in this case, causes the system to automatically load
 *        the subfile with messages from the message queue specified
 *     SFLPGMQ controls which program message queue messages are pulled from
 *        It is being populated with the name of the main procedure from the
 *        program status data structure in the RPG program.
 *     SFLEND with indicators that always evaluate to TRUE, allows the
 *        system to automatically toggle the "+" sign that indicates if
 *        there are more records to display in the subfile.
A              R MSGCTL                   SFLCTL(MSGSFL)
A                                         SFLSIZ(2)
A                                         SFLPAG(1)
A                                         SFLDSP
A                                         SFLDSPCTL
A                                         SFLINZ
A N99                                     SFLEND
A                SDS_PROC                  SFLPGMQ
```

SFL016RG: RPG Program Using Message Handling APIs

```
     *
     *   To compile:
     *
     *              CRTRPGPGM PGM(XXX/SFL016RG) SRCFILE(XXX/QRPGLESRC)
     *
     *========================================================================
Fsfl016df  cf   e              workstn
F                                          infds(info)
     *
Dpsds          sds
D sds_proc         *proc                                    Procedure name
     *
Dinfo          ds
D cfkey                    369    369
     *
Dexit          C                      const(X'33')
Dcancel        C                      const(X'3C')
Denter         C                      const(X'F1')
     *
*** Procedure prototype declaration
     *     Think of this as the PLIST in the CALLING procedure
d    msgId         s              7A
d    msgLoc        s             20A    inz('SFLMSGF    *LIBL      ')
d    msgRplDta     s              1A    inz(' ')
d    msgRplDtaLen  s              4B 0  inz(0)
d    msgType       s             10A    inz('*DIAG')
d    msgQueue      s            276A    inz('*')
d    msgCallStack  s              4B 0  inz(0)
d    msgKey        s              4A    inz(' ')
d    msgErr        s              4B 0  inz(0)
d    msgrmv        s             10A    inz('*ALL')

c                   dou       (cfkey = exit) or (cfkey = cancel)
c                   write     msgctl
c                   exfmt     screen1
C                   eval      msgKey = *blanks
C                   exsr      rcvmsg

c                   select
c                   when      cfkey = enter
C                   if        first_name  'Kevin'
C                   movel(p)  'SFL0001'      msgId
C                   exsr      sndmsg
C                   endif

C                   if        last_name   'Vandever'
C                   movel(p)  'SFL0002'      msgId
C                   exsr      sndmsg
C                   endif
c
```

SFL016RG: RPG Program Using Message Handling APIs (continued)

```
c                       endsl

c                       enddo
  *
C                       eval      *inlr = *on
  *
  * Send message subroutine
  *
c       sndmsg          begsr

c                       call      'QMHSNDPM'
c                       parm                  msgId
c                       parm                  msgLoc
c                       parm                  msgRplDta
c                       parm                  msgRplDtaLen
c                       parm                  msgType
c                       parm                  msgQueue
c                       parm                  msgCallStack
c                       parm                  msgKey
c                       parm                  msgErr

c                       endsr

  *
  * Remove message subroutine
  *
c       rcvmsg          begsr

c                       call      'QMHRMVPM'
c                       parm                  msgQueue
c                       parm                  msgCallStack
c                       parm                  msgKey
c                       parm                  msgRmv
c                       parm                  msgErr

c                       endsr
```

SFL016CL: CL Program to Send Messages Instead of Message APIs

```
          PGM

          DCLF      FILE(SFL016DF) RCDFMT(*ALL)
          CHGVAR    VAR(&SDS_PROC) VALUE('SFL016CL')
START:    SNDF      DEV(*FILE) RCDFMT(MSGCTL)
          SNDRCVF   DEV(*FILE) RCDFMT(SCREEN1)
          RMVMSG    MSGQ(*PGMQ) CLEAR(*ALL)
```

→

SFL016CL: CL Program to Send Messages Instead of Message APIs (continued)

```
            IF        COND(&IN03 = '1' *OR &IN12 = '1') THEN(GOTO +
                        CMDLBL(END))

            IF        COND(&FIRST_NAME *NE 'Kevin') THEN(DO)
            SNDPGMMSG MSGID(SFL0001) MSGF(SFLMSGF) TOPGMQ(*SAME)
            ENDDO

            IF        COND(&LAST_NAME *NE 'Vandever') THEN(DO)
            SNDPGMMSG MSGID(SFL0002) MSGF(SFLMSGF) TOPGMQ(*SAME)
            ENDDO

            GOTO      CMDLBL(START)

END:        ENDPGM
```

6

DISPLAYING MULTIPLE
SUBFILES ON A SCREEN

In chapter 1, I explained that a maximum of 24 subfiles can be active at one time and that a maximum of 12 can be displayed on a base screen or a window at one time. Don't believe me? Go ahead and take another look. I'll wait…. See, I told you. Would I lie to you? Anyway, in this chapter, I'm going to show you how to display more than one subfile on a screen. Even though I won't be displaying 12 subfiles on a screen in my example, you can use the provided explanation to help you do so.

MULTIPLE LISTS OF DATA

There are many situations where you may want to display more than one subfile on a screen. For instance, if you want to present information about an item, you might display one subfile showing the open orders for a given item and another subfile, on the same screen, showing the open purchase orders for that same item.

A third subfile might display the inventory status of that item from each warehouse. You can see that this one screen packs plenty of data for the user to digest. Add the ability to drill down and view the details of the subfile records (a skill you've acquired from reading previous chapters), and you've created a very powerful and useful inquiry application.

HORIZONTAL OR VERTICAL?

There are two ways to display multiple subfiles on a screen. One is the over/under method, where one subfile is on top of the other. Figure 6.1 shows a screen with two active subfiles, one on top of the other.

```
   SFL014RG              Multiple Subfiles - Over/Under          2/29/00
                                                                12:04:55
      First Name          MI      Last Name
      Tony                A       Anthony
      Al                  C       Bert
      Jim                 L       Coker
      Harry               H       Harrison
      John                J       Johnson
      Jim                 B       Naisium
      Gary                R       Patterson

                                                              More...

      First Name          MI      Last Name
      Tony                A       Anthony
      Al                  C       Bert
      Jim                 L       Coker
      Harry               H       Harrison
      John                J       Johnson
      Jim                 B       Naisium
      Gary                R       Patterson

                                                              More...
   F3=Exit    F12=Cancel
```

Figure 6.1: Example of the over/under subfile method.

Notice the two "More…" constants indicating that each subfile has more records to display? That's the first clue that there's more than one subfile on the screen. The other clue is the space between the lists and the change in column headings.

The second method of displaying multiple subfiles is to display them side by side. This method is a little trickier to pull off because of how subfiles occupy space on a screen. The short answer to how to do this is to use windows. Figure 6.2 shows an example of side-by-side subfiles using windows without borders.

```
SFL015RG              Multiple Subfiles - Side by Side        2/29/00
                                                             12:07:45


       First Name            MI          Last Name
       Tony                  A           Anthony
       Al                    C           Bert
       Jim                   L           Coker
       Harry                 H           Harrison
       John                  J           Johnson
       Jim                   B           Naisium
       Gary                  R           Patterson
       Louis                 A           Saint
       Sam                   S           Samuelson
       Othello               K           Simpson
                           More...                         More...




   F3=Exit   F9=Toggle   F12=Cancel
```

Figure 6.2: Example of side-by-side subfiles using the windows method.

We're going to look at both methods. Let's start with the easier, or at least more intuitive, method first—the over/under method.

OVER/UNDER

Let's start with the DDS for this technique. (You can find the complete DDS [SFL014DF] at the end of this chapter.) In this example, I'm going to display two subfiles on a screen, but you can use the same technique to add up to 12 subfiles per screen. Once you understand the basic concepts, your only challenge with adding more subfiles is figuring where to put them.

My header will simply display a title line in row 1, the name of the program, and the date and time. My first subfile control record (Figure 6.3) will start on line 3 and contain the column headings for my first, or top, subfile. Notice that this is a load-all subfile. In fact, I not only use the load-all technique in this example, but I use it in all my multiple subfile applications. I'll explain more about this later in this chapter. My first subfile will contain the first name, middle initial, and last name from the Employee Master file and will list seven names per page. Nothing Earth shattering so far, right?

```
A                    R SF1CTL                      SFLCTL(SFL1)
A                                                   SFLSIZ(0050)
A                                                   SFLPAG(0007)
A                                                   OVERLAY
A   32                                              SFLDSP
A                                                   SFLDSPCTL
A   31                                              SFLCLR
A   90                                              SFLEND(*MORE)
A                      CURSOR        1   I   3   2DSPATR(ND)
A                                            3   5'First Name'
A                                                   DSPATR(HI)
A                                          3 30'MI'
A                                                   DSPATR(HI)
A                                          3 37'Last Name'
A                                                   DSPATR(HI)
A                      RRN1          4S 0H          SFLRCDNBR
```

Figure 6.3: Subfile control record format for over/under subfile example (top subfile).

The second subfile in the DDS (Figure 6.4) is identical to the first one except that the subfile control format starts on line 13, with the subfile record format directly under it at line 14, and the indicators are different. In my example, the subfiles are identical. This probably isn't what you would do in the real world, but for simplicity's sake, I'm displaying the same subfile two times on the same screen.

```
A                    R SF2CTL                      SFLCTL(SFL2)
A                                                   SFLSIZ(0050)
A                                                   SFLPAG(0007)
A                                                   OVERLAY
A   42                                              SFLDSP
```

Figure 6.4: Subfile control record format for over/under subfile example (bottom subfile).

176

```
A                                    SFLDSPCTL
A    41                              SFLCLR
A    90                              SFLEND(*MORE)
A              CURSOR      1   I 13  2DSPATR(ND)
A                             13  5'First Name's
A                                    DSPATR(HI)
A                             13 30'MI'
A                                    DSPATR(HI)
A                             13 37'Last Name'
A                                    DSPATR(HI)
A              RRN2         4S 0H    SFLRCDNBR
```

Figure 6.4: Subfile control record format for over/under subfile example
(bottom subfile) (continued).

Finally, I define my function key format, footer, to display the valid function
keys available to the user. There you have the DDS. Two subfiles defined on one
screen, each containing seven records per page. Notice that I use two different
sets of indicators for SFLCLR, SFLDSP, and SFLEND. This is simply so I can control the subfiles separately. Again, in the real world, you might have a case where
one subfile has more records than the other. One or both might even be empty. In
my example, they'll always be equal.

The (Tab) Key to Success

Before I move on to the RPG, I would like to explain another technique I use
with over/under subfiles. Notice that each of the subfile control formats contain
an input only (I) field, CURSOR, that's placed before the first column heading.
This field has been defined as non-display (DSPATR(ND)) because I don't want to
have it displayed on the screen. Its only purpose is for easy cursor movement.
I'm going to use CURSOR to allow the user to more easily travel between the two
subfiles. Because both subfiles are active, the user is able to move between the
two subfiles with one keystroke, using either the Tab key or Field Exit key.

This is important because control in a load-all subfile isn't passed back to the
program when the page keys are pressed. As a result, OS/400 decides which
subfile to page to by interrogating (not harshly) the cursor position on the screen.
If the cursor is positioned anywhere in the top subfile, the top subfile will be

177

affected when the page keys are pressed. If the cursor is positioned in the bottom subfile, the bottom subfile will be affected. Without my CURSOR field, the user will have to use the arrow keys, and potentially many keystrokes, to maneuver between the subfiles. If the cursor is located in the HEADER or FOOTER format, the controlled subfile depends on how you coded the RPG. That said, let's move on to the RPG.

Where's the EXFMT?

The RPG code (SFL014RG) looks much like a typical load-all subfile program except that I'm loading and displaying two subfiles instead of one. Figure 6.5 shows the F specs for the display file. Notice that there are two subfiles defined, SFL1 and SFL2.

```
Fsfl014df  cf   e              workstn sfile(sfl1:rrn1)
F                                      sfile(sfl2:rrn2)
F                                      infds(info)
```

Figure 6.5: F specs for the display file using the over/under method for multiple subfiles.

Up to this point, you may be accustomed to seeing a WRITE operation, which displays the function key format, and an EXFMT operation, which displays to and reads from the subfile control and record formats. The code in Figure 6.6 isn't much different. It just looks that way.

```
C                  write     header
C                  write     footer
C                  write     sf2ctl
C                  write     sf1ctl
C                  read      sf2ctl
C                  read      sf1ctl
```

Figure 6.6: I use only WRITE statements to display my subfiles.

The EXFMT operation actually performs a write followed by a read. In my example, I want to make both subfiles active at the same time. To do this, I'm going to write them both to the screen first and then read from both of them when the user presses a valid function or Enter key.

The rest of the RPG is very similar to what you've seen before with load-all subfiles. It isn't responsible for much because the DDS is controlling almost everything. Control is returned back to the RPG program so the RPG can process the whole screen, and not just an individual subfile.

Anything specific to one subfile (i.e. paging) will be accomplished by the DDS and is determined by the cursor location. When the cursor is located in a neutral spot (header or footer), the top subfile, SF1CTL, will be paged when the user presses the page keys. This is because that's the subfile control record that was written last. Otherwise, the subfile that contains the cursor will be the one that's paged through. I've simplified the RPG to allow you to concentrate on multiple subfile concepts. In the real world, you're probably not going to load each subfile with the exact same data, unless, of course, you really want to emphasize that data.

Keep It Simple

One question you may have is whether you can display multiple self-extending or page-at-a-time subfiles on a screen. The answer is yes. However, you're going to do a lot more work in your RPG program. Instead of the DDS determining which subfile should be paged, you'll have to do that in your RPG. It's not a big deal, but it is more work. You'll have to know where the cursor was when the user pressed the Page Up or Page Down key and process the correct subfile accordingly.

You may also have an issue if you're loading subfiles from the same data file. Maybe you're reading from a file and interrogating the data before determining which subfile to load. If you don't use the load-all technique, you're going to have fun trying to keep track of all the file pointers associated with each subfile. Recommendation: Use load-all subfiles when you're displaying multiple subfiles on a screen.

SIDE-BY-SIDE SUBFILES

The other way to display multiple subfiles on a screen is side by side. Subfiles, however, cannot reside side by side on the same screen. When you define DDS for a screen that will include a subfile, you have to concern yourself with the row in which you're defining each record format. What I mean by that is that you have the subfile control record that takes up the top three or four rows of the screen in a typical subfile layout. It could be more, it could be less, but in general, the top portion of the screen is the subfile control, or header, portion. By the way, you can just as easily reserve the bottom portion of the screen for the subfile control. It doesn't have to display above the subfile record format, but it can't overlap it. Now, back to my DDS.

Once you've defined the rows the subfile control record will consume, you define the subfile record format. This is typically the middle part of the screen and cannot overlap the subfile control record. As a result, if your subfile control header takes up rows 1 through 4, your subfile record format must start on row 5.

Finally, you usually display some sort of function key line and maybe a message line at the bottom of your screen. Again, these lines can't share the rows occupied by the subfile record format. Once you've defined which rows each format will occupy, the formats occupy every column in the row. You cannot have the subfile record format only using columns 1 through 40. Even if the actual fields you define in subfile record only take up 40 columns, the format itself consumes all the columns.

Given the information above, you may now be asking how you can display side-by-side subfiles. The answer is, you can't—sort of. The only way to display subfiles side by side is to use windows. The good news is that it's easy to place windows side by side on a screen. If each of those windows happens to be a subfile window, you're now able to place subfiles side by side. The bad news is that because these subfiles are separate windows, they cannot be active at the same time. Remember our windows chapter? You can display up to 12 windows on a screen at a time, but only one can be active at a time. However, I don't give up easily, and you shouldn't either. I'll show you a technique to make the side-by-side windowed subfiles appear as two active subfiles, side by side, on one screen.

Nothing up My Sleeves

For this technique, I'm going to use two load-all subfile windows and place them next to each other on the screen. The complete DDS for this technique is shown at the end of the chapter (SFL015DF).

Our DDS includes a header, footer, and two subfile windows. I got really tricky this time and didn't display the same data in each subfile. The first subfile will contain first names and middle initials, and the second will contain last names. Think of this application as a way to see how different combinations of first and last names look together.

Let's take a look at Figure 6.7. In my example, I really don't want to show the user that I'm displaying two separate windows. With that in mind, I'm going to explicitly define the window border as blanks. Remember that the WDWBORDER keyword is optional, but if you leave it out, you'll get IBM's default border. In this case, because I want no border (see Figure 6.2), I'm going to add a WDWBORDER keyword to define no border.

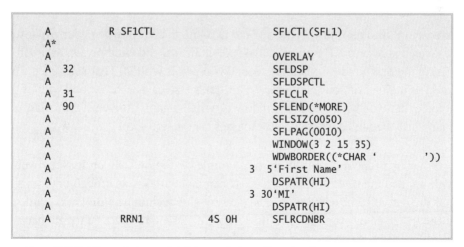

```
     A          R SF1CTL                    SFLCTL(SFL1)
     A*
     A                                      OVERLAY
     A   32                                 SFLDSP
     A                                      SFLDSPCTL
     A   31                                 SFLCLR
     A   90                                 SFLEND(*MORE)
     A                                      SFLSIZ(0050)
     A                                      SFLPAG(0010)
     A                                      WINDOW(3 2 15 35)
     A                                      WDWBORDER((*CHAR '        '))
     A                                3  5'First Name'
     A                                      DSPATR(HI)
     A                                3 30'MI'
     A                                      DSPATR(HI)
     A          RRN1          4S 0H         SFLRCDNBR
```

Figure 6.7: Subfile control record defining a window with no border.

The two windows are defined in much the same way. The difference is in the WINDOW keyword entry in the subfile control format. The only difference is the third parameter (see Figure 6.8), which tells you where to place (by column number) the upper, right-hand corner of the window. The window keywords have been defined appropriately to place the windows side by side.

```
A              R SF2CTL                    SFLCTL(SFL2)
A*
A                                          OVERLAY
A    42                                    SFLDSP
A                                          SFLDSPCTL
A    41                                    SFLCLR
A    90                                    SFLEND(*MORE)
A                                          SFLSIZ(0050)
A                                          SFLPAG(0010)
A                                          WINDOW(3 41 15 35)
A                                          WDWBORDER((*CHAR '        '))
A                                          USRRSTDSP
A                                      3  5'Last Name'
A                                          DSPATR(HI)
A              RRN2           4S 0H        SFLRCDNBR
```

Figure 6.8: Subfile control record for the second window.

Another technique I like to use with side-by-side windows is the USRRSTDSP keyword (see Figure 6.8). You were introduced to this keyword in chapter 4.

To recap, USRRSTDSP allows you, and not OS/400, to control when your windows are saved and restored. By using USRRSTDSP in the second window, OS/400 will not save the first window when the second window is written. That's not such a big deal to us in this example. However, USRRSTDSP also causes the second window not to be removed when the first window is written again. Conversely, the first window isn't removed when the user toggles back to the second window.

So, by using a function key (F9 in my example) to toggle back on forth between windows, and the USRRSTDSP keyword, I can make it look as though both windows are active at the same time. The side-by-side technique still works without the USRRSTDSP keyword, but you'll see a big difference when you toggle back and forth. Without USRRSTDSP, the windows will be removed and restored, which will cause the screen to "flash" each time the toggle (F9) key is pressed. By adding USRRSTDSP to the second subfile control record, the flash will disappear, and you'll only notice cursor movement between the two windows. Try running the programs both ways to see what I'm talking about.

The Toggle Technique

The RPG program for this technique is SFL015RG (as shown at the end of this chapter). As usual, the program doesn't get to have much fun. The DDS is the primary controller of what's going to happen. However, there are a few things that I want to show you in the RPG that are a bit different than what I've talked about before.

Take a look at the code in Figure 6.9. Field WHICH_ONE, defined in the D specs, will be used to determine which subfile window to control. As the user presses F9 to toggle between windows, the WHICH_ONE field will be set to a 1 or 2.

```
     Dwhich_one        S              1    inz('1')
```

Figure 6.9: Field WHICH_ONE will control which subfile is made active.

The mainline code in Figure 6.10 shows how I use the WHICH_ONE field. In my DOU loop, which processes the screen after I write my header and footer formats, I display both windows, but I'll determine which one is active based on the WHICH_ONE field. Because I initialized it to 1 in my D specs, the window on the left side will be active the first time through the loop.

```
     C                   dou       (cfkey = exit) or (cfkey = cancel)
     *
     C                   write     header
     C                   write     footer
     *
     C                   if        which_one = '1'
     C                   write     sf2ctl
     C                   exfmt     sf1ctl
```

Figure 6.10: Depending on the value of WHICH_ONE, the program will determine which subfile to make active.

```
C            else
C            write    sf1ctl
C            exfmt    sf2ctl
C            endif
```

Figure 6.10: Depending on the value of WHICH_ONE, the program will determine which subfile to make active (continued).

When the F9 toggle key is pressed, I determine the value of WHICH_ONE. If it's 1, I change it to 2; otherwise, I change it back to 1. This technique is illustrated by the code in Figure 6.11. Upon the next iteration through the DOU loop, the value of WHICH_ONE is interrogated to determine which window will be active.

```
C            when     cfkey = toggle
C            if       which_one = '1'
C            eval     which_one = '2'
C            eval     rrn1 = sflrrn
C            else
C            eval     which_one = '1'
C            eval     rrn2 = sflrrn
C            endif
```

Figure 6.11: When the F9 key is pressed, the program will set the appropriate variables in preparation for displaying a window.

There's another neat little trick you can use to control side-by-side subfile windows in the toggle logic. When I determine which window is currently active so I can toggle to the other window, I can also set the RRN associated with the window that will become active. If you go back to the DDS, you'll notice that I used the SFLRCDNBR keyword and associated it with the relative record number in each subfile record. If you remember, SFLRCDNBR allows you to display a given page of the subfile based on the current relative record number.

In the RPG D specs, I retrieve the relative record number of the first subfile record on the page (see Figure 6.12), I'm finally using something else from the file information data structure. In addition to the indicator that tells me which key the user pressed, I can get the relative record number of the first subfile record on the page. What this allows me to do is remember which page was displayed when the user pressed the toggle key to go the next subfile. When he toggles back, I want the subfile to stay in the same place it was when he left.

```
    D sflrrn                    378    379B 0
```

Figure 6.12: Use the relative record number to remember which page you are on when you leave one subfile and make another one active.

In my toggle logic, I not only set WHICH_ONE to the appropriate value, but I also set the RRN variable (which is used in the SFLRCDNBR keyword) for the window that's about to be displayed as it was before it was made inactive. For example, if I page through the left subfile and end up on page 4 and then toggle to the right subfile, I want page 4 to stay on the screen when I toggle back. Without the SFLRRN value from the file information data structure, the subfile will always revert to what it was set to in the SFLBLD routine (in this case, 1). By adding this little technique, the subfile will stick to where it was when it was last active. Again, I invite you to try side-by-side subfiles with and without the SFLRRN value from the INFDS to see the difference.

Another way to retrieve the subfile relative record number from the first subfile record on the page is to use the SFLSCROLL keyword. This keyword and a five-byte zero-decimal hidden field in your DDS will provide the same information as the D spec in Figure 6.12. Figure 6.13 shows how to code the SFLSCROLL keyword. When control is passed back to your program, the RETRN field will contain the same information as that contained in SFLRRN from Figure 6.12; that is, the relative record number of the first record on the page. If you decide to use SFLSCROLL instead of the file information data structure, note that SFLSCROLL and SFLRCDNBR can't be used on the same field and SFLSCROLL can't be used if SFLPAG and SFLSIZ are equal.

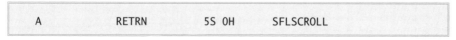

```
    A              RETRN          5S 0H      SFLSCROLL
```

Figure 6.13: Use SFLSCROLL to pass information back to the program.

HOCUS POCUS

There you have it—a couple of ways to display multiple subfiles on a screen. The over/under technique is fairly straightforward and allows you to easily implement multiple, active subfiles on a screen using traditional subfile techniques. Side-by-side subfiles aren't too difficult to implement, but they can't be made active at the same time. However, using a little finesse such as a toggling technique, the USRRSTDSP keyword, and the relative record number value from the file information data structure, you can create elegant side-by-side subfiles that look to the user as if they're all active at the same time.

CODE EXAMPLES

The following code examples are used in this chapter.

SFL014DF: Display File for the Over/Under Subfile

```
A                                    DSPSIZ(24 80 *DS3)
A                                    CA03
A                                    CA12
A*
A          R HEADER
A*
A                                    OVERLAY
A                                    1 26'Multiple Subfiles - Over/Under'
A                                       DSPATR(HI)
A                                    1  3'SFL014RG'
A                                    1 71DATE
A                                       EDTCDE(Y)
A                                    2 71TIME
A*
A          R SFL1                    SFL
A*
A            DBFNAM    R        O  4  5REFFLD(PFR/DBFNAM *LIBL/SFL001PF)
A            DBMINI    R        O  4 31REFFLD(PFR/DBMINI *LIBL/SFL001PF)
A            DBLNAM    R        O  4 37REFFLD(PFR/DBLNAM *LIBL/SFL001PF)
A*
A*
A          R SF1CTL                  SFLCTL(SFL1)
A                                    SFLSIZ(0050)
A                                    SFLPAG(0007)
A                                    OVERLAY
A   32                               SFLDSP
```

SFL014DF: Display File for the Over/Under Subfile (continued)

```
A                                           SFLDSPCTL
A  31                                        SFLCLR
A  90                                        SFLEND(*MORE)
A              CURSOR       1   I  3  2DSPATR(ND)
A                                    3  5'First Name'
A                                           DSPATR(HI)
A                                    3 30'MI'
A                                           DSPATR(HI)
A                                    3 37'Last Name'
A                                           DSPATR(HI)
A              RRN1        4S  OH            SFLRCDNBR
A*
A           R SFL2                           SFL
A*
A              DBFNAM       R      O 14  5REFFLD(PFR/DBFNAM *LIBL/SFL001PF)
A              DBMINI       R      O 14 31REFFLD(PFR/DBMINI *LIBL/SFL001PF)
A              DBLNAM       R      O 14 37REFFLD(PFR/DBLNAM *LIBL/SFL001PF)
A*
A*
A           R SF2CTL                         SFLCTL(SFL2)
A                                           SFLSIZ(0050)
A                                           SFLPAG(0007)
A                                           OVERLAY
A  42                                        SFLDSP
A                                           SFLDSPCTL
A  41                                        SFLCLR
A  90                                        SFLEND(*MORE)
A              CURSOR       1   I 13  2DSPATR(ND)
A                                   13  5'First Name'
A                                           DSPATR(HI)
A                                   13 30'MI'
A                                           DSPATR(HI)
A                                   13 37'Last Name'
A                                           DSPATR(HI)
A              RRN2        4S  OH            SFLRCDNBR
A           R FOOTER
A*
A                                           OVERLAY
A                                   22  3'F3=Exit'
A                                           COLOR(BLU)
A                                       +3'F12=Cancel'
A                                           COLOR(BLU)
```

SFL014RG: RPG Program for the Over/Under Subfile

```
     *
     *  To compile:
     *
     *            CRTRPGPGM PGM(XXX/SFL014RG) SRCFILE(XXX/QRPGLESRC)
     *
     *====================================================================
Fsf1014df  cf   e           workstn sfile(sfl1:rrn1)
F                                   sfile(sfl2:rrn2)
F                                   infds(info)
Fsf1001lf  if   e         k disk
     *
Dinfo           ds
D cfkey               369     369
D sflrrn              378     379B 0
     *
Dexit           C                   const(X'33')
Dcancel         C                   const(X'3C')
Denter          C                   const(X'F1')
     *
C               exsr      sflbld
     *
c               dou       (cfkey = exit) or (cfkey = cancel)
     *
C               write     header
C               write     footer
C               write     sf2ctl
C               write     sf1ctl
C               read      sf2ctl
C               read      sf1ctl
     *
C               select
     *
C               when      (cfkey = exit) or (cfkey = cancel)
C               eval      *inlr = *on
     *
C               endsl
     *
C               enddo
     *
     ****************************************************************
C     sflbld    begsr
     ****************************************************************
     *
     * Load-all subfile.  Clear both subfiles before loading.
     *
C               eval      *in31 = *on
C               eval      *in41 = *on
C               write     sf1ctl
C               write     sf2ctl
C               eval      *in31 = *off
```

SFL014RG: RPG Program for the Over/Under Subfile (continued)

```
C                   eval      *in41 = *off
C                   z-add     0           rrn1
C                   z-add     0           rrn2
 *
 * Read the records from file and load both subfiles.
 *
C     *loval        setll     sfl001lf
C                   read      sfl001lf
C                   dow       not %eof
C                   eval      rrn1 = rrn1 + 1
C                   eval      rrn2 = rrn2 + 1
C                   write     sfl1
C                   write     sfl2
C                   read      sfl001lf
C                   enddo
 *
 * Since we are reading from the same file,
 * just check rrn1 to determine empty subfiles.
 *
C                   if        rrn1 > 0
C                   eval      *in32 = *on
C                   eval      *in42 = *on
C                   eval      rrn1  = 1
C                   eval      rrn2  = 1
C                   endif
 *
 * SFLEND indicator
 *
C                   eval      *in90 = *on
 *
C                   endsr
```

SFL015DF: Display File for the Side-by-Side Subfiles

```
A                                   DSPSIZ(24 80 *DS3)
A                                   CA03
A                                   CA12
A                                   CF09
A*
A           R HEADER
A*
A                                   OVERLAY
A                               1 25'Multiple Subfiles - Side by Side'
A                                   DSPATR(HI)
A                               1  3'SFL015RG'
A                               1 71DATE
A                                   EDTCDE(Y)
A                               2 71TIME
A*
```

SFL015DF: Display File for the Side-by-Side Subfiles (continued)

```
A               R SFL1                        SFL
A*
A                  DBFNAM    R      O  4  5REFFLD(PFR/DBFNAM *LIBL/SFL001PF)
A                  DBMINI    R      O  4 31REFFLD(PFR/DBMINI *LIBL/SFL001PF)
A*
A               R SF1CTL                      SFLCTL(SFL1)
A*
A                                             OVERLAY
A   32                                        SFLDSP
A                                             SFLDSPCTL
A   31                                        SFLCLR
A   90                                        SFLEND(*MORE)
A                                             SFLSIZ(0050)
A                                             SFLPAG(0010)
A                                             WINDOW(3 2 15 35)
A                                             WDWBORDER((*CHAR '       '))
A                                     3  5'First Name'
A                                             DSPATR(HI)
A                                     3 30'MI'
A                                             DSPATR(HI)
A                  RRN1           4S OH       SFLRCDNBR
A*
A               R SFL2                        SFL
A*
A                  DBLNAM    R      O  4  5REFFLD(PFR/DBLNAM *LIBL/SFL001PF)
A*
A               R SF2CTL                      SFLCTL(SFL2)
A*
A                                             OVERLAY
A   42                                        SFLDSP
A                                             SFLDSPCTL
A   41                                        SFLCLR
A   90                                        SFLEND(*MORE)
A                                             SFLSIZ(0050)
A                                             SFLPAG(0010)
A                                             WINDOW(3 41 15 35)
A                                             WDWBORDER((*CHAR '       '))
A                                             USRRSTDSP
A                                     3  5'Last Name'
A                                             DSPATR(HI)
A                  RRN2           4S OH       SFLRCDNBR
A               R FOOTER
A*
A                                             OVERLAY
A                                    22  3'F3=Exit'
A                                             COLOR(BLU)
A                                    22 13'F9=Toggle'
A                                             COLOR(BLU)
A                                    22 25'F12=Cancel'
A                                             COLOR(BLU)
```

190

SFL015RG: RPG Program for the Side-by-Side Subfiles

```
FSFL015df  cf   e                workstn sfile(sfl1:rrn1)
F                                        sfile(sfl2:rrn2)
F                                        infds(info)
Fsfl001lf  if   e         k disk
*
Dinfo           ds
D cfkey               369    369
D sflrrn              378    379B 0
*
Dexit           C                const(X'33')
Dcancel         C                const(X'3C')
Denter          C                const(X'F1')
Dtoggle         C                const(X'39')
*
Dwhich_one      S          1     inz('1')
*
C               exsr     sflbld
*
c               dou      (cfkey = exit) or (cfkey = cancel)
*
C               write    header
C               write    footer
*
C               if       which_one = '1'
C               write    sf2ctl
C               exfmt    sf1ctl
C               else
C               write    sf1ctl
C               exfmt    sf2ctl
C               endif
*
C               select
*
C               when     cfkey = toggle
C               if       which_one = '1'
C               eval     which_one = '2'
C               eval     rrn1 = sflrrn
C               else
C               eval     which_one = '1'
C               eval     rrn2 = sflrrn
C               endif
*
C               when     (cfkey = exit) or (cfkey = cancel)
C               eval     *inlr = *on
*
C               endsl
*
C               enddo
*
************************************************************************
```

SFL015RG: RPG Program for the Side-by-Side Subfiles (continued)

```
C     sflbld        begsr
     ****************************************************************
     *
     * Load-all subfile.  Clear both subfiles before loading.
     *
C                   move      *on           *in31
C                   move      *on           *in41
C                   write     sf1ctl
C                   write     sf2ctl
C                   move      *off          *in31
C                   move      *off          *in41
C                   z-add     0             rrn1
C                   z-add     0             rrn2
     *
     * Read the records from file and load both subfiles.
     *
C     *loval        setll     sfl0011f
C                   read      sfl0011f
C                   dow       not %eof
C                   eval      rrn1 = rrn1 + 1
C                   eval      rrn2 = rrn2 + 1
C                   write     sfl1
C                   write     sfl2
C                   read      sfl0011f
C                   enddo
     *
     * Since we are reading from the same file,
     * just check rrn1 to determine empty subfiles.
     *
C                   if        rrn1 > 0
C                   eval      *in32 = *on
C                   eval      *in42 = *on
C                   eval      rrn1  = 1
C                   eval      rrn2  = 1
C                   endif
     *
     * SFLEND indicator
     *
C                   eval      *in90 = *on
     *
C                   endsr
```

7

SUBFILES AND DATA QUEUES —A PERFECT COMBINATION

This next technique came to me when I was asked to create a subfile application that works like the Program Development Manager (PDM). If you've ever looked at PDM on the AS/400, you may have marveled at what a cool subfile application it is. PDM is extremely flexible. It allows you to position to any place in a subfile-like panel, page forward or backward from that position, change a record on any page of the subfile, and process all changed records only when the Enter key is pressed. On their own, each feature is simple to code in an RPG subfile program. But the real fun begins when you combine the features.

I worked for a software development house that wanted the IBM look and feel on all of its screens. The thinking was that users familiar with the AS/400 would be comfortable using the interactive screens in our software and would require less training. It seemed simple enough at first, but as you will soon see, incorporating all the features included with PDM into a subfile application is no small task. In fact, PDM isn't even a subfile application; its displays are written using the User

Interface Manager (UIM), the language used for many native OS/400 commands and all of the help panels on the AS/400.

See Figure 7.1 for a typical PDM screen.

```
                         Work with Objects Using PDM                    MYSYSTEM

    Library . . . . .   VANDEVER          Position to . . . . . . . .
                                          Position to type  . . . . .

    Type options, press Enter.
      2=Change        3=Copy        4=Delete      5=Display      7=Rename
      8=Display description         9=Save       10=Restore     11=Move ...

    Opt   Object      Type        Attribute   Text
          QCLLESRC    *FILE       PF-SRC      ILE CL Source
          QCLSRC      *FILE       PF-SRC      Old CL source
          QDDSSRC     *FILE       PF-SRC      DDS Source
          QRPGLESRC   *FILE       PF-SRC      ILE RPG Source
          QTESTSRC    *FILE       PF-SRC      Internet Test Program Src


                                                                        Bottom
    Parameters or command
    ===>
    F3=Exit          F4=Prompt         F5=Refresh        F6=Create
    F9=Retrieve      F10=Command entry F23=More options  F24=More keys
```

Figure 7.1: Example of a PDM screen.

THE DILEMMA

Well, what do you do if you're an RPG programmer who likes the look, feel, and flexibility of PDM, but doesn't know how to obtain them using UIM? Do you learn UIM? You could, but if you already know RPG, is learning a new language the most effective use of your time? This was the dilemma I faced.

I'm not against learning UIM, but I thought that there must be a more efficient way to get the same results using RPG and subfile processing. After some research, I recommended to my programming group that we use data queues to add the necessary flexibility to our subfile applications. Data queues are the way to get the features and flexibility you're looking for—without having to learn UIM.

DATA QUEUES 101

Data queues are a type of system object (type *DTAQ) you can create and maintain using OS/400 commands and APIs. They're AS/400 objects that can be used to send and receive multiple record-like strings of data. Data may be sent to and received from a data queue from multiple programs, users, or jobs, making them an excellent mechanism for sharing data. They provide a fast means of asynchronous communication between two jobs because they use less system resources than database files, message queues, or data areas. Data queues have the ability to attach a sender ID to each entry being placed on the queue. The sender ID, an attribute of the data queue that's established when the queue is created contains the qualified job name and current user profile. Another advantage to using data queues is the ability to set the length of time a job will wait for an entry before continuing its processing. A negative wait parameter will tell the job to wait indefinitely for an entry before processing. A wait parameter of 0 to 99,999 will tell the job to wait that number of seconds before processing.

High-level language programs (HLLs) can send data to a data queue using the Send to a Data Queue (QSNDDTAQ) API and receive data using the Receive from a Data Queue (QRCVDTAQ) API. Data queues can be read in FIFO sequence, in LIFO sequence, or in keyed sequence. The technique I use for building PDM-like subfile applications requires a keyed data queue. Keyed data queues allow the programmer to specify a specific order in which entries on the data queue are received or to retrieve only data queue entries that meet a criterion. That is, the programmer can receive a data queue entry that's equal to (EQ), greater than (GT), greater than or equal to (GE), less than (LT), or less than or equal to (LE) a search key.

WHY SHOULD I USE A DATA
QUEUE IN A SUBFILE PROGRAM?

The reason behind using data queues in a subfile program stems from a combination of user requirements and an interest in selecting the most efficient solution for that combination. I wanted to provide the PDM look and feel by allowing users to position to anywhere in the subfile using the position-to field and to page up or down from that new position. This is easily accomplished using a page-at-time subfile.

However, I also wanted the data that was changed on subfile records to be saved, regardless of where the user navigated in the subfile, until the user was ready to process them by pressing the Enter key. This is accomplished easily in a load-all or self-extending subfile, but not in a page-at-a-time subfile.

With page-at-a-time subfiles, you have to clear and build one new page of subfile records every time the user pages and uses a position-to field. Any previously changed records are not saved. I needed a way to combine the flexibility of the page-at-a-time subfile with the capability to process the changed records only when desired. I needed a place to store and reuse changed subfile records until the user was ready to process them. Using data queues to accomplish this task instead of data structures, files, or arrays frees you from some additional work.

During an interactive job, the data queue APIs can provide better response time and decrease the size of the program, as well as its process activation group (PAG). In turn, this can help overall system performance. In addition, data queues allow the programmer to do less work. When you receive an entry from a data queue using the QRCVDTAQ command, it's physically removed from the data queue. The programmer doesn't have to add code to deal with unnecessary entries. Here's what you do.

I use the data queue to store a replica of the changed subfile record. Each time a subfile record is changed and the Enter key or Page key is pressed, the changed subfile record is stored in the data queue. I do this because I build the subfile one page at a time and need to know which records were previously changed. Once records are no longer displayed on the screen, they're not part of the subfile. When the user positions through the subfile by scrolling or by keying something in the position-to field, the program will check to see if each record read from the data file exists in the data queue before loading it to the subfile. If the record exists in the data queue, it's written to the subfile, along with the earlier changes, and marked as changed. When the user is ready to process all the changed records by pressing the Enter key with nothing in the position-to field, the records will be processed appropriately from the data queue. I have modified my original master file maintenance application using these principles. You can check out the CL, DDS, and RPG that make this work at the end of this chapter.

THE DDS—THE SAME AS IT EVER WAS

Before I get to the RPG, I need to say a few things about the DDS and CL. For this application to have the necessary flexibility, the RPG program—and not OS/400—must completely control the subfile. Of course, you know what that means. For this to happen, the subfile page (SFLPAG) and subfile size (SFLSIZ) values must be equal. The subfile will never contain more than one page, but, as you'll see, the program will make it appear that the subfile contains much more than one page of data. You should otherwise recognize the DDS as our Master File Maintenance DDS and understand what it's doing. The complete DDS is included at the end of this chapter (see SFL011DF).

CONTROL LANGUAGE— SO LITTLE CODE, SO MUCH CONTROL

It's important to note that even though entries are removed from a data queue after they're received, the space containing the entry isn't. Over the long run, performance will suffer because the data queue's size will increase. For this reason, I delete and re-create the data queue each time the program is called. Even if you build your data queues in QTEMP, as I do, it's best to delete and re-create them in case the user calls the program more than once before signing off. Program SFL011CL accomplishes this task. Again, you can find this program at the end of the chapter.

ABRACADABRA! THE SUBFILE'S NEVER MORE THAN ONE PAGE

Now that the setup issues have been covered, let's perform some magic. Let's start with the RPG program, which is our Master File Maintenance program from chapter 4, with a few additions thrown in. Rather than spending time rehashing the basic subfile techniques you've already mastered, I'll concentrate on how the program uses a data queue to make the subfile appear to be larger than it really is.

The program's first task is to load the subfile with one page of records (in this case, nine). This code is shown in Figure 7.2.

```
     *
     * Load data to subfile
     *
     C                   do        sflpag
     C                   read      sfl0011f                        90
     C                   if        *in90
     C                   leave
     C                   endif
     *
     C                   eval      option = *blanks
     C                   exsr      rcvque
     C                   eval      rrn1 = rrn1 + 1
     C                   if        rrn1 = 1
     C                   eval      savlnam = dblnam
     C                   eval      savfnam = dbfnam
     C                   endif
     C                   write     sfl1
     C                   eval      *in74 = *off
     C                   enddo
```

Figure 7.2: Loading the subfile with one page of records.

Notice that each time a record is read from the data file, the RCVQUE subroutine is executed. For the initial subfile load, this subroutine won't accomplish anything— (I will explain this later). However, after the initial load, the RCVQUE subroutine plays a vital part in the subfile load routine.

Once the subfile is initially loaded and displayed, the user can do several things. He can scroll through the subfile; add, change, display, or delete records; position to another place in the subfile; or exit the program.

The code listed in Figure 7.3 shows that no matter what the user decides to do, the ADDQUE subroutine is executed each time the Enter key or a valid function key (other than F3 or F12) is pressed. This subroutine uses the READC op code to find changed records in the subfile and add them to the data queue using the QSNDDTAQ API.

```
 * If ENTER key is pressed and position-to non blank,
 * reposition the subfile to close to what was entered.
 *
C                       when       (cfkey = enter) and (ptname  *blanks)
C                       exsr       addque
C       ptname          setll      sfl0011f
C                       exsr       sflbld
C                       clear                  ptname
 *
 * If ENTER key is pressed and position-to is blank,
 * process screen to interrogate options selected by user
 *
C                       when       (cfkey = enter) and (ptname = *blanks)
C                       exsr       addque
C                       exsr       prcsfl
C       savkey          setll      sfl0011f
C                       exsr       sflbld
 *
 * Roll up - load the data Q's before loading subfile
 *
C                       when       (cfkey = rollup) and (not *in90)
C                       exsr       addque
C                       exsr       sflbld
 *
 * User presses F6, throw the add screen, clear, and rebuild subfile
 *
C                       when       cfkey = add
C                       movel(p)   'Add    '       mode
C                       exsr       addque
C                       exsr       addrcd
C       dblnam          setll      sfl0011f
C                       exsr       sflbld
 *
 * Roll down - load the data Q's before loading the subfile.
 *
C                       when       (cfkey = rolldn) and (not *in32)
C                       exsr       addque
C                       exsr       goback
C                       exsr       sflbld
 *
C                       when       *inkl
C                       leave
```

Figure 7.3: Each time a valid function key, other than F3 or F12, is pressed, the changed records are added to the data queue.

Table 7.1 gives an explanation of the QSNDDTAQ parameters. The data queue entry will contain the option selected by the user and the key of the data file.

Figure 7.4 shows the contents of the data queue when the user selects a 4 next to a record, then pages down to see another page. When he paged down, an entry was added to the data queue that consisted of the option (4) and the value in DBIDNM, which is the key to the data file, the key to the data queue, and a hidden field in the subfile.

Table 7.1: Required QSNDDTAQ API Parameters.

Parameter	Explanation
QUEUE	Name of the data queue
LIB	Library containing the data queue
LEN	Length of the data being written to the data queue
DATA	The actual data being written to the data queue

```
                            Data Queue Display - TAA        2/02/00  12:14

   Queue: SFL011DQ    Lib: QTEMP        Nbr of Entries:     1  Seq: *KEYED
   Max Entry Length:    256  Key Length:     7  Force: *NO    Sender ID: *NO
         Text:
   Entry: 00001      Enqueue Date: 02/02/00    Enqueue Time: 12:07:36
   Posn   ....+....1....+....2....+....3....+....4....+....5....+....6....
     1   0000004                              40000004
    33   (DBIDNM as the key)              (OPTION followed by DBIDNM)
    97
   161
   225
```

Figure 7.4: The contents of the data queue after the user places a 4 in the option field and presses the page-down key.

The ADDQUE subroutine, shown in Figure 7.5, keeps track of all records changed through the subfile. For example, if the user decides to delete two records on the next page after selecting a 4 to delete a record on the current page, the ADDQUE subroutine sends the two changed records to the data queue before rebuilding the subfile in the page forward (SFLBLD) routine. Now there are three entries in the data queue, and nothing has been deleted. The same logic holds true if the user decides to position to another part of the subfile using the position-to field.

```
*****************************************************************
*   ADDQUE - Add subfile data to Data Queues
*****************************************************************
*
C       addque        begsr
*
* Read the changed subfile records and write them to the data Q's
* The first data queue is keyed by whatever the unique key of the file
* is.  If no unique key in the file, use the relative record number.
* This queue is used to save options selected on a specific subfile
* line.  The second queue is keyed by option, and is used to process
* like options together when the enter key is selected
*
C                     readc     sfl1
*
C                     dow       not %eof
*
C                     eval      len = qlen
*
C                     call      'QSNDDTAQ'
C                     parm                      queue
C                     parm                      lib
C                     parm                      len
C                     parm                      data
C                     parm                      keyln
C                     parm                      key
*
C                     readc     sfl1
C                     enddo
*
C                     endsr
```

Figure 7.5: This routine writes the changed records to the data queue.

Now we can get to the details of the RCVQUE routine, as shown in Figure 7.6.

```
*****************************************************************
*   RCVQUE - Check DATAQUEUE before writing to subfile
*****************************************************************
*
C       rcvque        begsr
*
* Read the data Q by the whatever the unique key from the
* physical file to see if there is a saved option.  If so, display
* the saved option when the subfile is displayed.
*
```

Figure 7.6: This routine removes entries from the data queue.

```
C                    eval      order = 'EQ'
C   *
C                    call      'QRCVDTAQ'
C                    parm                     queue
C                    parm                     lib
C                    parm                     len
C                    parm                     data
C                    parm                     wait
C                    parm                     order
C                    parm                     keyln
C                    parm                     key
C                    parm                     sndlen
C                    parm                     sndr
C   *
C                    if        len > *zero
C                    eval      *in74 = *on
C                    endif
C   *
C                    endsr
```

Figure 7.6: This routine removes entries from the data queue (continued).

This subroutine attempts to receive an entry from the keyed data queue using the same key as the record read from the database file (DBIDNM). The QRCVDTAQ API does this for you. The order is set to EQ (equal) so you will retrieve an entry only if there's one matching the record just read from the file. If the length is greater than 0 (len > 0), an entry was retrieved from the data queue. You then set on indicator 74, which conditions SFLNXTCHG in your DDS, to mark the record as changed when the subfile record is written. By doing this, subsequent READC operations will pick up the record the next time the page is processed.

Table 7.2 shows an explanation of the parameters for QRCVDTAQ.

If a matching entry exists in the data queue, the entry in the data queue—not the data from the database file—is written to the subfile. With this, the user can page and position through the subfile and store any changed records in the data queue. Whenever a record is read from the file, the data queue is checked to see if that record exists. If it does, it's displayed along with the previously selected option. If our user wanted to page up to see the first page after having selected two records for delete on the second page, he could do so. He would see a "4" in the original record he selected for delete, and the data queue would now contain the two records from the second page.

If the user presses the Enter key and the position-to field is empty, the ADDQUE routine executes one last time to load any changes to the current page, and the PRCSFL routine is executed. The PRCSFL routine (shown in Figure 7.7) in this example is a little different than the one in my original Master File Maintenance program. This subroutine uses the RCVDTAQ API instead of READC to process all the changed records. Remember hat changed records will reside in the data queue, not the subfile, which never contains more than

Parameter	Explanation
QUEUE	Data queue name
LIB	Library containing the data queue
LEN	Length of entry received from the data queue
DATA	Data received from the data queue
WAIT	How long to wait for data (a negative number will cause the program to wait indefinitely)
ORDER	How to get the keyed data (EQ, GE, LT, etc.)
KEYLN	Length of the key to the data queue
KEY	The key field used to retrieve data
SNDLEN	Length of the sender ID information
SNDR	The sender ID information

Table 7.2:
Required QRCVDTAQ API Parameters When Working with Keyed Data Queues.

one page of data. By setting the key value, DBIDNM, to one and the order to GE (greater than or equal to), you're sure to retrieve all entries in the data queue. Figure 7.7 shows the RCVDTAQ API in action in the PRCSFL routine. This API will be run until the length (LEN) parameter is 0. That will happen when no more entries exist in the data queue.

```
    * Receive data queue records until the queue is empty LEN = 0
    *
C                       eval      dbidnm = 1
C                       eval      order = 'GE'
    *
C                       dou       len = *zero
    *
```

Figure 7.7: How to process all the changed records from a subfile by going through the data queue.

```
C                       call      'QRCVDTAQ'
C                       parm                     queue
C                       parm                     lib
C                       parm                     len
C                       parm                     data
C                       parm                     wait
C                       parm                     order
C                       parm                     keyln
C                       parm                     key
C                       parm                     sndlen
C                       parm                     sndr
 *
 *    If length is greater than zero, there was a record read.
 *    Process that record and receive from the second dataq to
 *    keep them in cinc.
 *
C                       if        len > *zero
```

Figure 7.7: How to process all the changed records from a subfile through the data queue (continued).

Each time an entry is received, the data is run through a select routine to determine which function needs to be performed. In the case of this program, depending on the option taken, a display screen, an update screen, or a delete confirmation subfile will appear, just as it did in my earlier example.

Controlling the subfile within the RPG program and using data queues to store and retrieve changed subfile records allows you to create an extremely flexible subfile application that will furnish your users with everything they ever wanted in a subfile program. Besides, it's a great way to make a page-at-time subfile look like a lot like a load-all subfile.

CODE EXAMPLES

The following code examples are used in this chapter.

SFL011CL: CL Program to Create the Temporary Data Queue

```
/*===========================================================*/
/*  To compile:                                              */
/*                                                           */
/*          CRTCLPGM PGM(XXX/SFL011CL) SRCFILE(XXX/QCLLESRC) */
/*                                                           */
/*===========================================================*/
PGM

    DLTDTAQ    DTAQ(QTEMP/SFL011DQ)
    MONMSG     MSGID(CPF2105)
    CRTDTAQ    DTAQ(QTEMP/SFL011DQ) MAXLEN(256) SEQ(*KEYED) +
                 KEYLEN(7)
    CALL       PGM(*LIBL/SFL011RG)

ENDPGM
```

SFL011DF: DDS Using the Data Queue Technique

```
     A*
     A                                      DSPSIZ(24 80 *DS3)
     A                                      PRINT
     A                                      ERRSFL
     A                                      CA03
     A                                      CA12
     A*
     A          R SFL1                      SFL
     A*
     A   74                                 SFLNXTCHG
     A            DBIDNM   R      H          REFFLD(PFR/DBIDNM *LIBL/SFL001PF)
     A            OPTION          1A  B 10  3VALUES(' ' '2' '4' '5')
     A            DBLNAM   R       O 10  7REFFLD(PFR/DBLNAM *LIBL/SFL001PF)
     A            DBFNAM   R       O 10 31REFFLD(PFR/DBFNAM *LIBL/SFL001PF)
     A            DBMINI   R       O 10 55REFFLD(PFR/DBMINI *LIBL/SFL001PF)
     A            DBNNAM   R       O 10 60REFFLD(PFR/DBNNAM *LIBL/SFL001PF)
     A          R SF1CTL                    SFLCTL(SFL1)
     A*
     A                                      CF06
     A                                      SFLSIZ(0012)
     A                                      SFLPAG(0012)
     A                                      ROLLUP
     A                                      ROLLDOWN
     A                                      OVERLAY
     A N32                                  SFLDSP
     A N31                                  SFLDSPCTL
     A   31                                 SFLCLR
     A   90                                 SFLEND(*MORE)
     A            RRN1            4S OH      SFLRCDNBR
     A                                  9  7'Last Name'
     A                                      DSPATR(HI)
     A                                  9 31'First Name'
```

SFL011DF: DDS Using the Data Queue Technique (continued)

```
A                                           DSPATR(HI)
A                                       9 55'MI'
A                                           DSPATR(HI)
A                                       9 60'Nick Name'
A                                           DSPATR(HI)
A                                       1  2'SFL011RG'
A                                       1 71DATE
A                                           EDTCDE(Y)
A                                       2 71TIME
A                                       1 24'Subfile Program with Update      '
A                                           DSPATR(HI)
A                                       4  2'Position to Last Name . . .'
A               PTNAME       20A  B     4 30CHECK(LC)
A                                       9  2'Opt'
A                                           DSPATR(HI)
A                                       6  2'Type options, press Enter.'
A                                           COLOR(BLU)
A                                       7  4'2=Change'
A                                           COLOR(BLU)
A                                       7 19'4=Delete'
A                                           COLOR(BLU)
A                                       7 34'5=Display'
A                                           COLOR(BLU)
A*
A               R PANEL1
A                                       1  2'SFL004RG'
A               MODE          6  O      2  2DSPATR(HI)
A                                       1 24'Subfile Program with Update      '
A                                           DSPATR(HI)
A                                       1 71DATE
A                                           EDTCDE(Y)
A                                       2 71TIME
A               DBIDNM       R     O    4 23REFFLD(PFR/DBIDNM *LIBL/SFL001PF)
A                                           DSPATR(HI)
A               DBFNAM       R     B    6 23REFFLD(PFR/DBFNAM *LIBL/SFL001PF)
A                                           CHECK(LC)
A               DBLNAM       R     B    8 23REFFLD(PFR/DBLNAM *LIBL/SFL001PF)
A                                           CHECK(LC)
A               DBMINI       R     B   10 23REFFLD(PFR/DBMINI *LIBL/SFL001PF)
A                                           CHECK(LC)
A               DBNNAM       R     B   12 23REFFLD(PFR/DBNNAM *LIBL/SFL001PF)
A                                           CHECK(LC)
A               DBADD1       R     B   14 23REFFLD(PFR/DBADD1 *LIBL/SFL001PF)
A                                           CHECK(LC)
A               DBADD2       R     B   16 23REFFLD(PFR/DBADD2 *LIBL/SFL001PF)
A                                           CHECK(LC)
A               DBADD3       R     B   18 23REFFLD(PFR/DBADD3 *LIBL/SFL001PF)
A                                           CHECK(LC)
A                                      23  2'F3=Exit'
A                                           COLOR(BLU)
A                                      23 12'F12=Cancel'
```

SFL011DF: DDS Using the Data Queue Technique (continued)

```
A                                        COLOR(BLU)
A                                  4  3'Customer Number . :'
A                                  6  3'First Name. . . . .'
A                                  8  3'Last Name . . . . .'
A                                 10  3'Middle Initial. . .'
A                                 12  3'Nick Name . . . . .'
A                                 14  3'Address Line 1. . .'
A                                 16  3'Address Line 2. . .'
A                                 18  3'Address Line 3. . .'
A          R PANEL2
A*
A                                  1  2'SFL004RG'
A          MODE       6   O  2  2DSPATR(HI)
A                                  1 24'Subfile Program with Update       '
A                                     DSPATR(HI)
A                                  1 71DATE
A                                     EDTCDE(Y)
A                                  2 71TIME
A          DBIDNM     R    O  4 20REFFLD(PFR/DBIDNM *LIBL/SFL001PF)
A                                     DSPATR(HI)
A          DBFNAM     R    O  6 20REFFLD(PFR/DBFNAM *LIBL/SFL001PF)
A                                     DSPATR(HI)
A          DBLNAM     R    O  8 20REFFLD(PFR/DBLNAM *LIBL/SFL001PF)
A                                     DSPATR(HI)
A          DBMINI     R    O 10 20REFFLD(PFR/DBMINI *LIBL/SFL001PF)
A                                     DSPATR(HI)
A          DBNNAM     R    O 12 20REFFLD(PFR/DBNNAM *LIBL/SFL001PF)
A                                     DSPATR(HI)
A          DBADD1     R    O 14 20REFFLD(PFR/DBADD1 *LIBL/SFL001PF)
A                                     DSPATR(HI)
A          DBADD2     R    O 16 20REFFLD(PFR/DBADD2 *LIBL/SFL001PF)
A                                     DSPATR(HI)
A          DBADD3     R    O 18 20REFFLD(PFR/DBADD3 *LIBL/SFL001PF)
A                                     DSPATR(HI)
A                                 23  2'F3=Exit'
A                                     COLOR(BLU)
A                                 23 12'F12=Cancel'
A                                     COLOR(BLU)
A                                  4  3'Customer Number:'
A                                  6  3'First Name . . :'
A                                  8  3'Last Name. . . :'
A                                 10  3'Middle Initial :'
A                                 12  3'Nick Name. . . :'
A                                 14  3'Address Line 1 :'
A                                 16  3'Address Line 2 :'
A                                 18  3'Address Line 3 :'
A*
A*
A          R WINDOW1              SFL
A*
A          DBIDNM     R    H      REFFLD(PFR/DBIDNM *LIBL/SFL001PF)
```

SFL011DF: DDS Using the Data Queue Technique (continued)

```
A              DBLNAM    R         O  6  2REFFLD(PFR/DBLNAM *LIBL/SFL001PF)
A              DBFNAM    R         O  6 26REFFLD(PFR/DBFNAM *LIBL/SFL001PF)
A*
A          R SF2CTL                    SFLCTL(WINDOW1)
A*
A                                      SFLDSP
A N41                                  SFLDSPCTL
A  41                                  SFLCLR
A N41                                  SFLEND(*MORE)
A                                      SFLSIZ(0009)
A                                      SFLPAG(0008)
A                                      WINDOW(4 10 16 52)
A            RRN2          4S 0H
A                                   5  2'Last Name'
A                                      DSPATR(HI)
A                                   5 26'First Name'
A                                      DSPATR(HI)
A                                   2  2'Press ENTER to confirm your choice-
A                                      s for delete.'
A                                      COLOR(BLU)
A                                   3  2'Press F12=Cancel to return to chan-
A                                      ge your choices.'
A                                      COLOR(BLU)
A*
A          R FKEY1
A*
A                                  23  2'F3=Exit'
A                                      COLOR(BLU)
A                                     +3'F6=Add'
A                                      COLOR(BLU)
A                                     +3'F12=Cancel'
A                                      COLOR(BLU)
A*
A          R FKEY2
A*
A                                  23  2'F3=Exit'
A                                      COLOR(BLU)
A                                     +3'F12=Cancel'
A                                      COLOR(BLU)
```

SFL011RG: RPG Program Using the Data Queue Technique

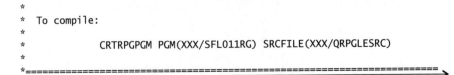

```
*
*   To compile:
*
*           CRTRPGPGM PGM(XXX/SFL011RG) SRCFILE(XXX/QRPGLESRC)
*
*========================================================================
```

SFL011RG: RPG Program Using the Data Queue Technique (continued)

```
Fsfl011df  cf   e              workstn
F                                         sfile(sfl1:rrn1)
F                                         sfile(window1:rrn2)
F                                         infds(info)
Fsfl0011f  if   e         k disk          rename(pfr:lfr)
Fsfl001pf  uf a e         k disk
 *
 * Information data structure to hold attention indicator byte.
 *
Dinfo           ds
D cfkey               369      369
 *
 * Constants and stand alone fields
 *
Dexit           C                         const(X'33')
Dcancel         C                         const(X'3C')
Dadd            C                         const(X'36')
Denter          C                         const(X'F1')
Drollup         C                         const(X'F5')
Drolldn         C                         const(X'F4')
Dsflpag         C                         const(12)
Dsflpag_plus_1  C                         const(13)
Dqlen           C                         const(256)
Ddisplay        C                         const('5')
Dchange         C                         const('2')
Ddelete         C                         const('4')

Dlstrrn         S              4  0 inz(0)
Dlstrrn2        S              4  0 inz(0)
Dcount          S              4  0 inz(0)
Dnew_id         S                   like(dbidnm)
Dsavlnam        S                   like(dblnam)
Dsavfnam        S                   like(dbfnam)
 *
 * Data Queue variables
 *
Dlib            S             10   inz('QTEMP')
Dqueue          S             10   inz('QUEUE1')
Dlen            S              5  0 inz(256)
Dkeyln          S              3  0 inz(7)
Dwait           S              5  0 inz(0)
Dsndlen         S              3  0 inz(0)
Dorder          S              2    inz('EQ')
Dsndr           S             10    inz('          ')
 *
 * Data structure to be loaded to data queue.
 *
D data           DS
D  option                      1
D  dbidnm               2      8s 0
D  key                  2      8s 0
```

209

SFL011RG: RPG Program Using the Data Queue Technique (continued)

```
D  filler                  9    256   inz(*blanks)
 *
 *
D
 *
 ******************************************************************
 *  Main Routine
 ******************************************************************
 *
C      *loval          setll     sfl0011f
C                      exsr      sflbld
 *
C                      dou       cfkey = exit
 *
C                      write     fkey1
C                      exfmt     sflctl
 *
C                      select
 *
 * If ENTER key is pressed and position-to non blank,
 * reposition the subile to closet to what was entered.
 *
C                      when      (cfkey = enter) and (ptname   *blanks)
C                      exsr      addque
C      ptname          setll     sfl0011f
C                      exsr      sflbld
C                      clear                       ptname
 *
 * If ENTER key is pressed and position-to is blank,
 * process screen to interrogate options selected by user
 *
C                      when      (cfkey = enter) and (ptname = *blanks)
C                      exsr      addque
C                      exsr      prcsfl
C      savkey          setll     sfl0011f
C                      exsr      sflbld
 *
 * Roll up - load the data Q's before loading subfile
 *
C                      when      (cfkey = rollup) and (not *in90)
C                      exsr      addque
C                      exsr      sflbld
 *
 * User presses F6, throw the add screen, clear, and rebuild subfile
 *
C                      when      cfkey = add
C                      movel(p)  'Add  '         mode
C                      exsr      addque
C                      exsr      addrcd
C      dblnam          setll     sfl0011f
C                      exsr      sflbld
```

SFL011RG: RPG Program Using the Data Queue Technique (continued)

```
 *
 * Roll down - load the data Q's before loading the subfile.
 *
C                     when      (cfkey = rolldn) and (not *in32)
C                     exsr      addque
C                     exsr      goback
C                     exsr      sflbld
 *
C                     when      *inkl
C                     leave
 *
C                     endsl
 *
C                     enddo
 *
C                     eval      *inlr = *on
 *
 *****************************************************************
 *  ADDQUE - Add subfile data to Data Queues
 *****************************************************************
 *
C       addque        begsr
 *
 * Read the changed subfile records and write them to the data Q's
 * The first data queue is keyed by whatever the unique key of the file
 * is.  If no unique key in the file, use the relative record number. This
 * queue is used to save options selected on a specific subfile line.   The
 * second queue is keyed by option, and is used to process like options
 * together when the enter key is selected
 *
C                     readc     sfl1
 *
C                     dow       not %eof
 *
C                     eval      len = qlen
 *
C                     call      'QSNDDTAQ'
C                     parm                  queue
C                     parm                  lib
C                     parm                  len
C                     parm                  data
C                     parm                  keyln
C                     parm                  key
 *
C                     readc     sfl1
C                     enddo
 *
C                     endsr
 *
 *****************************************************************
 *  RCVQUE - Check DATAQUEUE before writing to subfile
```

SFL011RG: RPG Program Using the Data Queue Technique (continued)

```
********************************************************************
*
C         rcvque        begsr
*
* Read the data Q by the whatever the unique key from the
* physical file to see if there is a saved option.  If so, display
* the saved option when the subfile is displayed.
*
C                       eval      order = 'EQ'
*
C                       call      'QRCVDTAQ'
C                       parm                    queue
C                       parm                    lib
C                       parm                    len
C                       parm                    data
C                       parm                    wait
C                       parm                    order
C                       parm                    keyln
C                       parm                    key
C                       parm                    sndlen
C                       parm                    sndr
*
C                       if        len > *zero
C                       eval      *in74 = *on
C                       endif
*
C                       endsr
*
********************************************************************
*   PRCSFL - process the options taken in the subfile.
********************************************************************
*
C         prcsfl        begsr
*
C                       eval      *in41 = *on
C                       write     sf2ctl
C                       eval      *in41 = *off
C                       eval      rrn2 = *zero
*
* Receive data queue records until the queue is empty LEN = 0
*
C                       eval      dbidnm = 1
C                       eval      order = 'GE'
*
C                       dou       len = *zero
*
C                       call      'QRCVDTAQ'
C                       parm                    queue
C                       parm                    lib
C                       parm                    len
C                       parm                    data
```

SFL011RG: RPG Program Using the Data Queue Technique (continued)

```
C                     parm                    wait
C                     parm                    order
C                     parm                    keyln
C                     parm                    key
C                     parm                    sndlen
C                     parm                    sndr
 *
 *  If length is greater than zero, there was a record read.
 *  Process that record and receive from the second dataq to
 *  keep them in cinc.
 *
C                     if        len > *zero
 *
C                     select
 *
 *  process the edit program or subroutine
 *
C                     when      option = change
C                     movel(p)  'Update'     mode
C                     exsr      chgdtl
C                     if        (cfkey = exit) or (cfkey = cancel)
C                     leave
C                     endif
 *
 * when a 4 is entered write the record the the confirmation screen,
 * set on the SFLNXTCHG indicator to mark this record as changed,
 * and update the subfile.  I mark this record incase F12 is pressed
 * from the confirmation screen and the user wants to keep his
 * originally selected records
 *
C                     when      option = delete
C                     eval      rrn2 = rrn2 +1
C                     write     window1
 *
 *  process the display program or subroutine
 *
C                     when      option = display
C                     movel(p)  *blanks      mode
C        dbidnm       chain     sfl001pf
C                     exfmt     panel2
C                     if        (cfkey = exit) or (cfkey = cancel)
C                     leave
C                     endif
 *
C                     endsl
 *
C                     endif
 *
C                     enddo
 *
 *
```

213

SFL011RG: RPG Program Using the Data Queue Technique (continued)

```
*  If records were selected for delete (4), throw the subfile to
*  screen.  If enter is pressed execute the DLTRCD subroutine to
*  physically delete the records, clear, and rebuild the subfile
*  from the last deleted record (you can certainly position the
*  database file where ever you want)
*
C                   if        rrn2 > *zero
C                   eval      lstrrn2 = rrn2
C                   eval      rrn2 = 1
C                   exfmt     sf2ctl
C                   if        (cfkey  exit) and (cfkey  cancel)
C                   exsr      dltrcd
C        dblnam     setll     sfl0011f
C                   endif
C                   endif
*
C                   endsr
*
*****************************************************************
*   SFLBLD - Build the List
*****************************************************************
*
C        sflbld     begsr
*
*  Clear subfile
*
C                   eval      rrn1 = *zero
C                   eval      *in31 = *on
C                   write     sf1ctl
C                   eval      *in31 = *off
*
*  Load data to subfile
*
C                   do        sflpag
C                   read      sfl0011f                            90
C                   if        *in90
C                   leave
C                   endif
*
C                   eval      option = *blanks
C                   exsr      rcvque
C                   eval      rrn1 = rrn1 + 1
C                   if        rrn1 = 1
C                   eval      savlnam = dblnam
C                   eval      savfnam = dbfnam
C                   endif
C                   write     sfl1
C                   eval      *in74 = *off
C                   enddo
*
C                   if        rrn1 = *zero
```

214

SFL011RG: RPG Program Using the Data Queue Technique (continued)

```
C                       eval        *in32 = *on
C                       endif
 *
C                       endsr
 *
 *******************************************************************
 *   GOBACK - page backward one page
 *******************************************************************
 *
C       goback          begsr
 *
C       savkey          setll       sfl001lf
 *
 * Re-position files for rolling backward.
 *
C                       do          sflpag_plus_1
C                       readp       sfl001lf
C                       if          %eof
C       *loval          setll       sfl001lf
C                       leave
C                       endif
 *
C                       enddo
 *
C                       endsr
 *
 *******************************************************************
 *   CHGDTL - allow user to change data
 *******************************************************************
 *
C       chgdtl          begsr
 *
 * chain to data file using selected subfile record
 *
C       dbidnm          chain       sfl001pf
 *
 * If the record is found (it better be), throw the change screen.
 * If F3 or F12 is pressed, do not update the data file
 *
C                       if          %found
C                       exfmt       panel1

C                       if          (cfkey  exit) and (cfkey  cancel)
C                       update      pfr
C                       endif

C                       endif

C                       endsr
 *
 *******************************************************************
```

SFL011RG: RPG Program Using the Data Queue Technique (continued)

```
*   ADDRCD - allow user to add data
********************************************************************
*
C       addrcd          begsr
*
* set to last record in the the file to get the last ID number
*
C       *hival          setgt     sfl001pf
C                       readp     sfl001pf
*
* set a new unique ID and throw the screen
*
C                       if        not %eof
C                       eval      new_id = dbidnm + 1
C                       clear                     pfr
C                       eval      dbidnm = new_id
C                       exfmt     panel1
*
* add a new record if the pressed key was not F3 or F12
*
C                       if        (cfkey  exit) and (cfkey  cancel)
C                       write     pfr
C                       endif
*
C                       endif
*
C                       endsr
*
********************************************************************
*   DLTRCD - delete records
********************************************************************
*
C       dltrcd          begsr
*
* read all the records in the confirmation subfile
* and delete them from the data base file
*
C                       do        lstrrn2         count
C       count           chain     window1
C                       if        %found
C       dbidnm          delete    pfr                         99
C                       endif
C                       enddo
*
C                       endsr
*
*
*
C       savkey          klist
C                       kfld                      savlnam
C                       kfld                      savfnam
```

8

EMBEDDED SQL AND DYNAMIC SORTING SUBFILES

Previously written books about subfiles have usually included a chapter on using the Open Query File (OPNQRYF) command with subfiles. If you haven't had a chance to use OPNQRYF before, its strength lies in its ability to sort and select data in a batch environment. I've used it, though, with subfile programs, and it works just fine, especially if you use optimizing techniques.

In my opinion, however, OPNQRYF doesn't really add anything to the subfile itself. Whether you use physical files, logical files, or open query files, you want to do what's best to trim down your data before you load your subfile. Once the subfile is loaded, the method used to sort and select the data is usually long forgotten. Regardless of how you prepare your data before loading your subfile, it's just not that exciting as far as the subfile is concerned. I'm not saying that logical files and open query files aren't exciting. But for the purpose of this book, I want to concentrate on things that make the subfile itself more powerful, or, as in the case of data queues in the previous chapter, make the subfile appear as something it's not.

You're probably wondering why I dedicated a chapter to *not* talk about open query files. I didn't. I'm actually getting to a point. What if you had a tool that allowed you the same selection and sorting capabilities as database files and open query files, but also added something to the subfile application itself? Wouldn't that be awesome? Well, that's just what you get with embedded Structured Query Language (SQL).

Embedding SQL into your RPG program not only allows you to sort and select the data as you want, but also provides the user with some added power. Let's say multiple users from different departments are going to use your subfile program, but they each want to see the data in a different order. You can certainly accomplish this by including enough logical files in your program to cover every possible sorting criterion, but that may amount to a large amount of logical files—especially if the user wants secondary and tertiary sorts. Besides, this may also create unnecessary access path administration by the system if all the logical files are created for this one application. It also makes for an ugly subfile-build routine in your RPG program.

Another way to allow the dynamic sorting of subfiles is to use open query files. You could create one open query for each possible sort or dynamically create the open query based on what the user wants to do. Either way, you would be passing parameters back and forth between the RPG and CL program to either build the open query file command or select which specific open query file command to use. I've messed around with the latter method, and the CL can get a bit cumbersome if you try to give the user complete flexibility by allowing him to sort on more than one field at a time. Now don't get me wrong—I love users—but that's a lot of work just to provide each of them with a different view of the same data.

Well, if you have the SQL licensed program installed, SQL is the answer. By embedding SQL into your RPG, you can dynamically build your SELECT statement, based on how the user wants to sort the data, all in one neat little subroutine. You can also use techniques that allow you to provide this capability very efficiently, and with a couple of minor changes, for data on other AS/400s. Let's see how it's done.

WHAT IS A SELECT STATEMENT?

Before I get into how to use SQL within an RPG program, I want to talk about the specific SQL statement I'm going to build. It's not the intent of this chapter to completely explain SQL, but a brief discussion of the SELECT statement is in order. You have a number of ways in RPG to retrieve data from a data file. You can use the CHAIN operation for random access or any one of the read operation variations such as READ, READE, or READPE for multiple record retrieval within some sort of loop.

In SQL, the way to retrieve data from a database file is by using the SELECT statement. The SELECT statement is used for random, as well as multiple, record retrieval. When coding the SELECT statement, you provide the fields you want to select (unlike with CHAIN and READ operations, which retrieve all the fields all the time). If you want all the fields, you use an "*". These are required fields. You have to specify the fields you want and the file you want to retrieve from. If I want to see FIELDA and FIELDB from FILEA, I would code my select statement as follows:

```
SELECT fieldA, FieldB FROM FileA
```

If I wanted all fields from FILEA, I would code the SELECT statement as follows:

```
SELECT * FROM FileA
```

There are a few other parameters included with the SELECT statement that I'll use in my example. They are the WHERE and ORDER BY clauses. The WHERE clause allows for selection criteria from within your select. For example, if I want to select last name and first name from our Name Master file, but I only want to retrieve the last name if it's equal to "Vandever," I could do the following:

```
SELECT dblnam, dbfnam FROM sfl001pf WHERE dblnam = 'Vandever'
```

 You can use the ORDER BY clause to sort the data you retrieve. If I wanted to retrieve first and last names from my file, but only if the last name is "Vandever," and wanted the list sorted by first name, I could code the following:

```
SELECT dblnam, dbfnam FROM SFL001PF WHERE dblnam = 'Vandever' ORDER BY dbfnam
```

There are a few other parameters that can be used with the SELECT statement, but I'm not going to cover them here. My example is going to take a basic SELECT statement and dynamically build the ORDER BY clause depending on what the user chooses to do on the screen. Now let's check out some code.

DISPERSE — THERE'S NOTHING TO SEE HERE

The DDS for this subfile is standard load-all fair. There's nothing new related to subfiles in it. I have coded a window record format to allow the user to select fields on which to sort. I could have made this window a subfile window, but there are only four fields from which to choose. Instead, I decided to make the selection window a regular format, and not a subfile. You can find the complete listing for this display file at the end of this chapter (SF013DF). Notice that for the second chapter in a row, the RPG is at center stage.

LOOK, MOM! NO F SPECS!

Well, that "No F Spec" statement isn't exactly true. There is one F spec, but it's used only for the display file. There are no F specs for the data files. I will introduce them in the embedded SQL. The subfile-related code in this program (SF013RG) should look familiar to you. It's a basic load-all subfile program used to list the names from our file. What this program will allow the user to do is display a window using the F4 key and select a field on which to sort. When the user presses the Enter key after selecting a field, the data will sort by that field and be redisplayed on the screen. Take a moment to look at the code, and I'll explain what the embedded SQL is doing.

BEHIND OPTION 14

Before I dig into the RPG code, I want to talk about the compile options you'll need to make this work. First of all, this source member is type SQLRPGLE, not RPGLE, as in the previous examples. This tells the compiler there are going to be embedded SQL statements in this RPG code.

The command used to create a program with a SQLRPGLE-type source member is Create SQL RPG ILE Program (CRTSQLRPGI). This command will verify, validate, and, if you choose, prepare the embedded SQL statements during compile time. When using this command, you'll need to consider some compile options. Figure 8.1 shows some of the parameters you may want to tinker with when compiling SQLRPGLE source code.

```
*  COMPILING. In order to compile this program you will need
*             to use options that allow it to work correctly
*             between machines. These options are--
*
*             COMMIT = *NONE
*             RDB    = Machine name that you will connect to.
*             DLYPRP = *YES
*             SQLPKG = The name & library that you want to
*                      use for the package. This will put the
*                      package on the RDB machine that you
*                      specify.
*             RDB    = Machine name that you will connect to.
*             DLYPRP = *YES
*             SQLPKG = The name & library that you want to
*                      use for the package. This will put the
*                      package on the RDB machine that you specify.
```

Figure 8.1: Compiling with embedded SQL is a little different than compiling with just RPG.

The Relational DataBase (RDB) parameter tells you which database you're using. This can be the name of your local DB2 database, or, if you're networked using Distributed Relational Database Architecture (DRDA), it can contain the name of a remote AS/400 database. If you use a remote database in the RDB parameter, you'll need to tell the compiler where to create the SQL package. You do this by entering a library and package name in the SQLPKG parameter.

The Delay Preparation (DLYPRP) parameter asks you if you want to delay preparation of your SQL statement until the program is run. I answer *YES to this parameter because I don't want to perform redundant access path validation. If I enter *NO in this parameter, access path validation is performed at compile time and again when the cursor is opened later during run time. By entering *YES, the validation is completed only at run time.

There are many other parameters in the CRTSQLRPGI command—I have mentioned a few here that I commonly deal with—but I suggest you peruse them for yourself to see if there's anything of interest to your specific implementation of this technique.

THE D SPECS

Now that you know how to compile an RPG program containing embedded SQL, you probably would like to know how to code one. First, I'll create the basis for my dynamic selection capability. I do this with the help of D specs.

I define a stand-alone field, SELCT1, as being 500 bytes long to hold my initial SQL statement. (I selected the number 500 at random, but you need a variable large enough to hold your SQL statement.) I initialize this field with my SQL statement, as shown in Figure 8.2.

```
Dselct1              S              500A    INZ('SELECT dblnam, dbfnam, -
D                                            dbmini, dbnnam -
D                                            FROM yourlib/sfl001pf -
D                                            ORDER BY ')

Dselct2              S              500A    INZ(' ')
```

Figure 8.2: The D specs used to build the initial SELECT statement.

I then define a second stand-alone field, SELCT2, also 500 bytes long, to hold the user-defined SQL statement, which will be made up of the initial SQL statement from SELCT1 plus the selection criteria assigned by the user. I also define a stand-alone field called ORDER and initialize it to DBLNAM, which is the name of the last name field in our database file. The order variable will be used to append the field selected by the user to the ORDER BY clause in the SELCT1 variable.

RULES AND REGULATIONS

All blocks of SQL code must begin with a "/" in position 7, followed by the EXEC SQL statement, and end with a "/" in position 7, followed by the END-EXEC command. You place all your SQL code between the EXEC and END-EXEC. Each line will be signified by a "+" in position 7. Figure 8.3 marks the first section of embedded SQL. The CONNECT RESET statement will connect to the local DB2 database. If you were going to connect to a database on another machine, you would do so by replacing the RESET parameter with the name of the remote database.

```
C/EXEC SQL
C+ CONNECT RESET
C/END-EXEC
```

Figure 8.3: Embedded SQL to connect to your local database.

YOU'VE GOT TO PREPARE, DECLARE, AND OPEN

Now let's look at the rest of the mainline routine. First, I'm going to execute the PREP subroutine. This is where the dynamic SQL statement will be built. We'll start with Figure 8.4, which is the PREP subroutine.

```
C       prep            begsr
 *
 * Prepare the SQL statement for validation, since the program was
 * compiled with DLYPRP (*YES), it will wait until it is used before
 * it prepares the cursor.
 *
C                       eval      selct2 = selct1 + ' ' + order
 *
C/EXEC SQL
C+    PREPARE sel FROM :selct2
 *
 * Declare the SQL cursor to hold the data retrieved from the SELECT
```

Figure 8.4: The PREP subroutine prepares the SQL statement for validation.

```
    *
    C+ DECLARE MYCSR SCROLL CURSOR FOR SEL
    *
    * Open the SQL cursor.
    *
    C+ OPEN MYCSR
    C/END-EXEC
    *
    C                          endsr
```

Figure 8.4: The PREP subroutine prepares the SQL statement for validation (continued).

The first thing I do is create the dynamic SQL statement based on what the user selected. Because this is the first time through, I use the default value for the ORDER variable. I set this in the D specs. Subsequent times through this subroutine, the user will have selected a field to sort the data in, and that data will be placed in the ORDER variable. Once I've appended the data in order to my original select statement defined in my D specs, I have a complete select statement that will retrieve my data and order it appropriately.

Now I'm going to use that select statement and retrieve my data. I use the prepare statement to prepare a statement called SEL using the new SELECT2 variable I just created. The prepare statement will validate the SQL statement contained in the SELECT2 variable. Next I declare a cursor called MYCSR using the declare statement. I am going to allow this cursor the ability to scroll and create it from the SEL statement I just prepared in the previous statement. Finally, I'll open the cursor using the OPEN command.

Before I go on, let me explain cursors a little. When SQL runs a select statement, the resulting rows create a result table. A cursor provides a way to access that result table. It's kind of like a subfile in its own right. The cursor is used within an SQL program to maintain a position in the result table. SQL uses the cursor to work with the data in the result table and make it available to your program. Your program may contain several cursors, although each must have a unique name.

There are two types of cursors: serial and scrollable. A serial cursor is defined without use of the SCROLL keyword. This type of cursor allows you to fetch each row once and only once. If you want to retrieve a row more than once, you need

224

to close the cursor and reopen it. This kind of cursor is perfect for a load-all subfile because you want to see the data only once before loading it into your subfile. It's the subfile that will allow for data scrolling in this case.

The scrollable cursor is what I've defined in my program, even though it's a load-all subfile. The advantage of a scrollable cursor is that you can move back and forth throughout the rows of data. Using different parameters in a FETCH statement, you can read the next or prior row, navigate to the first or last row, read the same row over again, or position any number of rows forward or backward from the current row. This type of cursor can be used if you're building your subfile one page at a time. The data remains in the cursor and is loaded into your subfile only one page at a time.

You have now successfully validated the select statement contained in your variable using the PREPARE command, created a scrollable cursor that will contain the result table from your select statement using the DECLARE command, and opened the cursor using the OPEN command. You're now ready to load the subfile from the cursor.

HERE, BOY! FETCH!

Take a look at Figure 8.5. Instead of loading the subfile directly from the database file, I am going to load it from the cursor using the SQL FETCH command.

```
     *
     * Process the records in the SQL cursor until the return not = 0
     *
     C                     dou        sqlcod  0
     *
     * Get the next row from the SQL cursor.
     *
     C/EXEC SQL
     C+    FETCH NEXT FROM MYCSR
     C+        INTO :dblnam, :dbfnam, :dbmini, :dbnnam
     C/END-EXEC
     *
     C                     if         sqlcod = 0
```

Figure 8.5: Retrieve records from the cursor using the FETCH statement instead of reading from a data file.

```
C                         eval      rrn1  = rrn1  + 1
C                         write     sfl1
C                         endif
   *
C                         enddo
```

Figure 8.5: Retrieve records from the cursor using the FETCH statement instead of reading from a data file (continued).

Notice that my FETCH command is inside my DO loop. I use the FETCH NEXT command and place the results into my display file field names. Because this is a scrollable cursor, I use the NEXT parameter. As I mentioned before, however, you don't have to use a scrollable cursor when using a load-all subfile. I did simply because I wanted to show you some of the parameters you can use with a scrollable CURSOR.

I use the SQLCOD to determine whether to write to the subfile record format. If you're astute, and I know you are, you may have noticed that SQLCOD isn't defined anywhere in the program or the display file. So where did it come from? Well, when you embed SQL in your program and use the CRTSQLRPGI command to create the program, a data structure not unlike the file information data structure is included in your program. It's filled with all sorts of information on the SQL statements embedded inside your program.

One example of that information is the error code returned when an SQL statement is run. Contained in the SQLCOD variable, it's set to zero upon successful execution of an SQL statement. For more information on the SQL Data Area (SQLDA), look in IBM's SQL AS/400 Programming manual. For this program, the only data I use from the SQLDA is contained in the SQLCOD variable. Once my subfile is loaded, I'm ready to display it. Now we can go back to the mainline.

LET'S KICK IT UP A FEW NOTCHES!

When displaying the subfile the first time, you'll see the data sorted by last name. That's because I initialized the ORDER variable to the last name field. Now that the user has the data in his control, he can press F4 to sort the data another way.

When F4 is selected, a number of subroutines will be executed. First the SORT subroutine is executed, which will determine what to place in the ORDER variable. Then the CLEAN subroutine is executed. This simply closes the MYCSR. Once the sort criterion is determined and the cursor is closed, the PREP and SFLBLD routines are executed again. We've already seen what they do. Figure 8.6 shows what happens when F4 is pressed.

```
     * prompt to selection sorting criteria
     *
C                       when      cfkey = prompt
C                       exsr      sort
C                       exsr      clean
C                       exsr      prep
     *
C                       exsr      sflbld
```

Figure 8.6: When F4 is pressed, this block of code sorts, cleans, and prepares the SQL statement before loading the subfile.

The last thing I want to take a look at is the SORT subroutine. There's no new, exciting subfile code in this routine. Nor is there even any SQL. However, there is some code in here that may interest you. Figure 8.7 marks the SORT subroutine.

```
C    sort         begsr
     *
C                 exfmt     window1
     *
C                 select
     *
C                 when      tab1  *blank
C                 movel(p)  'dblnam'      order
C                 clear                   tab1
     *
C                 when      tab2  *blank
C                 movel(p)  'dbfnam'      order
C                 clear                   tab2
     *
C                 when      tab3  *blank
C                 movel(p)  'dbmini'      order
```

Figure 8.7: This routine determines the field to sort by.

```
C                    clear                      tab3
*
C                    when      tab4    *blank
C                    movel(p)  'dbnnam'         order
C                    clear                      tab4
*
C                    endsl
*
C                    endsr
```

Figure 8.7: This routine determines the field to sort by (continued).

It's in this subroutine that I will determine which field to append to the ORDER BY clause in my dynamic SQL statement. A window is displayed that lists the fields contained in the subfile. The user can select one of these fields and press Enter. The program then determines which field was selected and places that field in the ORDER variable. Figures 8.8 through 8.10 show what it all looks like.

```
SFL013RG              Dynamic Sort with Embedded SQL          2/10/
                                                             12:44:

Last Name            First Name          MI   Nick Name
Anthony              Tony                A    Triple A
Bert                 Al                  C    Alphabet Man
Coker                Jim                 L    Da AS/400 Guru
Harrison             Harry               H    Happy
Johnson              John                J    JJ
Naisium              Jim                 B    Sweaty
Patterson            Gary                R    The All-Knowing One
Saint                Louis               A    Missouri
Samuelson            Sam                 S    The snake
Simpson              Othello             K    Don't call me OJ
Stevenson            Steve               S    Mike
Tessential           Quinn               C    Important
Thompson             Tom                 T    Triple T
Vandever             Corina              B    Wife of Subfile Man
Vandever             Felicia             R    Cub
Vandever             Kalia               M    Koo
Vandever             Kelly               M    FaderHead
                                                            More

F3=Exit     F4=Prompt    F12=Cancel
```

Figure 8.8: The initial display sorted by last name.

When the user presses F4 to request a change in sort order, the screen shown in Figure 8.9 is displayed.

```
SFL013RG                Dynamic Sort with Embedded SQL          2/10/
· · · · · · · · · · · · · · · · · · · · ·                        12:44:
:  Select a sort field    :
:                         :   Name              MI    Nick Name
:     Last Name           :                     A     Triple A
:     First Name          :                     C     Alphabet Man
:  1  Middle Initial      :                     L     Da AS/400 Guru
:     Nick Name           :                     H     Happy
:                         :                     J     JJ
:                         :                     B     Sweaty
:                         :                     R     The All-Knowing One
:  F3=Exit   F12=Cancel   :                     A     Missouri
:                         :                     S     The snake
:· · · · · · · · · · · · · · · · · · · · : lo    K     Don't call me OJ
   Stevenson              Steve               S     Mike
   Tessential            Quinn               C     Important
   Thompson              Tom                 T     Triple T
   Vandever              Corina              B     Wife of Subfile Man
   Vandever              Felicia             R     Cub
   Vandever              Kalia               M     Koo
   Vandever              Kelly               M     FaderHead
                                                            More
   F3=Exit    F4=Prompt    F12=Cancel
```

Figure 8.9: The user has pressed F4 and chosen to sort by middle initial.

After the user makes his choice and presses Enter, the file will be redisplayed, now resorted based on the user's selection (see Figure 8.10).

```
SFL013RG                Dynamic Sort with Embedded SQL          2/10/
                                                                12:47:
   Last Name             First Name          MI    Nick Name
   Saint                 Louis               A     Missouri
   Anthony               Tony                A     Triple A
   Naisium               Jim                 B     Sweaty
   Vandever              Corina              B     Wife of Subfile Man
   Bert                  Al                  C     Alphabet Man
   Tessential            Quinn               C     Important
   Harrison              Harry               H     Happy
   Johnson               John                J     JJ
   Simpson               Othello             K     Don't call me OJ
   Coker                 Jim                 L     Da AS/400 Guru
   Vandever              Kevin               M     Subfile Man
   Vandever              Kalia               M     Koo
   Vandever              Kelly               M     FaderHead
   Vandever              Felicia             R     Cub
   Patterson             Gary                R     The All-Knowing One
   Samuelson             Sam                 S     The snake
   Stevenson             Steve               S     Mike
                                                            More
   F3=Exit    F4=Prompt    F12=Cancel
```

Figure 8.10: The list is now sorted by middle initial.

Pretty simple, huh? Well, if you really want to separate this technique from what's easily implemented using logical files and open query files, you can allow the user to select more than one field. If the user wants to sort by first name, last name, and nickname, you allow him to enter a 1 next to first name, a 2 next to last name, and a 3 next to nickname. You'll then place logic in your SORT routine to interrogate all the fields selected, place them in the correct order, and place that information in the ORDER variable. So instead of the ORDER variable containing one field to append to the ORDER BY clause, it would now contain three.

VOILA!

What a slick technique! No open query files, and no access paths to maintain. You've just seen how to use embedded SQL and subfiles to select and sort data dynamically. This chapter wasn't meant to fully explain SQL and SQL programming. Rather, it was intended to introduce embedded SQL to you and show how it can be used to work with subfiles to create a very flexible subfile and an efficient application while maintaining an easily maintainable program. If you're interested in learning more about SQL programming, I suggest you dig into IBM's AS/400 SQL Programming manual. You'll learn all sorts of advanced techniques, such as allocating storage and loading the SQLDA using the SQL DESCRIBE command, as well as implementing optimizing techniques to make your programs scream. Combining embedded SQL and subfile programming will allow you to take your applications to new heights. Enjoy.

SUMMARY AND CODE EXAMPLES

The following are the SQL steps taken in program SFL013RG:

1. Place the input SQL statement into a host variable.

2. Connect to the appropriate database—local or remote.

3. Issue a PREPARE statement to validate and prepare the dynamic SQL. If DLYPRP (*YES) is specified on the CRTSQLRPGI command, the preparation is delayed until the first time the statement is used.

4. Declare a cursor for the statement name.

5. Open the cursor (declared in step 4) that includes the name of the dynamic SELECT statement.

6. FETCH a row.

7. When end of data occurs, close the cursor.

8. Handle any SQL return codes that might result.

SFL013DF: Display File for Dynamically Sorting Subfile

```
A*
A                                        DSPSIZ(24 80 *DS3)
A                                        PRINT
A                                        ERRSFL
A                                        CA03
A                                        CA12
A                                        CF04
A*
A           R SFL1                       SFL
A*
A             DBLNAM    R       O  5  2REFFLD(PFR/DBLNAM *LIBL/SFL001PF)
A             DBFNAM    R       O  5 26REFFLD(PFR/DBFNAM *LIBL/SFL001PF)
A             DBMINI    R       O  5 50REFFLD(PFR/DBMINI *LIBL/SFL001PF)
A             DBNNAM    R       O  5 55REFFLD(PFR/DBNNAM *LIBL/SFL001PF)
A*
A*
A           R SF1CTL                     SFLCTL(SFL1)
A*
A                                        SFLSIZ(0050)
A                                        SFLPAG(0017)
A                                        OVERLAY
A N32                                    SFLDSP
A N31                                    SFLDSPCTL
A  31                                    SFLCLR
A  90                                    SFLEND(*MORE)
A             RRN1         4S 0H         SFLRCDNBR
A                                      4  2'Last Name'
A                                        DSPATR(HI)
A                                      4 26'First Name'
A                                        DSPATR(HI)
A                                      4 50'MI'
A                                        DSPATR(HI)
```

SFL013DF: Display File for Dynamically Sorting Subfile (continued)

```
A                                      4 55'Nick Name'
A                                          DSPATR(HI)
A                                      1  2'SFL013RG'
A                                      1 26'Dynamic Sort with Embedded SQL'
A                                          DSPATR(HI)
A                                      1 71DATE
A                                          EDTCDE(Y)
A                                      2 71TIME
A*
A          R FKEY1
A*
A                                     23  2'F3=Exit'
A                                          COLOR(BLU)
A                                         +3'F4=Prompt'
A                                          COLOR(BLU)
A                                         +3'F12=Cancel'
A                                          COLOR(BLU)
A          R WINDOW1
A*
A                                          WINDOW(*DFT 11 25)
A            TAB1        1   B  3  2
A                                      3  5'Last Name'
A            TAB2        1   B  4  2
A                                      4  5'First Name'
A            TAB3        1   B  5  2
A                                      5  5'Middle Initial'
A            TAB4        1   B  6  2
A                                      6  5'Nick Name'
A                                     10  1'F3=Exit'
A                                          COLOR(BLU)
A                                     10 11'F12=Cancel'
A                                          COLOR(BLU)
A                                      1  3'Select a sort field'
A                                          DSPATR(HI)
```

SFL013RG: RPG Program for Dynamically Sorting Subfile

```
*********************************************************************
*
*  To compile:
*
*          CRTSQLRPGI PGM(XXX/SFL013RG) SRCFILE(XXX/QRPGLESRC)
*
*
* COMPILING. In order to compile this program you will need
*            to use options which allow it to work correctly
*            between machines. These options are--
*
```

SFL013RG: RPG Program for Dynamically Sorting Subfile (continued)

```
*                    COMMIT = *NONE
*                    RDB    = Machine name that you will connect to.
*                    DLYPRP = *YES
*                    SQLPKG = The name & library that you want to
*                             use for the package. This will put the
*                             package on the RDB machine that you
*                             specify.
***************************************************************
Fsfl013df  cf    e             workstn
F                                    sfile(sfl1:rrn1)
F                                    infds(info)
*
* Information data structure to hold attention indicator byte.
*
Dinfo            ds
D cfkey                   369     369
*
* Constants for attention indicator byte
*
Dexit           C                    const(X'33')
Dprompt         C                    const(X'34')
Dcancel         C                    const(X'3C')
Denter          C                    const(X'F1')

Dorder          S              8     INZ('dblnam')

Dselct1         S            500A    INZ('SELECT dblnam, dbfnam, -
D                                    dbmini, dbnnam -
D                                    FROM i013kmv/sfl001pf -
D                                    ORDER BY ')

Dselct2         S            500A    INZ(' ')
*
* Establish the connection to the remote machine. The -842 return
* code indicates that the connection is already established. If
* you want to connect to the local machine, use CONNECT.

C/EXEC SQL
C+ CONNECT RESET
C/END-EXEC
*
C               exsr      prep
C               exsr      sflbld
*
C               dou       (cfkey = exit)
*
C               write     fkey1
C               exfmt     sflctl
*
C               select
```

233

SFL013RG: RPG Program for Dynamically Sorting Subfile (continued)

```
     * prompt to selection sorting criteria
     *
C                     when       cfkey = prompt
C                     exsr       sort
C                     exsr       sflbld
     *
C                     when       cfkey = cancel
C                     leave
     *
C                     endsl
     *
C                     enddo
     *
C                     exsr       clean
     *
     *   Disconnect the current connection.
     *
C/EXEC SQL
C+    DISCONNECT CURRENT
C/END-EXEC
     *
C                     eval       *inlr = *on
     *
     ******************************************************************
     * Prepare SQL cursor
     ******************************************************************
     *
C     prep            begsr
     *
     * Prepare the SQL statement for validation, since the program was
     * compiled with DLYPRP (*YES), it will wait until it is used before
     * it prepares th cursor.
     *
C     selct1          cat(p)     order:1        selct2
     *
C/EXEC SQL
C+    PREPARE sel FROM :selct2
C/END-EXEC
     *
     * Declare the SQL cursor to hold the data retrieved from the SELECT
     *
C/EXEC SQL
C+ DECLARE PREMCSR SCROLL CURSOR FOR SEL
C/END-EXEC
     *
     * Open the SQL cursor.
     *
C
C/EXEC SQL
C+ OPEN PREMCSR
C/END-EXEC
```

SFL013RG: RPG Program for Dynamically Sorting Subfile (continued)

```
 *
C                     endsr
 *
 *********************************************************************
 * Clean up before exiting
 *********************************************************************
 *
C     clean         begsr
 *
 *   Close the SQL cursor after all processing is complete.
 *
C/EXEC SQL
C+    CLOSE premcsr
C/END-EXEC
 *
C                     endsr
 *
 *********************************************************************
 * Build the subfile
 *********************************************************************
 *
C     sflbld        begsr
 *
 * Clear the subfile
 *
C                     eval      *in31 = *on
C                     write     sflctl
C                     eval      *in31 = *off
C                     eval      rrn1 = 0
 *
 * Process the records in the SQL cursor until the return not = 0
 *
C                     dou       sqlcod  0
 *
 * Get the next row from the SQL cursor.
 *
C/EXEC SQL
C+    FETCH NEXT FROM premcsr
C+      INTO :dblnam, :dbfnam, :dbmini, :dbnnam
C/END-EXEC
 *
C                     if        sqlcod = 0
C                     eval      rrn1  = rrn1  + 1
C                     write     sfl1
C                     endif
 *
C                     enddo
 *
C                     if        rrn1 = 0
C                     eval      *in32 = *on
C                     else
```

SFL013RG: RPG Program for Dynamically Sorting Subfile (continued)

```
C                   eval      rrn1 = 1
C                   endif
 *
C                   eval      *in90 = *on
 *
C                   endsr
 *
 ********************************************************************
 * SORT - prompt to select sort criteria
 ********************************************************************
 *
C     sort          begsr
 *
C                   exfmt     window1
 *
C                   select
 *
C                   when      tab1   *blank
C                   movel(p)  'dblnam'       order
C                   clear                    tab1
 *
C                   when      tab2   *blank
C                   movel(p)  'dbfnam'       order
C                   clear                    tab2
 *
C                   when      tab3   *blank
C                   movel(p)  'dbmini'       order
C                   clear                    tab3
 *
C                   when      tab4   *blank
C                   movel(p)  'dbnnam'       order
C                   clear                    tab4
 *
C                   endsl
 *
C                   exsr      clean
C                   exsr      prep
 *
C                   endsr
 *
```

9

No Aversion to Recursion

Up to this point, you've learned how to display, modify, add, and delete data from database files using subfile applications. The techniques in this book work very well for independent data records, such as our Name Master file, where every record exists independently of any other record in the file. Well, you're going to see data in the real world (you probably already have) that doesn't nicely conform to a straightforward independent database file.

Sometimes, data from a file can mean different things depending on how it's read. Files containing a company's organizational structure or components for manufacturing parts are often stored in an awkward fashion. These files tend to be stored in a hierarchical structure and are difficult to organize in a subfile application. This chapter will show you how to use ILE and RPG IV to easily display hierarchical data in a subfile application.

ILE and RPG IV not only introduced new programming techniques to us, but they also forced (I mean that in a good way) us to change the way we think about designing applications. One new feature to the RPG language that has opened our minds up as much as any is the subprocedure. You might ask, "why subprocedure? What happened to the procedure?" Well, in V3R1 ILE RPG, you had the ability to write one procedure per module, and that procedure was considered the main procedure. Since V3R2 (CISC) and V3R6 (RISC), you're now allowed to define more than one procedure per module. You can have from zero to one main procedure, and zero to many subprocedures. Subprocedures allow a module to have multiple entry points.

For example, you might have a pricing module with many specific pricing subprocedures, each accomplishing a different pricing task. Programs outside this module would now have the ability to call any or all of the pricing subprocedures contained in that module. Subprocedures allow you to better separate, organize, and reuse your RPG code without the performance impact of traditional program calls. They're different from main procedures in that they don't load in a bunch of extra code that you won't use. For example, when you code a main procedure, which is in essence any RPG program you write, the RPG logic cycle code is loaded even if you don't use it. In fact, a subprocedure can't even load the RPG logic cycle (I can almost hear the non-cycle advocates cheering).

This book obviously isn't intended to provide you an in-depth look at subprocedures; for that, I recommend IBM's *ILE RPG for AS/400 Programmers Guide* or *The RPG Programmer's Guide to RPG IV and ILE* by Richard Shaler and Robin Klima. However, to give you a better understanding of subprocedures, I do think a summary of the benefits is in order.

GETTING TO KNOW SUBPROCEDURES

This isn't your father's RPG. Here are a few of the specifics about subprocedures that you'll find important as you implement them in your programs.

- Subprocedures support local variables. That's right, local variables. Whatever is defined inside the subprocedure is visible to only that subprocedure. Think of the possibilities!

- Parameters can be passed by reference (as parameters are normally passed between programs), by value, or by read-only reference. Passing a parameter by value protects that parameter from being changed. Passing a parameter by read-only reference is much like passing by value because the data cannot be modified. That they can be passed by reference, though, is an added benefit.

- Variable-length and optional parameters can be defined and passed (or not passed in the case of optional parameters).

- A subprocedure is prototyped. This allows the parameters to be checked at compile time instead of at run time, allowing for more stability in your applications.

- Subprocedures can be exported so they're available for use by other modules. Imagine that—write once, use many times.

- Subprocedures are called by using the CALLP operation code, but they can also be used as expressions, just as you would use built-in functions, to return a value.

- Last but certainly not least, subprocedures support recursive calls. I didn't believe it at first either, but it's true. In fact, it's this last feature of subprocedures that brings me to my connection to subfiles (it took a while to get there, but it's worth it, as you'll see).

THE ORG CHART

A recursive call is generated when a subprocedure calls itself, or calls another procedure, which in turn calls the subprocedure again. Get that? Each recursive call creates another entry on the invocation stack with new storage allocation. But beware: It's easy to start chewing up system resources.

So when is it appropriate to use recursion? Or more specifically, when is it appropriate to use recursion with subfiles? If you have experience with C, you probably programmed, as an assignment in school, a recursive call to calculate factorials. You remember factorials, don't you? The factorial of 5 (5!) is 5 x 4 x 3 x 2 x 1 or 120. I remember coding a C program that would allow me to type a number on the command line and get its factorial. I accomplished this using recursive calls.

Now that may be fine for a programming assignment in school, but you're probably interested in a real-life business reason to employ recursive calls. The best time to take advantage of recursion is when your data is stored in a hierarchical level as opposed to the relational level we're accustomed to. In a relational database, you have a parent/child relationship. That is, you have a master file with a one-to-many relationship with detail records contained in a detail file. As RPG programmers, we're pretty adept at displaying or printing information stored in a relational database structure. A hierarchical structure (also known as a recursive structure) doesn't have this parent/child relationship. In this structure, the data is independent of the rest of the data while also possibly being associated with it. This is true in a company's chain of command. A person may be a manager or supervisor of other managers and supervisors. That means that a person may be listed in the hierarchy as both manager and subordinate.

Using a relational database system, it would be difficult to list the chain of command starting with person X. It wouldn't be too hard to find out who reports to person X, but what if I want to list the person who reports to the person who reports to person X? And what about the person who reports to the person who reports to the person who reports to person X? How do you know how many levels to go?

You can start to picture the subfile build routine already, can't you? Because this data is stored in recursive fashion, it makes sense that I should use a recursive method to display it. So what I'm going to do is pass an employee's ID number and list his chain of command with recursive calls to the subfile load procedure. I'll mark each new level of command by indenting the names. Figure 9.1 shows what the displayed data will look like.

I'm going to CHAIN to the SFL002PF file to get an employee's subordinate. After displaying the subordinate, I'll check to see if that employee has a subordinate by calling the same procedure again, recursively. I'll drill down through the subordinate tree until I get to the last level in the chain of command—you know, the ones who do all the work. The code will then go back through the recursive calls to check each level in the tree until finally returning to the first level, where it will read the next record and, if necessary, start all over again. Let's take a look at the code to give you a better picture.

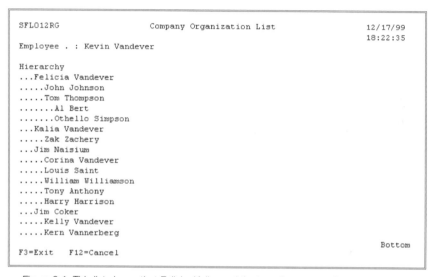

```
SFL012RG                Company Organization List              12/17/99
                                                               18:22:35
Employee . : Kevin Vandever

Hierarchy
...Felicia Vandever
.....John Johnson
.....Tom Thompson
.......Al Bert
.......Othello Simpson
...Kalia Vandever
.....Zak Zachery
...Jim Naisium
.....Corina Vandever
.....Louis Saint
.....William Williamson
.....Tony Anthony
.....Harry Harrison
...Jim Coker
.....Kelly Vandever
.....Kern Vannerberg

                                                               Bottom
F3=Exit    F12=Cancel
```

Figure 9.1: This list shows that Felicia, Kalia, and the two Jims report directly to Kevin.

ONE FIELD IS WORTH 1,000 BYTES...OKAY, 60

The DDS is of typical load-all nature. The only interesting thing to note here (other than the inherently interesting subfile specifications) is the 60-byte field, SUBNAM, listed in the subfile record format and shown in Figure 9.2. You can find the complete DDS (SFL012DF) at the end of this chapter.

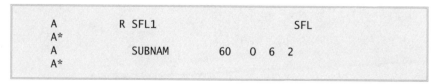

```
A            R SFL1                        SFL
A*
A              SUBNAM        60   0  6  2
A*
```

Figure 9.2: Defining a field for name and indent concatenation.

I define a field of this size to allow me to concatenate the first and last name and indent that name the appropriate level within the chain of command. Again, Figure 9.1 shows how it will look. By using one long field name, I'm able to indent the name a little more to the right for each level in the chain, without knowing how many levels actually exist.

In my example, you're limited in the number of levels you can go by the number of positions available on the display screen—you can only indent so far to the right. However, you could add a field to the subfile called level and show the level of command followed by the name, without indenting and without the one long field name. I chose to indent the names to further illustrate the effect of recursive calls.

RPG (RECURSION, PROCEDURES, AND GREEK?)

Close the Greek-to-English translation book. This isn't Greek. It's good old RPG. Well, maybe it's not so old, but it is good and it is RPG. The example you have in this chapter (SFL012RG at the end of the chapter) is of a subprocedure that calls itself to build a subfile.

Before we dig into it, I want to mention some compile options and a couple of ways you can define them. Figure 9.3 shows some comments about how to compile this module.

```
* To compile:
*
*       CRTBNDRPG  PGM(XXX/SFL012RG) SRCFILE(XXX/QRPGLESRC) +
*                  DFTACTGRP(*NO) ACTGRP(*CALLER)
*
*=================================================================

* Turn on source statement debugging.  Stop the generation of
* debug points for IO statements.  Optionally, these could be
* specified on the compile command.   V4R4 feature
*
H OPTION(*SRCSTMT *NODEBUGIO)
```

Figure 9.3: Compilation parameters along with compilation options defined in a header specification.

When using ILE concepts such as subprocedures, you're not allowed to use the default activation group. Therefore, you must specify that you won't use the default activation group by using DFTACTGRP *NO in the option parameter. Additionally, you may want to specify an activation group. If you don't, you'll probably use QILE. I like to use *CALLER, which uses the activation group of the person calling the program. I don't want to say much here except that using *NEW is very bad as far as performance goes. I would stick with *CALLER unless you have specific, predefined (named) activation groups—in which case you could use them. If you don't know what activation groups are or aren't sure how to use them properly, you may want to obtain information on them before using this technique. You can get that information from the aforementioned IBM manuals.

Another technique you can use to change or override the compile options is to define them in the header specification (H spec). Remember the H spec? You probably thought it left with RPG II, but it didn't. In fact, it's more powerful than ever. The H spec in Figure 9.3 shows another way to define compile options. In this example, I'm telling the compiler that I want source statement debugging, *SRCSTMT, and that I don't want to generate IO break points, *NODEBUGIO. These parameters could have also been entered during compilation using the OPTION keyword in the CRTBNDRPG command. This might come in handy if you have strict default compile parameters in your shop but need specific compile options for your program. You can easily define them in the H spec.

PROPER PROTOTYPING PROMOTES PREDICTABLE PARAMETERS

For the most part, the F and D specs look pretty normal. I'm using two data files in this example: our Name Master file and a new subordinate file, SFL002PF. The subordinate file will contain two fields per record: the employee ID and a subordinate ID.

I'm going to be using one subfile to display the records and will include my usual information data structure to contain the key that was pressed by the user.

There's something new to look at here, though. The last set of D specs, as shown in Figure 9.4, defines a prototype for the subprocedure I'm going to use.

```
    * Prototype for NextLevel procedure:
    * Receives two parameters, returns none
   D NextLevel         pr
   D    level                      3  0 value
   D    employee                   7  0 value
```

Figure 9.4: Prototyping defines the parameters and the optional return value of the subprocedure.

As mentioned earlier, prototyping a subprocedure allows the parameter to be validated at compile time instead of run time. To prototype a subprocedure, start with the name (NEXTLEVEL in this case) and "PR" in positions 24 and 25 of the first D spec. Optionally, you can define the specifications of a return value on this line (remember that subprocedures can return a value). In this example, I'm not using a return value, so none is defined.

The next two lines of my prototype are simply the parameter definitions. I'm going to pass the level and an employee ID to the subprocedure. Notice the keyword VALUE in both instances. Because I want to pass these values along, but don't want the subprocedure to have the ability to change them, I pass them by value. RPG programmers are accustomed to passing parameters by reference, which allows us to manipulate them. In this case, I don't want to manipulate the parameters. I just want to read their values. That's it. Your subprocedure is prototyped.

CALLP VERSUS EXSR

Now, let's get into the code a little. The mainline routine accepts the employee ID from the user who's calling the program. It then gets the name associated with that ID and formats it for display in the heading. If the employee ID isn't found, I state so in the NAME field and display the screen. If the ID was found and formatted for display, I'm now ready to start building my subfile. Figure 9.5 marks the mainline code that does just that.

```
      * Clear the subfile, then call the recursive NextLevel procedure
     C                   exsr      clrsfl
     C                   callp     NextLevel (1 : P_employee)
     C                   eval      *in90 = *on
     C                   if        rrn1 = 0
     C                   eval      *in32 = *on
     C                   endif
     C                   endif
```

Figure 9.5: After the subfile is cleared, the NEXTLEVEL subprocedure is called to load the subfile.

First, I execute the CLRSFL routine that, you guessed it, clears my subfile and gets it ready for loading. Then I call my NEXTLEVEL subprocedure using the CALLP operation. Notice the difference in syntax between the CALLP and the traditional CALL. The parameters are passed in the CALLP by placing them inside parentheses and separating them by colons. In this case, I'm passing the level, which is 1 the first time through, and the employee ID that was passed in by the user. Remember the prototype? It's important to note that my parameters must match by data type, not by variable name. It doesn't matter if you send constants, fields, or expressions, as long as they match the data types defined in the prototype.

This one call to the NEXTLEVELsubprocedure will start the recursive process and build the subfile. Think of it as the subfile build routine you've seen throughout this book. Although the internals of the subfile build routine are quite different from that of the NEXTLEVEL subprocedure, as far as your mainline routine is concerned, they're the same. That is, you're going to call the NEXTLEVEL subprocedure, and when control returns back to the mainline, your subfile is ready to be displayed.

After the call to the subprocedure, I set on my SFLEND indicator, *IN90, check to see if any records were written to the subfile, and execute the DO loop to display the subfile. Again, this isn't much different from the subfile program mainline routines throughout this book, with the exception of the CALLP versus the EXSR. Now the fun begins. Let's take a look at how to drill down through the chain of command by using a recursive subprocedure.The subprocedure in program SFL012RG (NEXTLEVEL) is a type of SFLBLD routine, which you've seen in previous chapters. That is, its purpose is to build the subfile. But this subprocedure will work quite differently from what you've seen before.

245

The P Spec

Let's start our dissection of this subprocedure with the Procedure specification (P spec). The P spec's only purposes are to begin and end a subprocedure. The first line and the last lines of a subprocedure will always be P specs. The beginning of a subprocedure is denoted by a P spec, containing the name of the subprocedure, followed by a "B" in position 24. The end of the subprocedure is marked by a P spec containing an "E" in position 24. Figure 9.6 shows the P specs from NEXTLEVEL.

```
 *
 * Procedure interface.  Describes procedure parameters.
 * VALUE keyword causes paramters to be passed by value, not reference.
 * Begin subprocedure NextLevel
P NextLevel        B
 .
 .
 .
 *
 * End the procedure
P                  E
```

Figure 9.6: The beginning and ending P specs for the NEXTLEVEL procedure.

Variables Close to Home

The next thing you'll see in a subprocedure is the procedure interface, defined by D specs. Each subprocedure will contain its own D specs housing at least one procedure interface. The procedure interface is signified by a "PI" in positions 24 and 25 (see Figure 9.7). Its purpose is to define the parameters of the subprocedure, and it must match the prototype defined earlier. You could say it is used to "interface" between the subprocedure and its prototype.

```
D                 pi
D   level                     3 0 value
D   employee                  7 0 value

 *
 * Local variables - visible only within this subprocedure.
D SaveSubord     s                    like(employ)
```

Figure 9.7: D specs from the NEXTLEVEL procedure.

Following the procedure interface, you can define any local variables you want to use in this subprocedure. Yes, this is RPG, and I mentioned local variables without having to size myself for a straight jacket. Any variables you define inside the subprocedure are available only within the subprocedure. Just like almost every other programming language in the world, RPG now supports local variables. In my example, I define a variable (SAVESUBORD) to save the subordinate number for return from recursive calls. Additionally, any local variables that are defined are local to the specific running of a subprocedure. Any subsequent calls to the same subprocedure (that would be recursion) will create new local variables scoped to that instance of the subprocedure.

SUBMERGING SUBFILES INTO SUBPROCEDURES

Let's build the subfile. Each recursive call to a subprocedure will represent a new level in the chain of command. If you take a look at the structure of my sub-procedure, it's built around a DOW loop (as shown in Figure 9.8) that will find all the subordinates for the employee ID passed as a parameter to the subprocedure. Once the record is found, it's formatted using a couple of EVAL statements. The first EVAL will simply fill SUBNAM with the ".". The second EVAL will use the %SUBST built-in-function, concatenate the first and last name, and indent it according to the level of command I'm processing. After each successful write to the subfile within the DOW loop, the NEXTLEVEL procedure is called again, passing the current level plus one and the subordinate's ID, which was obtained with the previous read to SFL002PF. This will allow me to determine if the subordinate has any subordinate entries in the file before reading the next record for the current employee.

```
     *
     * Loop until EOF is encountered.  Test V4R2 %EOF function rather
     * than indicator.
     C                     dow       not %eof

     * Look up master record for the current subordinate.  Notice, no
     * chain indicators!  Using V4R2 %found function instead.
     C     subord          chain     sfl001pf
     C                     if        not %found
     C                     eval      subnam = *blanks
     C                     eval      subnam = 'Employee information not found'
```

Figure 9.8: The DOW loop within subprocedure NEXTLEVEL with a recursive call to itself to build the subfile.

```
C                      else

*   fill the subnam subfile field with '....................'
*   Use %TRIM BIF to strip leading and trailing spaces from database fields.
*   Assign INTO the subnam field through the %subst function, indenting based
*   upon the current level.
C                      eval      subnam = *all'.'
C                      eval      %subst(subnam : Level+2)=%trim(dbfnam) +
C                                  ' ' + %trim(dblnam)

*   Update the global RRN counter, and write the new subfile record.
C                      eval      rrn1 = rrn1 + 1
C                      write     sfl1
C                      endif
*
*   Save the subordinate in the local variable, and recursively
*   call NextLevel, updating the level number, and passing the
*   current subordinate as the input employee.
C                      eval      SaveSubord = Subord
C                      callp     NextLevel (Level + 1 : subord)
*
*   Get next subordinate for the current employee.
C     pf2key           setgt     sfl002pf
C     Employee         reade     sfl002pf
C                      enddo
```

Figure 9.8: The DOW loop within subprocedure NEXTLEVEL with a recursive call to itself to build the subfile (continued).

Only when I come back from 1 to many recursive calls to the NEXTLEVEL subprocedure will I find the next direct subordinate for the current employee. I do this using the current employee (employee) and the last subordinate used before the call to NEXTLEVEL (SAVSUBORD). Each subsequent call to NEXTLEVEL will have the employee passed to it. The subordinate in one level of the NEXTLEVEL subprocedure becomes the employee when passed in the next call to NEXTLEVEL.

This may seem a little confusing at first, but if you look at one instance of a subprocedure at a time and realize that it's building the subfile for one level of the chain, you can then start to understand how each subsequent call works. It's simply our SFLBLD routine with a little twist…and another…and another….

WARNING

Each recursive call to a subprocedure creates a new invocation of that subprocedure, and with it, automatic storage for the local data items. Because of this, infinite recursion could quickly chew up system resources. Make sure your subprocedure has some condition to stop it from calling itself infinitely. In my example, the data file will ensure that the subprocedure will eventually stop calling itself. As you use this technique, you should make sure that you condition your subprocedure so it won't get into an infinite recursive call loop. That would be bad.

CODE EXAMPLES

The following code examples are used in this chapter.

SFL012DF: Display File for Recursive Subfile Build Routine

```
      A*
      A                                    DSPSIZ(24 80 *DS3)
      A                                    PRINT
      A                                    ERRSFL
      A                                    CA03
      A                                    CA12
      A*
      A            R SFL1                  SFL
      A*
      A              SUBNAM       60   0  6  2
      A*
      A            R SF1CTL                SFLCTL(SFL1)
      A*
      A                                    SFLSIZ(0050)
      A                                    SFLPAG(0016)
      A                                    OVERLAY
      A N32                                SFLDSP
      A N31                                SFLDSPCTL
      A  31                                SFLCLR
      A  90                                SFLEND(*MORE)
      A              RRN1         4S 0H
      A                                 1  2'SFL012RG'
      A                                 1 28'Company Organization List'
      A                                    COLOR(WHT)
      A                                 1 71DATE
      A                                    EDTCDE(Y)
```

SFL012DF: Display File for Recursive Subfile Build Routine (continued)

```
A                               2 71TIME
A                               3  2'Employee . :'
A           NAME        41   0  3 15
A                               5  2'Hierarchy'
A                                  COLOR(WHT)
A*
A           R FKEY1
A*
A                              23  2'F3=Exit'
A                                  COLOR(BLU)
A                              23 12'F12=Cancel'
A                                  COLOR(BLU)
```

SFL013RGF: RPG Program for Recursive Subfile Build Routine

```
*=================================================================
*
* Subfile program demonstrates Version 4 features and functionality
*
* To compile:
*
*     CRTBNDRPG  PGM(XXX/SFL012RG) SRCFILE(XXX/QRPGLESRC) +
*                DFTACTGRP(*NO) ACTGRP(*CALLER)
*
*=================================================================

* Turn on source statement debugging.  Stop the generation of
* debug points for IO statements.  Optionally, these could be
* specified on the compile command.   V4R4 feature

H OPTION(*SRCSTMT *NODEBUGIO)

* Display file uses field "rrn1" as the subfile relative record
* number for subfile "sfl1".  Data structure "info" is used as
* the file information data structure for this display file.

Fsfl012df  cf   e              workstn
F                                        sfile(sfl1:rrn1)
F                                        infds(info)

* sfl001pf = Employee master file
* sfl002pf = Employee /Subordinate file
Fsfl001pf  if   e       k disk
Fsfl002pf  if   e       k disk

* Information data structure to hold attention indicator (AID) byte.
* AID byte contains a code identifying the function
* key used to return control to the program from the display file.
```

SFL013RGF: RPG Program for Recursive Subfile Build Routine (continued)

```
* For more information see the DATA MANAGEMENT GUIDE.
Dinfo             ds
D cfkey                    369    369

* Constants to compare to AID - F3, F12, F6, and ENTER keys.
* Other values documented in DATA MANAGEMENT GUIDE.
Dexit            C                   const(X'33')
Dcancel          C                   const(X'3C')
Dadd             C                   const(X'36')
Denter           C                   const(X'F1')
*
* Input parameter: Employee number
D In_Employee     s            7a

* Prototype for NextLevel procedure: Receives two parameters
D NextLevel       pr
D   level                     3  0 value
D   employee                  7a    value

* Inpput parameter list - receives an employee number to start display
C     *entry        plist
C                   parm                      In_Employee

* Get master record for input employee
C     in_employee   chain       sfl001pf
C                   if          not %found
C                   eval        name = *blanks
C                   eval        name = 'Employee not found.'
C                   eval        *in32 = *on

* If found, Trim blanks and form First /Last name field
C                   else
C                   eval        name = (%trimr(dbfnam) + ' ' +
C                                       %trimr(dblnam))

* Clear the subfile, then call the recursive NextLevel procedure
C                   exsr        clrsfl
C                   callp       NextLevel (1 : in_employee)
C                   eval        *in90 = *on
C                   if          rrn1 = 0
C                   eval        *in32 = *on
C                   endif
C                   endif
*
* Simply redisplay subfile until user hits Exit or Cancel
C                   dou         (cfkey = exit) or (cfkey = cancel)
C                   write       fkey1
C                   exfmt       sfl1ctl
C                   enddo
*
```

SFL013RGF: RPG Program for Recursive Subfile Build Routine (continued)

```
 * Close files and terminate.
C                   eval      *inlr = *on
 ********************************************************************
C    clrsfl       begsr
 *
 * Clear the subfile by activating SFLCLR and writing the subfile control
 * format.  Reset the subfile relative record number.
C                   eval      *in31 = *on
C                   eval      rrn1 = 0
C                   write     sf1ctl
C                   eval      *in31 = *off
 *
C                   endsr
 ********************************************************************
 * Recursive NextLevel subprocedure.  Drills down through the subordinate
 * tree, populating the subfile as it goes.

 * Begin subprocedure NextLevel
P NextLevel      B
 *
 * Procedure interface.  Describes procedure parameters.
 * VALUE keyword causes paramters to be passed by value, not reference.
D                  pi
D    level                       3  0 value
D    employee                    7a    value


 *
 * Local variables - visible only within this subprocedure.
D SaveSubord      s               like(employ)

 *
 * Key list for SFL002PF
C    pf2Key       klist
C                 kfld                      employee
C                 kfld                      SaveSubord

 *
 * Position to first subordinate record for this employee and read it.
C    employee     setll     sf1002pf
C    employee     reade     sf1002pf

 *
 * Loop until EOF is encountered.  Test V4R2 %EOF function rather
 * than indicator.
C                   dow       not %eof

 * Look up master record for the current subordinate.  Notice, no
 * chain indicators!  Using V4R2 %found function instead.
C    subord       chain     sf1001pf
C                   if        not %found
```

SFL013RGF: RPG Program for Recursive Subfile Build Routine (continued)

```
s   C                     eval      subnam = *blanks
    C                     eval      subnam = 'Employee information not found'
    C                     else

    *   fill the subnam subfile field with '...................'
    *   Use %TRIM BIF to strip leading and trailing spaces from database
    *   fields. Assign INTO the subnam field through the %subst function,
    *   indenting based upon the current level.
    C                     eval      subnam = *all'.'
    C                     eval      %subst(subnam : 2*(Level+1))=%trim(dbfnam) +
    C                                      ' ' + %trim(dblnam)

    *   Update the global RRN counter, and write the new subfile record.
    C                     eval      rrn1 = rrn1 + 1
    C                     write     sfl1
    C                     endif
    *
    *   Save the subordinate in the local variable, and recursively
    *   call NextLevel, updating the level number, and passing the
    *   current subordinate as the input employee.
    C                     eval      SaveSubord = Subord
    C                     callp     NextLevel (Level + 1 : subord)
    *
    *   Get next subordinate for the current employee.
    C    pf2key           setgt     sfl002pf
    C    Employee         reade     sfl002pf
    C                     enddo
    *
    *   End the procedure
    P                     E
```

SFL002PF: Physical File for Subordinate File

```
A                                           UNIQUE
A             R PFR2
A               EMPLOY        7  0
A               SUBORD        7  0
A             K EMPLOY
```

APPENDIX

SOFTWARE INSTALLATION INSTRUCTIONS

The CD-ROM you receive with this book contains all of the source code presented in each chapter. To install the code on your AS/400, you'll need a PC with file transfer capability attached to your AS/400. You can use a PC that's running a product such as PC Support or Client Access, or you could use a PC connected to your AS/400 through TCP/IP and use FTP. The following applies to the source files:

1. All files are ASCII text.

2. The base names of the files on the CD are named according to the names specified in the chapters.

3. When you upload a file, you should transfer it to a source physical file, such as QRPGLESRC, from which it can be compiled. The appropriate source member can be determined by positions 7 and 8 of the name. For example SFL001RG.TXT is an RPG program (as determined by RG in positions 7 and 8) and should be placed in a source file such as QRPGLESRC. The source member distinctions are as follows:

   a. RG = RPG and should be placed in a source file such as QRPGLESRC.

   b. DF = Display File, PF = Physical File, and LF = Logical file and should all be placed in a source file such as QDDSSRC.

   c. CL = CL Program and should be placed in a source file such as QCLLESRC.

4. The code should be aligned properly. For example, the form type in an RPGLE program should be in column 6. If any alignments are incorrect due to uploading, please adjust the code as necessary prior to compiling. Also, you will have to fill in the appropriate type, such as RPGLE, CLP, and DSPF before compiling. The download will not do that for you.

The code in this book is to be used as templates for your own code. For that reason, data for each of the program files is not included. If you want to compile and execute these programs, you will have to create data files and populate them with data.

INDEX

A

active subfiles, maximum number of, 24, 118

active windows, displaying multiple subfiles and, 180-181

Add Record subroutine, 78

ADDQUE subroutine for data queue subfiles, 198-199, **199**, 200, **201**

ASSUME vs. OVERLAY keyword, 131, **131**, 134

B

blank subfile records for adding/modifying data, 79, 84-85, **84**

borders (WDWBORDER keyword), 118-119, 129-130

    for displaying multiple subfiles, 181

Bottom... screen display indicator, 15

    message subfiles and, 156

build routine (*See* subfile build routine [SFLBLD])

C

call stack entries for message subfiles, 152*(t)*

CALLP operation, 239, 244-245, **245**

CD-ROM companion disk, xvi-xvii, 255-256

CHAIN operation, 23, 67

    in dynamic sort subfiles, 219

    in modifying files using subfiles, 81-82, 86

Change Physical File (CHGPF) command, 3

CL program to open message subfiles, 166-168, **167**, 171-172

CLEAN subroutine for dynamic sort subfiles, 227, **227**

clear subfile (CLRSFL) subroutine (*See also* subfile clear [SFLCLR] keyword), 35

clearing (initializing) a subfile, 5

    message subfiles and, 154

command attention (CA) indicators, 18

command function (CF) indicators, 18

compile options

    in dynamic sort subfiles, 221-222

    in recursive calls, 242-243, **242**

CONNECT RESET command, 223, **223**

Note: boldface numbers indicate illustrations; (t) indicates a table.

Note: boldface numbers indicate illustrations; (t) indicates a table

Note: boldface numbers indicate illustrations; (t) indicates a table